MODEST MANSIONS
Design Ideas for Luxurious Living in Less Space

by Donald Prowler

Illustrations by Jean Farquhar,
except where otherwise noted

Rodale Press, Emmaus, Pa.

CONTENTS

ACKNOWLEDGMENTS vi
INTRODUCTION viii

Part 1
Chapter 1 THE CASE FOR THE MODEST MANSION 1
Chapter 2 A SELECTIVE HISTORY OF THE COMPACT
HOME 19

Part 2
Chapter 3 PLANNING THE COMPACT HOME 41
Chapter 4 CONSTRUCTING THE COMPACT HOME 85
Chapter 5 COMPLETING THE COMPACT HOME 130
Chapter 6 IMPROVING YOUR PRESENT HOME 160

Part 3
Chapter 7 PUTTING IT ALL TOGETHER 184

Appendix 1 CONSTRUCTION REGULATIONS 234
Appendix 2 DIMENSIONAL STANDARDS 240

ANNOTATED BIBLIOGRAPHY 259
PHOTOGRAPH CREDITS 268
INDEX 270

ACKNOWLEDGMENTS

Like most worthwhile projects, *Modest Mansions* proved far more work than anyone anticipated. But because of the support, encouragement, and assistance of many friends, I never found it a burden. To these people—and to the many talented architects and designers who freely donated their time, their ideas, and their photographs—I offer my most sincere thanks.

The editorial baton on this book passed from Carol Hupping—who initiated the project and started me in the right direction—to Joe Carter and Ray Wolf—who nurtured it—and finally to the very capable hands of Roger Rawlings. Roger's enthusiastic participation in the project has resulted in a more accessible and coherent whole. His help is much appreciated.

Jean Farquhar assisted throughout this project, doing invaluable work as illustrator, reader, and researcher. Her patience and perseverance were unflagging; I am deeply grateful to her.

I also want to thank Doug Kelbaugh for his critical reading of the manuscript in its earliest stages; Bill Glennie for his patient retrieval of apparently lost word processor text files (a new trauma of the microcomputer age); and Alan Morrison and his staff at the Furness Library of the University of Pennsylvania for their expertise, on which I drew throughout the project.

Most importantly, I want to thank my wife, Mady, and our children, Matthew and Rachel. Nothing would have been possible without them. Their love and understanding have made our own modest mansion a source of inspiration.

INTRODUCTION

The premise of this book, like its subject, is a modest one. I believe Americans should reduce the size, and increase the quality, of their homes. Many people already are selecting smaller homes because of economic necessity and other circumstances that we will discuss in Chapter 1. The question is: Can small homes provide the amenities we have come to expect? Can we have small size and high quality in our homes simultaneously? The answer is a resounding yes! This book tells how.

Too often, homeowners equate large rooms with comfort. This is unfortunate, because some of the most pleasant rooms of all are modestly sized and modestly furnished. Think, for example, of a sunlit breakfast nook, a cozy sleeping loft, or a cool screened porch. Home designers must learn to capture the spirit of these spaces for tomorrow's high-quality compact dwellings.

In most houses, we occupy only a small fraction of the usable space at any one time. Nevertheless, year in and year out, we heat or cool the unused portions of these houses, paint and repaint the excess surfaces, and fill the oversized rooms with possessions we may not necessarily cherish. This has never made sense, but it is now becoming economically insupportable as well as socially unrealistic. This book is offered as an affirmation that "small" can be beautiful, practical, and desirable in home design.

How big is a "small" house? This is a question I have been asked repeatedly as I worked on this book. Indeed, most of the homes discussed in the book are small. In some ways, however, the question misses the point. The real trademark of a well-designed compact home is the efficient use of space, not the total number of square feet. Consider the following: If we build a 1,000-square-foot house for one person, are we really constructing a compact home? It certainly would be a small house by contemporary standards—1,000 square feet is appreciably below the average size for new houses in the United States—but would it be space efficient? In fact, for one person, 1,000 square feet is fairly lavish.

This example underscores the fact that square footage is not the central issue in compact-home design. Above all else, a home must meet the physical and psychological needs of its inhabitants. Most people understand these priorities. In my experience as an architect, I have found that few, if any, clients begin with a fixed opinion about the square footage they require in their homes. Rather, they have preconceptions about the type and number of rooms they desire, or the activities they want the rooms to accommodate, and they hope these rooms can be shoehorned into the number of square feet their budgets will allow.

A well-designed compact home—a modest mansion—meets its inhabitants' needs without resorting to shoehorns and without breaking its owners' budgets. Anyone concerned with space efficiency in new or existing homes—whether they are architects, owner/builders, or would-be homeowners—can benefit from understanding the principles of compact-home design. One fruitful way to approach these principles is to ask why one home feels more spacious and livable than another home of the same size. This is precisely the question *Modest Mansions* addresses.

The book is divided into three parts. Part 1, comprising Chapters 1 and 2, demonstrates that compact living has a rich history and is today at the center of a converging set of economic, social, and design trends. This section makes the case for "downsizing the American dream."

The core of the book is Part 2, which encompasses Chapters 3 through 6. Chapters 3, 4, and 5 address the issues of planning, constructing, and completing the compact home. Chapter 6 explains how to make an existing home more space efficient. In

a

b

c

Photo 0-1. *The terms "small," "compact," and "modest" are interrelated. a. Small objects (such as the author's young son) are physically diminutive. b. Compact objects pack large capabilities in miniaturized form. c. Modest mansions are often small, always compact, and, above all, well designed.*

each chapter, a number of design principles are introduced, usually accompanied by at least one photograph or illustration in which the principle is applied. Most of the homes shown in the book are unique—some are striking statements of the owners' personal tastes. They have been selected to demonstrate that besides providing shelter, a compact home can also be a rich expression of the aspirations of its owners. This should underscore the point that a compact home need not be plain: The size of the home does not restrict your design options. One goal of this book is to encourage design exploration, and I hope many of the homes shown will pique your interest not only about modest mansions but also about architecture in general.

Chapter 7 constitutes the third part of the book. It presents 11 exemplary compact homes built in recent years. Each of the homes embodies design principles discussed in the previous chapters; studying these homes will give you many ideas that you may be able to incorporate in your own design. Several illustrations accompany the description of each home.

The book concludes with two appendixes. The first provides information about construction regulations that may affect compact-home design. The second is a summary of practical standards for the dimensions of compact homes.

A word about illustrations is in order. Photography can lie: Wide-angle lenses, special lighting, and darkroom tricks can distort real dimensions, thereby making comparisons of different

Photo 0-2. *Many of the homes shown in the book are personal expressions of the owners' tastes. Such homes underscore the range of design options available for compact dwellings. (Design by Kevin Wilkes)*

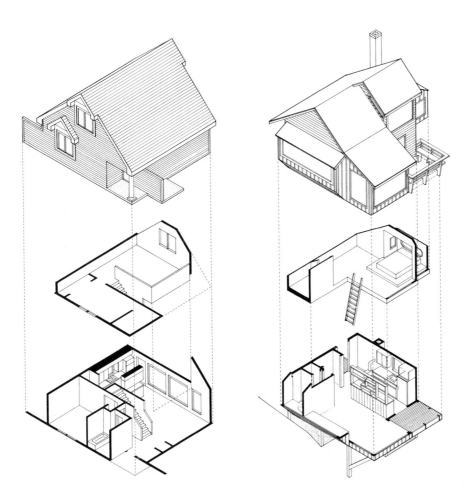

Figure 0-1. *The isometric drawings in Chapters 2 and 7 are the same scale, allowing easy comparison of the different house designs.*

designs impossible. To partially remedy this situation, the floor plans in Chapters 2 and 7 have all been drawn at the same scale, one inch to 16 feet. Thus, you can easily compare the various designs to one another.

In some cases, an "isometric" drawing of a house accompanies a photograph or floor plan. An isometric drawing is an illustration in which a slanted floor plan of a room or building is projected vertically to provide a three-dimensional representation. If you are unaccustomed to thinking in three dimensions, you'll find it instructive to study the floor plans first, imagine how the rooms fit together, and then inspect the isometric drawings to see if your imagination is confirmed. The isometric drawings in

Chapters 2 and 7 are presented at the same scale to allow easy and accurate visual comparisons.

What this book is not, and does not claim to be, is a how-to-build book. Books to help you develop skills as a builder are listed in our bibliography; you should consult them when preparing to construct a new home or to renovate an existing home. But before then, you should devote appreciable time and attention to creating a well-conceived design. This is what *Modest Mansions* is about: It is a how-to-design book. It will help you design a new, space-efficient home, and it can help you improve the space efficiency of your existing home. By applying the architectural and space-planning ideas presented in this book, you can make any home—small or large—a more exciting, vibrant, and space-efficient place to live.

PART 1

Chapter 1

THE CASE FOR THE MODEST MANSION

Photo 1-1. *The Wisconsin log home of Laura Ingalls Wilder, author of* Little House on the Prairie. *An early compact home (c. 1860), it symbolizes the frontier spirit of rugged individualism, one source of the American dream of homeownership.*

Few needs are as basic as our need for shelter. The way a society responds to this need says a great deal about its values, resources, and environmental concerns. In the United States, the dream of homeownership—particularly, the dream of owning a single-family detached house—has been a driving force in millions of lives. It is a dream that grows naturally out of the American civic values of individualism, enterprise, and material success.

In their quest for the good life, Americans have supported a dynamic homebuilding industry as well as an active owner/builder tradition. The result since World War II has been an unprecedented period of new-home construction. Americans have built homes stocked with an ever-increasing array of amenities: larger rooms, two-car garages, built-in appliances, luxurious bathrooms, and central air conditioning. The lifestyle and material well-being implied by this housing boom would seem to indicate that the "American dream" is alive and well. But is it really? Or has the possibility of homeownership slipped from the grasp of many families?

Sky-high mortgage rates tell the story of the last few years. The price of a new home has increased faster than most people's ability to pay. To cope with this problem, Americans have begun turning to a wide range of solutions. We are implementing new building technologies and mechanized construction techniques; we are devising new financing methods; and, of central interest to

Figure 1-1. *If we came equipped with built-in shelters, we wouldn't have to worry about making mortgage payments. But we would be deprived of the pleasures involved in designing new homes. (Sketch by Malcolm Wells)*

this book, we are rethinking the way we design homes. One of the most important results of these changes is that new homes are getting smaller.

Dependable national statistics on the size and cost of new homes have been available only since 1963, when the United States Department of Commerce and the United States Census Bureau began to collect annual information about housing. Figure 1-2, derived from these data, shows the median and average costs of new homes in the United States over the last 20 years. One thing is immediately evident: The trend has been up, up, and away. The cost of residential construction has increased noticeably faster than the general inflation rate. One consequence is that new homeowners have had to set aside progressively larger slices of their incomes to make their mortgage payments. An even worse consequence is that each year fewer Americans have been able to qualify for mortgages: Many people have effectively been blocked from buying their own homes.

Figure 1-2. *The cost of new homes in the United States has been increasing steadily for years. As a result, more and more families are being priced out of the housing market. (Figure by Darla Hoffman)*

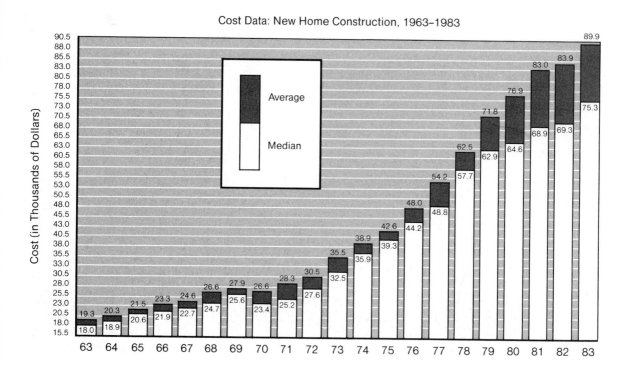

Cost Data: New Home Construction, 1963–1983

Smaller homes offer a way to reverse this trend, because they are less expensive both to build and to maintain. Fortunately, important demographic tendencies in America make a shift to smaller homes possible. In 1890, the average American household contained approximately five people. Today, the figure has been cut almost in half. There are numerous causes for this decrease, including the decision by many couples to have fewer children and the fact that many grandparents now live in their own homes or in retirement communities. The implications for home design are significant. Whereas yesterday's large families required extensive homes, today's smaller families can live quite comfortably in more compact dwellings.

The median size of new homes purchased in the United States during the last 20 years has varied considerably. (The "median" falls exactly in the middle of the scale: It is smaller than 50 percent of the new homes and larger than the other 50 percent. Tracking the median size rather than the average size

Figure 1-3. *The size of new homes has risen and fallen in recent years, reflecting the state of the economy. The trend in the future is almost certainly toward smaller homes. (Figure by Sandy Freeman)*

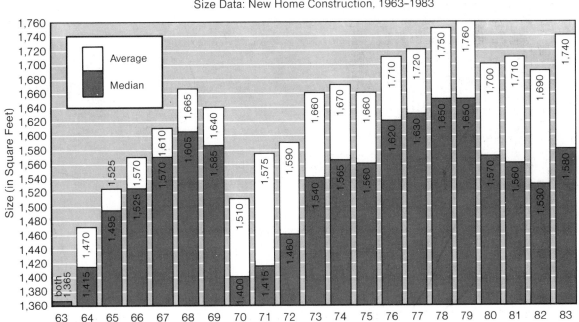

Size Data: New Home Construction, 1963–1983

gives a better indication of what is happening to the nation's housing, because the median is less skewed by the relatively small number of very large homes.) In 1963, both the median size and the average size of new American homes were 1,365 square feet (see Figure 1-3). From 1963 to 1968, there was a steady increase in both the median and the average, reflecting the typical American preference for large homes. However, a housing recession in 1969 caused the median and average to drop precipitously. Note that median home size was affected more than average home size, indicating there was still a market for large homes to accommodate high-income homebuyers. In 1971, home size again inched upward, and it continued rising in subsequent years—reaching and surpassing the previous highs of 1968. The gap between median and average home sizes stayed wide during this period.

In 1980, another drop in both median and average size occurred—reflecting difficult economic conditions brought on by a steep recession—and it continues to the present day. Is this just another temporary dip, or is it a sign of a long-term trend? Experts offer differing views. But there can be no doubt that the prevailing economic and social conditions make a return to sprawling home styles extremely improbable. It is more likely that homes will become progressively smaller in the coming years, inaugurating the age of well-designed compact homes: the age of the modest mansion.

The data in Figure 1-3 hold an important lesson for the compact homes of the future. Why did home size rebound so quickly after the 1969 dip? The answer is that many of the compact homes built at that time did not sell very well. There was considerable consumer resistance to the stripped-down, low-quality home designs that emerged from the 1969 housing recession. Potential homebuyers were turned off by compact homes that possessed neither the amenities they had come to expect nor the quality they had learned to demand. When the housing market improved after the recession, builders quickly returned to time-tested, larger designs.

Today, homeowners are turning once again toward compact houses, but we have learned that such houses must be carefully designed if they are to have lasting appeal. This is precisely what this book is about—how to design compact houses that are space efficient, high in quality, and beautiful. We will investigate techniques that can trim excess square footage from a home without sacrificing necessary living space and without skimping on the conveniences that Americans expect.

Economic Benefits

Affordability

Compact homes offer economic, social, and design benefits. Let's examine each of these, beginning with the most important economic benefit: affordability.

As a nation, we simply cannot afford to build millions of large new homes each year. The truth of this statement hardly needs to be defended. But consider just one piece of evidence. More and more American homeowners are improving their existing homes rather than building or purchasing new ones. The National Association of Home Builders (NAHB), the trade association of the homebuilding industry, reports that in 1980 for the first time, remodeling surpassed new-home construction in dollar volume. According to the NAHB, "America is spending more money to remodel and repair its inventory of existing homes than it is in building new ones." The reason for this trend is clear: New homes simply have become too expensive, so an increasing number of families are deciding to renovate their old homes and stay put.

If the situation is bad for families who can't afford to move out of their old homes into newer homes, things are worse for families who don't own any homes, old or new. For them, staying in their old home means staying in an apartment. What makes this particularly painful is that, in our society, getting a foothold on homeownership remains as important as ever: It is still the best single investment for most families. Our national commitment to homeownership has resulted in legislation that allows homeowners to take tax deductions both for the interest they pay on home mortgages and for the local property taxes they pay. Homeownership thus offers an enormous economic advantage over renting. As long as this is true, owning a home will remain the first rung on the ladder to financial security for most families. The problem today is that many young families can't reach this rung.

The percentage of Americans who can afford new homes has increased a bit recently, but it is still nowhere near historical maximums. Moreover, most economists have little hope the situation will improve significantly in the near future. As long as American homes remain oversized and overpriced, the outlook will be bleak. But compact homes could change this. Consider the following: The median new home contained 1,600 square feet in 1981, and it cost about $50 per square foot to purchase. If instead of buying such a house you purchased a home containing 1,200 square feet, you would save 400 square feet, or about $20,000 (400 square feet multiplied by $50).

This calculation is admittedly an oversimplification, but it makes an important point. Based on a 14 percent, 30-year mortgage, the monthly payment needed to amortize $20,000 is $237, or about $2,844 per year. Lowering the annual cost of mortgages by this amount would allow millions of additional families to qualify for mortgages. A Realtor's rule of thumb is that you should spend no more than one-quarter to one-third of your annual income on housing payments. Thus, if the annual cost of a mortgage were lowered by $2,844, you could qualify for a mortgage with a much lower income. For example, instead of needing to earn $40,000 a year to get a mortgage for the home you want, you might be able to get a mortgage with an income of $30,000. The bottom line, then, is that compact homes can bring the dream of homeownership back within the grasp of a large segment of the population, families who recently have been excluded from the dream.

Photo 1-2. *The once and future energy shortage: The 1973 oil embargo made energy conservation an important national goal. Fuel supplies have been up—and prices have been down—recently. But a return to energy shortages is a persistent danger.*

Energy Consciousness

Ever since the first OPEC oil embargo in 1973, Americans have had a heightened awareness of the importance of energy conservation and energy efficiency. Homebuyers are slowly learning to ask questions about a home's energy efficiency: Does the home have adequate insulation? Is the insulation properly installed? Is there an airtight vapor barrier? This new consciousness has also created an enormous interest in passive-solar, earth-sheltered, and superinsulated homes.

An obvious but often overlooked advantage to small-home construction is that it offers reduced energy consumption with-

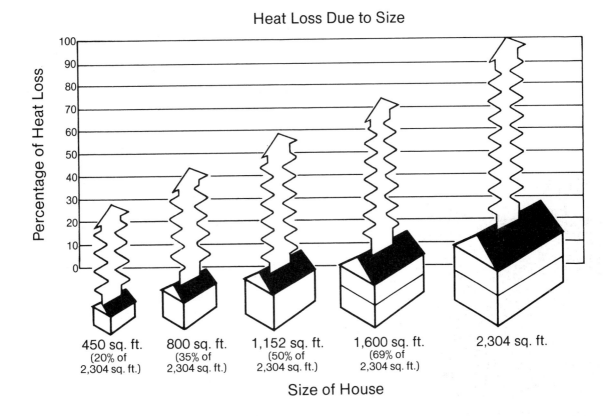

Heat Loss Due to Size

450 sq. ft. (20% of 2,304 sq. ft.)   800 sq. ft. (35% of 2,304 sq. ft.)   1,152 sq. ft. (50% of 2,304 sq. ft.)   1,600 sq. ft. (69% of 2,304 sq. ft.)   2,304 sq. ft.

Size of House

out recourse to special design techniques or unusual construction technologies. Building a home small is in itself a legitimate energy-saving strategy. The home contains fewer cubic feet of air needing to be warmed in winter or cooled in summer, and the exterior surfaces of the home are less extensive so less heat passes through them.

Figure 1-4 shows the amount of heat lost through exterior surfaces in several homes with floor plans varying in size from 450 square feet to 2,304 square feet. These homes represent common building shapes with typical proportions. Consistent assumptions have been made about insulation quality, air-change rates, the number and placement of windows, and geographical location. The results show clearly that smaller homes suffer less heat loss: They are, in other words, more energy efficient.

One subtlety to note is that while the amount of heat loss is tied to the size of a home, it is not directly proportional to that

Figure 1-4. *The smaller a house is, the smaller its heat loss. A 1,152-square foot home loses 59 percent as much heat as a 2,304-square-foot home, and a 450-square-foot home loses 28 percent as much. (Figure by Acey Lee)*

size. You might expect, for example, that reducing a home's size by 10 percent would reduce the heat loss in that home by 10 percent. But in fact, the reduction in heat loss will be somewhat less than this. The reason is that the ratio of exterior surfaces to floor area actually increases slightly as the home gets smaller. This simply means that, compared to a larger home, a small home has more square feet of wall and roof surface per square foot of floor space. Therefore, a small home loses slightly more heat *per square foot of floor space* than a large home does. But this result does not change the basic fact that small homes require less energy for heating and cooling than large homes do. Therefore, when you calculate total heat loss, small homes are the clear winners: They have smaller volumes and smaller exterior surfaces, so they require less heating in winter and less cooling in summer.

Small homes can boast other energy-related advantages as well. Because their heating needs are usually low, they are more easily heated by alternative heating systems, such as woodstoves or solar-energy systems, whose heat output is restricted. In addition, zones of temperature stratification can be minimized easily in small homes by using small fans, thereby providing greater comfort throughout the home. More about these subjects later.

Sustainability

As consumers, we are becoming increasingly aware of the price society pays for the excesses of industrial development. Each new product that industry creates seems to entail some new chemical waste that must be disposed of at the taxpayer's expense. Each problem that we solve through increased production seems to create another, perhaps even more intractable, problem. As a result of these experiences, we are learning to look at the long-term implications of the way we design houses; we are beginning to seek a sustainable future. The modest mansion responds to this concern as it treads softly on the landscape. It consumes less land, fewer raw materials, and less labor for construction and maintenance.

Not surprisingly, new-home construction consumes a considerable quantity of America's raw materials. In any given year, two-fifths of all the lumber and plywood used in the United States goes toward new-home construction. The NAHB has calculated

a

b

Photo 1-3. *One average-size new house requires all the lumber from an acre of timber forest.*

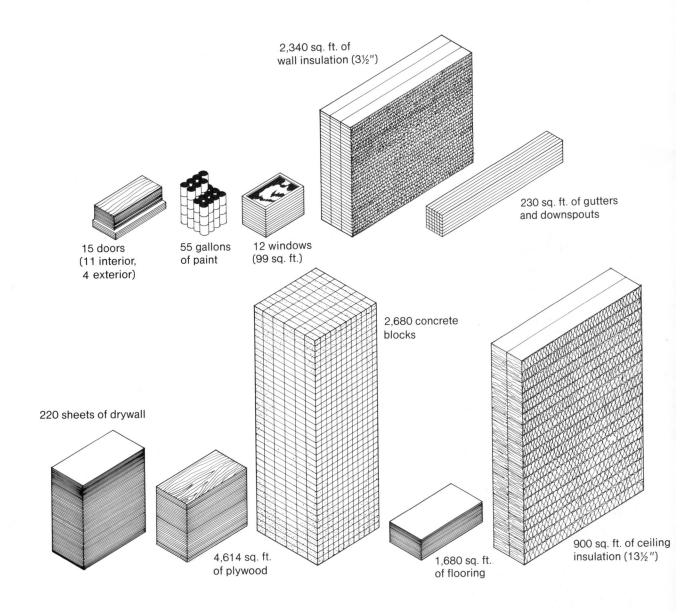

2,340 sq. ft. of
wall insulation (3½")

15 doors
(11 interior,
4 exterior)

55 gallons
of paint

12 windows
(99 sq. ft.)

230 sq. ft. of gutters
and downspouts

2,680 concrete
blocks

220 sheets of drywall

4,614 sq. ft.
of plywood

1,680 sq. ft.
of flooring

900 sq. ft. of ceiling
insulation (13½")

that a typical 1,710-square-foot home constructed in 1981 required—among other products—12,200 board feet of lumber, 302 pounds of nails, 55 gallons of paint, 99 square feet of glass, and 7,025 square feet of drywall (see Figure 1-5). To put this in perspective, consider that the average acre of timber forest in the United States

Figure 1-5. *Constructing an average-size home in the United States consumes large quantities of natural resources. (Figure by Acey Lee. Source: National Association of Home Builders)*

produces approximately 12,222 board feet of lumber when it is clear-cut, according to recent National Forest Service statistics. This means there is almost an exact one-to-one relationship: To build one average-size new home, we must clear one acre of forest.

A rough calculation reveals that a modest mansion of 1,140 square feet (one-third smaller than the NAHB's typical house) requires about 25 percent fewer board feet of lumber for construction. By building the smaller house, then, we can save one-quarter acre of forest. This statistic becomes all the more impressive if you extend it nationwide: If each of the roughly one million new homes constructed annually in this country achieved a similar lumber savings, we could save 250,000 acres of forest in one year alone. Clearly, as we learn to build modest mansions, we will dramatically reduce our exploitation of the earth's resources.

Figure 1-6. *The American family is getting smaller. This is just one of the factors leading toward smaller, more compact homes. (Figure by Acey Lee)*

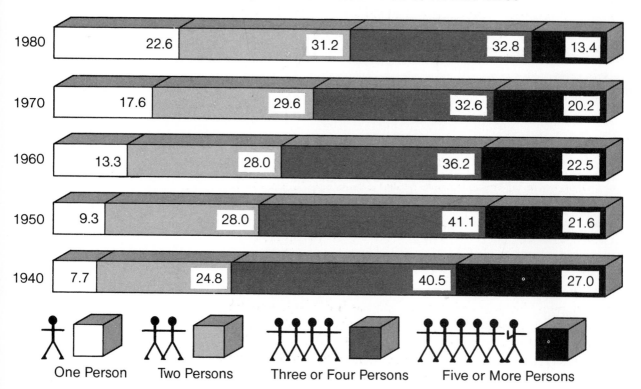

Percent of Population in Households of Various Sizes

Year	One Person	Two Persons	Three or Four Persons	Five or More Persons
1980	22.6	31.2	32.8	13.4
1970	17.6	29.6	32.6	20.2
1960	13.3	28.0	36.2	22.5
1950	9.3	28.0	41.1	21.6
1940	7.7	24.8	40.5	27.0

The same analysis applies to resources besides wood. If you build a brick home, reducing the total number of bricks needed by trimming the home's size can result in a significant savings of natural resources. It takes the energy equivalent of one gallon of oil to make and set in place eight bricks. Thus, if your modest mansion requires 800 fewer bricks than a larger home, you will save the equivalent of 100 gallons of oil. (The next time you see blocks of abandoned inner-city townhouses constructed with brick party walls, you should realize that those walls might as well be stacked gallons of oil. They represent an enormous waste of resources.)

There is no simple way to calculate all the resources consumed by housing of different sizes and configurations. The problem is too complex when all the relevant factors are taken into consideration, including the resources required to build, power, maintain, replace, and commute to and from homes in various locations. Nevertheless, compact homes unquestionably consume fewer total resources than their larger neighbors. Just as smaller, more fuel-efficient cars helped reduce our nation's energy appetite, modest mansions are an essential component of the sustainable society of the future.

Social Benefits

The New American Family

In the last 50 years, there has been a quiet revolution in the composition of the American family. For better or worse, the large family has become a thing of the past. Families today typically have fewer children: The population is increasing by 1 percent a year, compared to 3 percent annually in 1970. But the lowered birth rate is not the only cause of decreasing household size. The proliferation of single-parent families resulting from high divorce rates also is an important factor, as is the large number of senior citizens who live independently. The modest mansion addresses the housing needs of such modestly sized households.

Statistics from the United States Census Bureau highlight the transition in family size (see Figure 1-6). In 1940, 27 percent of all American households were composed of five or more people, while only 7.7 percent of all households were single-person families. By 1970, the figures were 20.2 percent and 17.6 percent, respectively. This trend toward smaller households continues today, and it has led to new living arrangements such as "accessory" apartments and "mingles" homes, phenomena we will look at more closely in Chapter 6.

Not only is the average family size decreasing, but the average age of Americans is going up. In 1980 for the first time, the percentage of households composed of people age 65 or older became greater than the percentage of households composed of people age 30 or younger. One result is that there are more and more couples whose grown children have "left the nest." These so-called "empty-nesters" find themselves rattling around large homes that were designed for more occupants. Increasingly, they are demanding smaller houses out of preference rather than financial necessity. In many cases, they are relatively affluent people, with discretionary income to spend on housing. They do not need large homes, but they are unwilling to settle for stripped-down, no-frills housing, either. So they are adding to the demand for high-quality small homes.

Builders and developers everywhere in the United States have begun to accommodate today's new, small households by providing a greater number of homes with only one or two bedrooms. This is a break with the recent past, when most builders assumed that the three-bedroom home was standard for residential design. But to make homes with fewer bedrooms function successfully, new design ideas are needed—the kind of ideas described in the chapters that follow.

Home Sweet Home

Even for the wealthiest families, the appeal of large homes may be declining. Throughout most of recorded history, a large home was the quintessential symbol of wealth and prestige. One's home was, literally, one's castle, a monument of stability and permanence. Today, while a large home is still a sign of wealth, it is no longer the unique status symbol it once was. As Paul Goldberger, the architecture critic for the *New York Times*, puts it, "Perhaps our society has come to believe that it is more a sign of wealth to be able to pick up a phone and command a quiche to appear than to control large amounts of space." Certainly it is evident that mobility and access to the latest technology have evolved as acceptable alternatives to spatial extravagance. A sleek sports car or the newest microcomputer are often substituted for the family homestead as symbols of success.

Information and people flow freely between locations today, so a large, permanent home no longer has the allure it once had as a base of operations. Frequently, an affluent family will trade one large home for two more compact homes. In such a case, one of the compact homes is generally near a city where the family members are employed, while the other home serves as a vacation retreat.

Looking toward the future, it is easy to imagine changes in how we live and work that could radically alter our conception of "house." For example, most economists and sociologists agree that our society is evolving from an industrial society, in which people are engaged primarily in heavy manufacturing, to an information society, in which the majority are engaged in channeling information and providing related services. If this evolution continues, could the house with its computer terminal become the primary workplace of the future? Some forecasters say so, and a few argue that houses will grow larger as we provide additional rooms for office work.

It is possible that some individuals will feel a need for increased office space in the home. But on the other hand, there's at least an equal likelihood that computerization will create a heightened need for human interaction: As we surround ourselves more with machines, we may feel a stronger need to be with people. As a result, we may turn to neighborhood facilities for recreation and social contact. This may well mean that computerized homes will be smaller, not larger, because rather than needing large recreation areas in our homes (dens, playrooms, and the like), we will make greater use of community facilities. Moreover, when we plug our computers into large-scale communications networks, the size of our immediate surroundings may seem less important to us. As a participant in such networks, you may come to feel that your "neighborhood" effectively includes millions of people sitting at terminals located throughout the United States and—

Photo 1-4. *What effect will the computerization of our homes have on home size? Computers may well reinforce the trend toward compact dwellings.*

eventually—all around the world. The expanded horizons created by computer networks may more than offset the compact dimensions of your home.

Design Benefits

Quality vs. Quantity

In my neighborhood, there is an ice cream parlor that features two brands of ice cream. One is a standard brand and the other is a premium brand, nationally known for its quality and taste. The store charges much less for the standard brand; you can get two scoops of it for the price of one scoop of the premium brand. Following a long-standing childhood habit, I always opted for two scoops. After a while, however, I began to wonder: Was the quantity I was purchasing making up for the quality I was missing? One day, I made the leap from two low-price scoops to one high-price scoop. To my delight, I am enjoying the one scoop more; it tastes better, and it has fewer calories.

American homebuyers often have made the same mistake in the housing market that I used to make in the ice cream parlor. They typically have chosen 2,000 square feet of poorly designed house instead of 1,000 square feet of well-designed house. The reason is easy to deduce. The frontier spirit of endless wide-open spaces has dominated our national consciousness, leading us to believe that bigger invariably means better. As a consequence, builders and homebuyers generally have chosen to maximize square footage at the expense of quality. At least until recently, homes were big, but too often they were not sensitively designed or well built. Fortunately, a change in this attitude seems imminent. Housing is coming to be viewed as an enormously valuable long-term resource rather than as a mere commodity. This means the time is near when the quality of a house will become more important than its size. As architect Douglas Kelbaugh puts it, we will soon see "a future that derives its excitement from authenticity rather than growth."

This book comes down squarely on the side of emphasizing quality and reducing size. American homes—like too many Americans themselves—are bloated. But the balloon frame is about to burst. Collectively, we need to go on a spatial diet that will achieve leaner, more finely tuned dwellings. One of the most important themes of this book is to make sure that you get your money's worth from your next home. Above all, if you decide to reduce the size of your next home, make sure that you gain a compensating increase in quality. Opt for a compact home, but make sure it is a well-designed, livable compact home.

Consider the following: An average American-made car has about a 10-year road life before it is scrapped. A good appliance may last 15 years before it starts to fizzle. Even a smoothly functioning nuclear power plant has a useful life of little more than 30 years before it must be decommissioned. Our homes, by comparison, can be expected to stand an average of well over 100 years. For this reason, building or buying a home is an event of truly historical significance, an event that should not be taken lightly. Most of America's wealth is invested in its building stock. With this in mind, can we morally do otherwise than to design and build homes of the highest quality we can attain?

Express Yourself

Our homes always have done far more than provide shelter: They reveal our characters and dispositions. Are you an extrovert, with pink flamingos in your yard and bright paint on your walls? Are you more conservative, with manicured lawns and traditional color schemes? Are you technologically inclined, with the latest solar panels prominently displayed on your roof? No matter what sort of person you are, your home certainly reflects your personality—or it reflects the public image you want to project.

In almost all locations and price ranges, a variety of house types is available. What makes people select one type over another? Sometimes objective factors are paramount: the price of a particular home, the quality of its construction, or the location. But in many cases, consumers base their final selections on more subjective factors. The image projected by the home is particularly important. You need only remember that many thoroughly American homebuyers prefer French Chateau or English Tudor styles to understand that complicated motivations are at work in home selection.

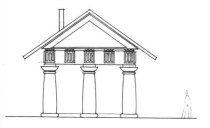

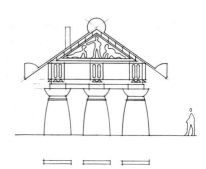

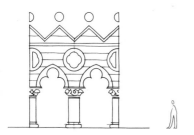

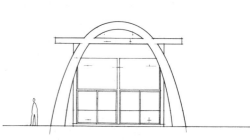

Figure 1-7. *The basic plan of a home does not necessarily dictate that home's appearance. This point is illustrated by six fanciful—and highly varied—facades for the same compact-house plan. ("Eclectic House," design and illustration by Venturi, Rauch and Scott Brown)*

Surprisingly, a small home may offer greater opportunities for self-expression than a large home would. Because less money is eaten up by gross square footage, more is available for other purposes. Thus, you can personalize the home, making it truly fit your individual needs. In addition, a small home is more amenable to playful flights of fancy: It is less constrained by limits of materials and spans; it is less restricted by traditions that dictate what is "correct." So do not be misled into believing that the limited size of a small home places limits on the design options open to you.

A related advantage is that a small home can be built by a do-it-yourselfer of only modest skills, thus opening even more avenues for self-expression. Owner/builders erect or contract approximately 20 percent of all the homes in America. The majority of these self-reliant individuals build homes of conventional design: Cape Cods, California bungalows, split-levels, ranch

houses, and the rest. But other owner/builders trade the simplicity of off-the-shelf styles for the freedom to express personal
tastes. Some of their most creative efforts are expressed in small
homes. This book is sprinkled with examples of homes conceived
by adventurous owner/builders. Unrestrained by market demand,
these individuals have built residences that are often the forerun-
ners of new housing trends: homes that serve as the laboratory in
which new design ideas are tested.

New Opportunities

Whenever social, economic, or technological innovations
require new design solutions, the first response invariably is to
apply existing designs to the new problem, whether or not they
are appropriate. Thus, the first automobiles were intended to
look like horseless carriages, and the first skyscrapers were meant
to resemble numerous one-story buildings stacked on top of each
other. It is altogether understandable that many of the first
generation of contemporary compact homes were designed to

Figure 1-8. *Old designs often are applied to new conditions. Early automobiles—such as this 1896 Oldsmobile—were designed to look literally like horseless carriages. (Courtesy of General Motors)*

look like shrunken versions of standard-size homes. It is also reasonable to expect that after some design evolution has taken place, tomorrow's compact homes will look different and function differently than today's homes.

This does not necessarily mean that a design revolution is in order. In fact, many of the ideas presented in this book are variations on time-proven concepts of home design. An analogy with automobiles is again useful: Today's new small cars have more similarities with large cars than dissimilarities. They possess four wheels, internal combustion engines, and steering wheels. Nevertheless, certain essential details have changed: Front-wheel drive has become common, for example, and styling has become boxier so shorter wheelbases can accommodate the same usable volume as before. Everything is almost the same, yet so many details are a little bit different. The evolutionary process that led to these changes in car design probably will be paralleled in the evolution of compact-home design.

Of course, it would be wrong to take the comparison with the automobile too far. Our homes are unique products of our economy and culture. The evolution of housing will follow its own internal logic, reflecting changing conditions in our society. But we can be certain of some things. Human dimensions will not change much, and our perception of human scale will not be fundamentally altered: The human being will remain the true measure of scale and appropriateness. In the past, new technologies such as central heating and cooling, the telephone, and the television influenced how we organized our houses, but they did not alter the fundamental spatial principles around which living spaces were designed. There is no reason to expect tomorrow's technologies to have any greater impact; our basic housing needs will remain the same. Homebuyers will continue to require houses that are comfortable, secure, imaginative, and affordable, and our standards of comfort and livability will be essentially the same as they are today.

In the following chapters, we will examine how the modest mansion can meet these requirements. We will explore design principles through which we can develop homes that will repay fully the 100-year investment of resources that each new home represents.

Chapter 2

A SELECTIVE HISTORY OF THE COMPACT HOME

Before designing our own modest mansions, we can learn a great deal by studying the successful (and unsuccessful) compact homes of the past. The first half of this chapter is an analysis of several traditional house types that embody useful principles of compact-home design. The second half is a brief survey of more recent compact-housing trends.

Throughout history, people have chosen to live in modestly sized homes for a variety of reasons. In most cases, the overriding motivation has been economic. But social, environmental, and cultural factors also have played a significant role. Scarce land and resources, or extreme climatic conditions, often have made compact homes the only viable option. In some cultures, ingenious spatial organizations have evolved to make small homes function both efficiently and graciously despite their restricted size.

Twentieth-century architectural conceptions of space—and modern mass-production techniques—have created new opportunities for compact housing. Some designers have foreseen the development of affordable, mass-produced, high-quality compact homes. For the most part, however, this prospect has yet to be realized.

Traditional Compact Homes

The homes we will examine first are all excellent examples of vernacular design—that is, designs that have evolved through the contributions of many builders, architects, and developers in a particular locale. During the evolution of such a design, a consensus emerges about the "right" way to construct a home, and thereafter it becomes unnecessary for each homebuilder to create an original set of plans. Individualism within this system arises from subtle elaborations on a basic tradition.

Photo 2-1. *A Trinity house in Philadelphia. Scarcity of downtown land led to the creation of this compact housing type.*

Today, we are not restricted to a narrow set of local building styles. In our heterogeneous, migratory society, the concept of vernacular housing has become blurred. For example, the Colonial and Cape Cod homes that can be found in almost all American communities are stripped-down versions of what were originally northeastern vernacular styles. These and many other vernacular styles have been uprooted and tossed randomly across the suburban landscape. As a result, we have inherited a broad array of acceptable housing choices.

The Trinity House

On the block where I live in Philadelphia, there stands a beautiful example of a vernacular modest mansion. Photo 2-1 shows the street facade of a classic early American "Trinity" rowhouse. The Trinity (also referred to as a Father, Son, and Holy Ghost) got its name from the fact that it is composed of three rooms—one room on each of its three main floors. Many such Trinities were constructed between 1800 and 1850 in the cities of the northeastern United States.

Each floor of a typical Trinity home is about 14 to 16 feet square. In a 16-foot by 16-foot Trinity, each room has just 256 square feet of living space, minus space for the stairway and fireplace. Some quick multiplication reveals that the entire house contains only 768 square feet—a modest home by any standards. Nor does the Trinity contain a large volume of cubic footage, for its ceilings are invariably low. This accentuates the feeling of compactness and also allows the stairway to be as small as possible, having a minimum number of steps. In a typical Trinity, a side-winding stairway occupies one corner of the plan, opening out directly into the room on each floor.

While a Trinity house feels small, it does not feel as constricted as you might expect. Because the floors are not divided into smaller spaces, the rooms seem reasonably sized. After all, many larger urban townhouses of the 19th century were no wider than a Trinity. Moreover, because of the Trinity's square floor plan, each room is fully as long as it is wide. There are no tiny, walled-off areas.

Some Trinity owners have increased the apparent size of their homes by clever use of basement or rooftop space. They excavate portions of their rear yards, for example, to create bright kitchens and dining areas in otherwise dark basements, or they build roof decks that afford much-appreciated views of the city skyline.

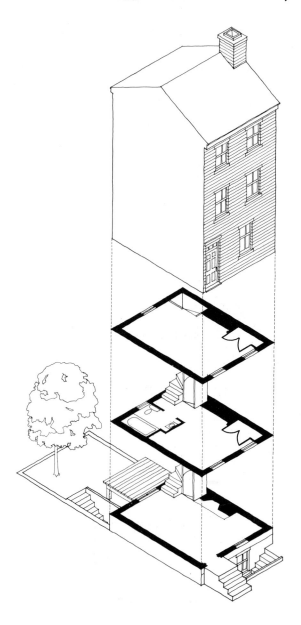

Figure 2-1. *Exploded isometric drawing of a typical Trinity house.*

Why did the Trinity become a popular house design of the last century? Of course, its modest size made it more affordable than its stately neighbors, but that is not the complete explanation. To understand the Trinity's popularity, you must realize that in many urban centers, the demand for space already was becoming a major problem by the early 19th century. The Trinity responded as much to the limited availability of land as to the high cost of housing. The home's compact size allowed maximum use of ground area, thus permitting individual homeownership: The Trinity spread upward rather than outward. The 20th-century high-rise condominium is a logical extension of this phenomenon.

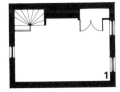

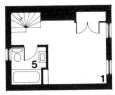

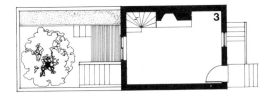

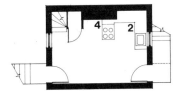

Figure 2-2. *Typical floor plans, Trinity house.*

1. Bedroom
2. Kitchen
3. Living Room
4. Dining Area
5. Bathroom

The Traditional Japanese House

The island nation of Japan has severely limited space available for housing, and access to raw materials is even more sharply limited. These factors led to the development of a unique compact vernacular house type. Unlike the vertical Trinity, the traditional Japanese house spreads horizontally, rarely rising more than one story. This seems to contradict the need to conserve scarce land and forests, but fear of the frequent earthquakes that plague Japan dictated low structures. The houses, therefore, needed to be extremely well designed—because they were spreading over such scarce and valuable land, every effort had to be made to ensure that each square foot of each house was well conceived. Compactness was a goal in all but the grandest dwellings.

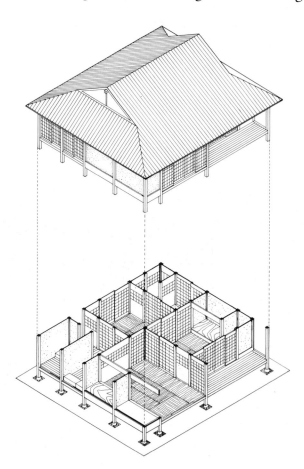

Figure 2-3. *Exploded isometric drawing of a traditional Japanese house.*

The traditional home that evolved from these constraints was designed with elegant simplicity and restraint. It was capped by a broad roof of gentle slope, with wide overhanging eaves that sheltered a verandah on one side of the main floor. The floor plan was generally rectangular, and—with the exception of guest rooms—few rooms had projections or bays. There was no attic or cellar, no chimneys or hearth, few closets, and little furniture—in fact, no beds, tables, or chairs.

The main floor of the house was raised a foot or more above the ground on foundation poles that rested on stones rammed into the earth. The floor itself was planned to correspond to a certain number of "tatami" floor mats, on which the residents sat and slept. These mats, which measured approximately three feet by six feet, were made of straw that was matted and bound together with string. Because the mats in each house had a precise size dictated by tradition, the number of mats used in a room determined that room's dimensions.

The house almost always was composed of several regularly shaped rooms fitted together like pieces of a jigsaw puzzle: that is, without corridors, closets, and the other in-between-spaces that connect rooms to each other in Western houses. Instead of interior walls, the rooms were delineated by "fusuma" (sliding partitions,

Figure 2-4. *Typical floor plan of a traditional Japanese house.*

1. Living/Dining/Sleeping Space
2. Entry
3. Bathroom
4. Storage
5. Porch
6. Tokonoma

Photo 2-2. *The dimensions of "tatami" floor mats influence the dimensions of rooms in traditional Japanese homes. Sliding screens called "shoji" connect the rooms.*

often richly painted and lacquered) and "shoji" (sliding doors covered with white paper, allowing light to be diffused throughout the house). Both fusuma and shoji were easily retracted or removed. In this way, the house could be transformed quickly from a collection of discrete rooms to a single living space for gatherings or ceremonial occasions. In addition, the partitions permitted diagonal views and shared light throughout the house, giving the house an appearance of greater size.

Subtle touches were employed to differentiate the zones in a single room. One ceiling beam might be lower than the other beams, for example, or a single tatami mat might be raised a few inches to denote a special ceremonial location. The exterior wall of one room, usually the guest room, had a recess that was divided into two bays two or three feet deep. The bay nearest the verandah was called the "tokonoma" and was a ceremonial space where prized possessions—such as painted scrolls, flower arrangements, or carvings—were displayed one at a time. In this way, a single object took on great symbolic and decorative importance, eliminating the need for other space-consuming ornamental furnishings.

The flexibility of the traditional Japanese house contrasts markedly with the more strictly defined use of space in the Trinity. The occupants of the Japanese house paid for this flexibility with a certain loss of privacy and thermal comfort. Nevertheless, the design tradition was so fundamental that the same spatial arrangements prevailed even in the houses of the rich. This should not be surprising, for even today the traditional Japanese house remains a masterful example of creative manipulation of limited floor space.

The Igloo

The igloo is the winter home of the nomadic Eskimo of the Canadian North. Few non-Eskimos would consider living in one of these small domes made of snow. But even so, we can learn important lessons from the principles of space efficiency used in the design of the igloo.

Photographs or illustrations rarely give a clue to the igloo's actual size. An igloo is usually composed of a main room about

15 feet in diameter attached to a long, narrow passageway that protects the entrance from intruding wind. Thus, with approximately 175 square feet of floor area, the igloo is similar in size to one floor of the typical Trinity house, or one large room in a traditional Japanese house. The top of the dome is, at most, ten feet high.

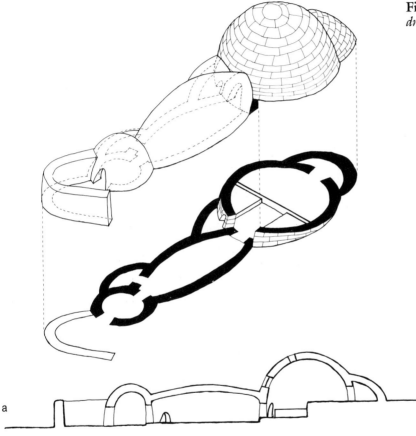

Figure 2-5. *Exploded isometric drawing of a typical igloo.*

a

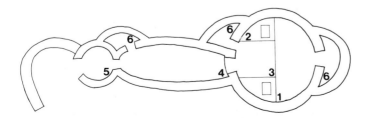

b

Figure 2-6. *a. Section of a typical igloo. b. Igloo floor plan.*

1. Sleeping Alcove
2. Kitchen Area
3. Living Space
4. Passageway
5. Entry
6. Storage

Igloos are constructed from blocks of snow about three feet long, 20 inches wide, and 6 to 10 inches thick. The blocks are slightly beveled so that when laid in a continuous spiral, they corbel in toward each other, thus allowing a dome to be formed without requiring the temporary supports normally needed in dome construction. The igloo's shape limits the exposure of the house to the arctic cold and wind, for it encloses a maximum volume in a minimum exterior surface area. This is one reason the igloo is so often cited as an example of environmentally harmonious residential design.

Unlike the conditions in Philadelphia or Japan, scarcity of land is not a constraint for the Eskimo. Miles and miles of empty tundra abound on which to build. The obvious constraints facing the igloo dweller are a limited variety of building materials, limited heating fuel, and extreme environmental conditions, notably prodigious cold, wind, and snow. Making your home compact is necessary when animal fat is the only available heating fuel.

The igloo's contours offer unique interior-design possibilities. In a simple but enlightened example of interior architecture, the Eskimo creates a raised sleeping alcove within the dome, thereby taking advantage of the home's thermal characteristics. The igloo's ice-sealed interior surface, lack of operable windows, and long entry tunnel make the structure quite airtight. Warm air stratifies in the upper reaches of the dome: The sleeping alcove thus provides a platform on which family members can benefit from the warmth. Of course, the alcove's 40° to 50°F temperatures would not be considered warm by people from more temperate climates, but in the arctic, they are most welcome.

The igloo also employs a subtle method of differentiating among interior spaces. A "kitchen" area, which is usually near the entrance, is located on a platform that is smaller and lower than the sleeping alcove. The main living area is at ground level, several inches lower than the kitchen platform. The interior of the igloo is thus divided into several "rooms" that are defined by variations in the floor level. In this way, the Eskimo takes full advantage of the vertical opportunities of the igloo's one-story design. In fact, by exploiting various levels within one volume, the Eskimo actually reveals a modernistic perception of space. The sleeping lofts and open-plan kitchens that characterize many current small-home designs have their spiritual ancestors in the platforms of the

igloo. They remind us that even the simplest building forms can benefit from consideration of the space-planning possibilities offered in the third dimension.

The Courtyard House

Versions of the courtyard house can be found throughout the hot climates of the world, from India and the Middle East to North Africa and parts of Latin America. In all cases, the basic design principle at work is essentially the same: A relatively small amount of interior space encloses an outdoor court that extends the usable area of the house and provides for outdoor living. Such an arrangement also maximizes the opportunities for cross-ventilation and air movement so vital to indoor comfort in hot climates.

The courtyard house usually is constructed from mud, adobe, concrete block, stone, or some other masonry material that shields

Photo 2-3. *An open courtyard provides light and ventilation in this Saudi Arabian house. Rooftop areas, like the courtyard itself, create opportunities for outdoor living.*

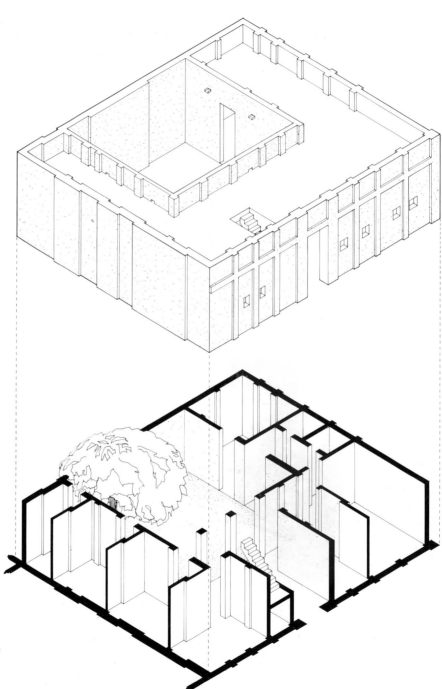

Figure 2-7. *Exploded isometric drawing of a Middle Eastern courtyard house.*

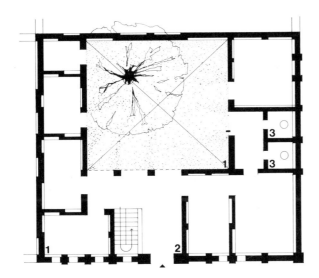

Figure 2-8. *Floor plan of a typical urban courtyard house in the Middle East.*

1. Courtyard
2. Entry
3. Bathroom
All other spaces are used for varying purposes at various times.

the house and courtyard from direct sunlight, thus helping to keep temperatures under control during the day. At night, the courtyard provides an escape from rooms that may be too warm for comfortable sleeping.

In the Trinity house, traditional Japanese house, and igloo, the goal of compact design led to the creation of small homes. This is not true for the courtyard house. In fact, the courtyard house explodes horizontally—its overall dimensions are not small, due to the central court. Yet the rooms and other interior spaces in the home are quite compact and actually include minimum amounts of enclosed space. This illustrates the fact that space efficiency is not confined to small homes: Even large homes can benefit from the principles of space-efficient design.

The most important lesson of the courtyard house can be found in its use of outdoor living space to increase the home's sense of spaciousness. Few weapons in the arsenal of the compact-home designer are more important than the creative manipulation of outdoor space. When the barriers between inside and outside are lowered, a compact home becomes much less confining.

Photo 2-4. *A typical Charleston "single" home with a two-story piazza that connects the home to the street.*

This lesson is eminently applicable in many parts of the southern and western United States, where outdoor living is quite desirable during much of the year. In fact, a distant relative of the courtyard house has evolved in Charleston, South Carolina. Called the Charleston "single" house, it does not have a courtyard—it does not superficially resemble the courtyard house at all. But below the surface, there is an important connection between the Charleston single and the courtyard house. Both designs capture outdoor space to extend the living area of the home.

The Charleston single is long and narrow, with its short end abutting the street. The house is one room wide, an arrangement that facilitates cross-ventilation. On the south or west side of the house is one or more stories of continuous porches, locally called "piazzas." To enter the house, you walk from the street up several steps to a piazza and then proceed into a central hallway. The piazzas provide an intermediate zone between the public street and the private parlor: They open the house to the outdoors, much as a courtyard would. Thus, although the courtyard house and the Charleston single are very different structures, they share an essential design approach.

The Recent Past

Having looked at several vernacular designs from around the world, we should turn now to more recent developments. In the last half century, two trends in design and construction have become apparent. On the one hand, custom-designed homes have never been more popular or more sought-after; on the other hand, more and more houses are being mass produced or at least partially prefabricated. Both of these trends have relevance for compact-home design.

Custom Homes

A custom home is one that is personalized for its occupant in some fashion. It may have been designed by an architect for a particular client, or it may be the unique creation of an owner/builder. Custom homes hold the potential for increasing the stock of housing ideas through great leaps rather than through gradual change. Occasionally, a particularly successful custom home leads the way, contributing to the creation of a new vernacular style.

We should be cautious about placing too much emphasis on the designs of particular architects or builders. Nevertheless, the contributions of several well-known architects to the development of compact-home design should be noted. Among the architects are Frank Lloyd Wright, LeCorbusier, Walter Gropius, and Mies Van der Rohe.

Frank Lloyd Wright's long, low prairie homes of the first decades of this century became the inspiration for generations of suburban ranch and split-level dwellings throughout the United States. In these homes, rooms were often connected freely to each other, providing an "open plan." In the words of the eminent architectural historian Henry-Russell Hitchcock, Wright "was the first to conceive of architectural design in terms of planes existing freely in three dimensions rather than in terms of enclosed blocks." Not surprisingly, Wright was an admirer of Japanese architecture and its use of continuous space. Wright also appreciated the need for affordable housing, but he never tolerated shoddy workmanship or careless detailing in his quest for low cost. In this respect, he was an early advocate of the modest mansion—small size but high quality.

In his SunTop design for Ardmore, Pennsylvania, Wright also was among the first American "high style" architects to argue that modest housing—and small attached housing, at that—was a reasonable concern for the cutting edge of design. A group of four of these homes was built in 1939, and it still stands in only slightly altered form. Excluding carport and basement, each unit has approximately 1,000 square feet of living space.

One of Wright's primary contributions to compact design was his demonstration that opening up partitions between rooms to let space "flow" creates new spatial relationships and living opportunities. In the last 30 years, this lesson has been so well assimilated that virtually everyone now understands how kitchens can open up to dining areas, how dens and living rooms can be joined, and how two-story spaces or light wells can tie two floors together. In fact, as a reaction to the pervasiveness of these techniques, some leading architects today are advocating a return

Photo 2-5. *Sun Top, designed by Frank Lloyd Wright, consists of four compact attached houses. The structure is shown here under construction in 1939 (a) and as it appears today (b).*

to the discrete, distinct rooms and traditional ornaments of earlier periods. But the influence of Wright's designs remains strong.

In 1931, the newly opened Museum of Modern Art (MOMA) in New York City held its first architectural exhibit, titled "The International Style: Architecture since 1922." The exhibit heralded the existence of a new "modern movement" in architecture that was characterized by—among other things—open plans, minimal ornamentation, the use of non-load-bearing exterior "curtain" walls, and flat or slightly sloped roofs. The International Style was

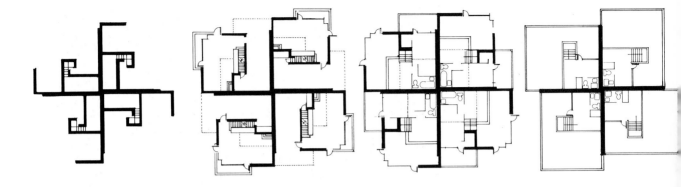

seen as a reaction against design tendencies in the late 1800s and early 1900s, when revivals of historical styles dominated architecture. Inspired by Frank Lloyd Wright and others, advocates of the International Style were seeking a new way of building, an approach that would be appropriate for the emerging industrialized, democratic societies of the 20th century.

At the MOMA show, designs by the French architect Le-Corbusier and the German architect/educators Walter Gropius and Ludwig Mies Van der Rohe—both of whom later moved to the United States and directly influenced a generation of American architects—were prominently displayed as models of the new style. Much of what most people associate with "modern" architecture—sleek, primary forms, asymmetrical compositions, the use of white or primary colors—has its roots in the International Style and the work of these masters.

The designs of LeCorbusier, Gropius, and Mies Van der Rohe hold significant lessons for today's compact-home designer. Perhaps most importantly, their designs share a desire to break down the exterior boundaries of the home. Like the anonymous creators of the courtyard house, they sought to extend the home into the landscape and the landscape into the home. For example, they used large picture windows, cantilevered balconies, and roof decks to extend the domain of the home. In Chapter 3, we will see just how well this technique is suited to the modest mansion.

All three men also foresaw innovations in the mass production of building components: They welcomed the potential for manufactured housing. LeCorbusier went so far as to character-

Figure 2-9. *Plan of Frank Lloyd Wright's Sun Top, showing the basement, first, second, and third floors. The structure contains four dwelling units. (Rendering by Bradley Lambersten)*

Photo 2-6. *This contemporary home in Rye, New York, draws on the principles of the International Style. (Design by Gwathmey-Siegal)*

ize the house as "a machine for living." Their interest was mostly symbolic, however; the building industry was not yet capable of producing the components they sought. It was not until some years later that manufactured housing began to become a reality.

Mass-Produced Housing

Since the turn of the century, the cost of housing has consistently tended to rise faster than the overall inflation rate. As a result,

America has increasingly turned to mass production as one means of keeping costs in bounds: House designs have been created on a mass-produced basis, and factory production techniques have been used to create relatively inexpensive building components as well as entire houses. Unfortunately, the mass-produced homes now on the market are often low in quality. While you may find a mass-produced home that is both affordable and well designed, your most certain route to a modest mansion is to create your own custom design.

One of the earliest efforts to apply mass production to house design was through the use of standardized, or "stock," house plans. A stock plan is a set of drawings that has been used many times by a given builder or that can be purchased from a plans service. In the early part of this century, when homebuilding was still largely a family activity, a variety of plans services marketed their products directly to the public. In fact, Sears, Roebuck and Co. was the largest seller of house plans in the country at that time.

In the 1920s, the American Institute of Architects (AIA), the national professional association of architects, decided it needed to play a greater role in shaping America's future housing. Therefore, the AIA created a nonprofit corporation called the Architects' Small House Service Bureau to provide what it considered high-quality stock house plans. The cost for the service was $5 per room—extraordinarily inexpensive by today's standards. However, because of the housing slump caused by the Great Depression, the bureau soon found itself with few clients, so it eased out of business. Today there are only a handful of nationally advertised sources of complete, inexpensive, small-house plans.

Figure 2-10. *Emblem of the Architects' Small House Service Bureau, which closed its doors during the Depression.*

As the Depression brought home construction to a halt, new visions of the homebuilding process evolved. There was a belief, powerfully held in the 1930s and 1940s, that technical efficiency could be the cornerstone of a prosperous society with adequate factory-built homes for all. Among the proponents of this belief was Buckminster Fuller. His early advocacy of mass-produced shelters foretold today's boom in manufactured housing and the widespread use of prefabricated building components such as roof and floor trusses. His vision took the form, for example, of mobile, mass-produced "Dymaxion" houses. Fuller also foresaw the use of prefabricated "plumbing cores"—self-contained units that would incorporate all the plumbing required for compact, space-efficient homes.

As compelling as Fuller's spirit and personal energy were, it is not easy to point to specific designs of his that have survived the test of time. His contribution was more that of a catalyst, a visionary who fomented change. It remains for a younger generation of designers to take up the challenge he laid down: to use technology and the efficiencies of mass production to create tomorrow's homes.

a

b

Photo 2-7. *a. This autonomous mobile dwelling, designed and built in 1979 by Michael Jantzen and Ted Bakewell, reflects Buckminster Fuller's vision of a compact structure created through the use of modern technology. b. The interior—just 440 square feet—is snug yet comfortable.*

One of the first attempts to apply mass-production techniques to whole structures came in the field of recreational vehicles. At first, small trailers were built. Slowly, these increased in size until the trailers had been transformed into full-fledged mobile homes, and a new industry was born. The mobile home industry has not lived up to the standards of quality envisioned by Fuller and others, however. A tradition of shoddy construction and poor design has beleaguered the industry, with the result that in the last several years the popularity of mobile homes has, for the first time, declined.

Photo 2-8. *The travel trailer is the forerunner of today's mobile and manufactured homes. The first all-aluminum Airstream trailer appeared in 1937.*

While sales of mobile homes have dipped, a related form of housing—manufactured homes—is becoming increasingly popular. The manufactured home is constructed of wood, much like a conventional house, except that most of the work is done in a factory. Typically, the home is constructed in two separate sections inside the factory; then the sections are towed to a house site, placed on a foundation, and attached to each other. It is a sobering fact that in 1981, of the homes constructed in this country for less than $40,000, an overwhelming 89 percent were either mobile or manufactured homes.

While the makers of manufactured homes would seem to have a unique opportunity to experiment with compact-design ideas, they generally have not taken advantage of this opportunity. On the whole, they have used their sophisticated production facilities merely to duplicate conventional site-built designs rather than to investigate new designs. As the industry matures, the manufactured home may yet lead the way to affordable, high-quality modest mansions. Today, however, a high-quality, off-the-shelf compact home is hard to find: If you want a modest mansion, you will have to either hire an architect or design it yourself with the aid of the principles set forth in the following chapters.

PART 2

Chapter 3

PLANNING THE COMPACT HOME

People often confuse goals with strategies when evaluating their housing needs. They do not realize, for example, that an eat-in kitchen represents just one strategy for achieving the goal of informal dining; or they forget that enclosing a bedroom and equipping it with a lockable door is only one of many strategies for achieving the goal of privacy.

It is essential that you begin the process of designing your home by determining your real goals. At least initially, try to define these goals as broadly as possible to allow the greatest variety of potential solutions to emerge. Only then will you find the most creative and appropriate solutions. This chapter provides compact-home design strategies: It describes six approaches you can take to organize space effectively in your modest mansion. After you have established your goals, you will be able to decide which approach—or which combination of approaches—is right for you.

Goals

One goal for every house should be design excellence. This is easily stated, but what, precisely, is an "excellent" design? Excellent in whose eyes? Benjamin Franklin said, "Eat to please yourself and dress to please others." What would he have prescribed for house design? We occupy the houses we build, but they also are constantly on display: They are both personal and public.

Most architects probably would agree that to qualify as "excellent," a house design should simultaneously address personal needs and shared needs. The needs are personal, in that the house should meet the particular requirements of a given site, budget, and occupant; they are shared, in that the house should be aesthetically pleasing to other members of the society in which it will stand.

We constantly "read" buildings as if they were books. For instance, many of us recognize a gable shape as a symbol for house—a child's drawing of a house almost invariably depicts a door under a gabled roof. We rarely stop to consider that in other cultures, the same shape has little significance and certainly does not represent "house." For the people in those cultures, the gable may be meaningless; for us, however, it is an extremely powerful symbol, representing something of great importance.

Figure 3-1. *Almost everyone in our culture—children included—immediately recognizes the gable shape as a symbol for "house." (Drawing by Matthew Prowler)*

Buildings are full of symbols of this type, symbols so basic that we rarely pause to recognize them consciously, although we constantly read them subconsciously. A building can embody symbols that we interpret as institutional and cold, or it can embody symbols that we associate with comfort and human warmth. Any building we design will transmit messages of this type—it will send pleasing or displeasing signals to the rest of the community. As a result, concern for the community's shared aesthetic values should underlie the design of any house. It is this concern that transforms a group of houses into a neighborhood.

In addition to considering shared needs, of course, a designer must also examine the personal needs that a house is intended to meet. One of the first steps in the design process is to create a list of these needs. In architectural parlance, this list is called a "building program." It might include a summary of the number and type of rooms you want; the general layout you prefer; the living arrangements and lifestyle you have in mind, and an approximate budget. It is helpful to make the building program quite explicit, so that later you can evaluate alternatives as they arise.

With the program in hand, you can begin translating its requirements into actual floor plans. Often, statements from the program will have immediate implications for your design. A gourmet cook will no doubt want a kitchen with ample preparation space and perhaps room to entertain, while a confirmed bachelor might decide to dispense with most interior partitions, because privacy is not a problem in a one-person home.

Some of the goals your design must fulfill are wholly objective: It must meet code requirements, size standards, and structural demands. Beyond these, however, a good design also should address certain subjective—although no less significant—goals. In fact, poor designs result most often from a failure to adequately satisfy these subjective necessities, not from any failure to meet objective requirements. In even the most lackluster buildings, the rooms are usually adequately sized and the stairways work, but the more intangible considerations have been overlooked.

Human "scale" is one of the most important subjective factors to bear in mind when designing a modest mansion. If you have ever visited a home under construction, you may have been surprised to find that its apparent size changed as detail, trim work, and furnishings were added. Many homeowners have been

a

b

Photo 3-1. *Whether a home is new or old, it almost inevitably exists within a community. For this reason, its design should reflect shared community needs as well as the owner's personal needs.*

Photo 3-2. *Gauging a home's size is difficult before it is finished. The apparent size will shift continually during the construction process.*

appalled at the apparently tiny size of their planned homes when the outlines were first staked out on the ground; yet in most cases, these same individuals have been totally satisfied with the size of their completed homes after moving in. We rely on visual clues provided by objects—elements whose size we know, such as chairs, windows, or telephones—to tell us how big the rooms in our homes really are. A bare room or an empty lot does not allow us to judge dimensions accurately.

The need to provide adequate visual clues is common to all homes, but it is especially important in a compact home. By manipulating people's sense of scale, we can make a small home feel much larger than it really is. Just as people involved in conversation maintain a polite distance of several feet between them, so, too, we expect certain distances to exist between our bodies and the interior surfaces of our homes. By varying these distances—raising or lowering ceilings, for example—we create new relationships between ourselves and our homes, with the result that our sense of space is altered.

A good compact-home design should be a mix of large- and small-scale elements: high and low ceilings, large and small windows, and so forth. However, while we can create impressions of larger size through the careful selection of these elements, we must make sure that this selection does not backfire, creating impressions of even smaller size. Several of the strategies discussed in this and other chapters concern the subject of manipulating scale.

Strategies

When designing a home, you should not simply decide on an arrangement of rooms and then select a structure to enclose those rooms. Instead, you should keep your overall goals in mind at all times and let the final form of the house evolve from these goals. Seen in this light, design is not a linear, step-by-step process—it is a cyclical process in which a decorating idea might suggest an attitude about privacy, which in turn might become a primary determinant of room arrangement, which then might change the decorating idea that you began with.

Each home design has a different starting point. If you start with an idea for an exposed post-and-beam structural system, you will find that the choice of this system affects the size of the home's rooms, and this may affect everything from room layout to window placement. If you start with a decision to orient the home toward the south for solar heat, you will find that the spatial arrangements and even the structural systems of the home will be affected profoundly by this orientation. Sometimes a design's starting point is the site, sometimes it is a choice of materials or an attitude about privacy—but whatever it is, the starting point should be constantly tested and challenged by other factors as they are encountered, allowing the design to develop and improve when the new factors are taken into account. You may even find that you'll want to reconsider your basic goals and change your building program as you go along. Programs often change, resulting in superior final designs.

Because designs evolve in this way, you should realize that the six strategies presented in this chapter are by no means mutually exclusive. In fact, it is impossible to pinpoint neatly where one strategy begins and another ends. Several or all of them may appear in a single home—some of the most handsome and successful small homes are skillful mixes of varied room organizations, construction methods, and interior-design ideas.

The strategies should not be taken uncritically. They are abstractions intended to help you clarify your design ideas within the context of your particular goals. Are you committed to full privacy, for example? If so, there may be a limit to how far you can go with the notion of combining space (strategy number three). Are you frustrated by small rooms, or do you have a collection of rowing oars you wish to display? Then shrinking space (strategy number one) probably has limited applicability for you. Each approach has its own advantages and disadvantages, which only you can weigh and evaluate for your own design.

Shrink Space

When Alice drinks the potion in *Through the Looking Glass*, she shrinks. Her legs do not fall off (a rather grisly method of getting smaller); instead, all the parts of her body are reduced proportionately. In a similar way, one of the most obvious approaches to small-home design is simply to take a design for a standard-size home and shrink the dimensions of the rooms.

This approach has considerable appeal. First of all, it is easily understood. What could be easier, you might think, than paring a few feet out of every room and then fitting all the rooms back together? Most traditional home designs have separate rooms for specific activities such as dining, studying, reading, and sleeping. By shrinking a design, you can retain these separate areas, thus preserving privacy for family members in each part of the home. Of the six strategies, shrinking is certainly the one that requires the least change in your living habits.

Sometimes shrinking spaces *is* as simple as it seems. But don't be fooled—you are unlikely to find that all rooms in a design will respond equally well. While some rooms have excess space and thus can afford to shrink a bit, others may already be as trim as they can be while remaining comfortable.

One remarkable example of shrinking as a design strategy can be found in Disneyland, of all places. The planners of that theme park consciously built 7/8-scale replicas of the Main Street buildings they were copying. They hoped (and they were right) that visitors would be made to feel larger than life when they walked through a town that is imperceptibly smaller than life. In Disneyland, at least, the result is quite exciting. A strategy suited for a theme park, though, may well need refinement before we apply it in the real world. Indiscriminately applying Disney-like shrinkage to your favorite large-home design is unlikely to result in a successful small home.

Another approach is to shrink parts of a design, not the whole—or to shrink different parts of a design at different rates. These alternatives provide results that are spatially quite similar, because the number of rooms is kept the same and their relationship to each other is retained. A mathematician would say these variations are "topologically" the same. Figure 3-2 shows the floor plans of two typical ranch homes. In both cases, the bedroom wing is the same size, but in one the living/dining area and the kitchen are two feet narrower, resulting in a smaller overall floor plan. Part of the house has been shrunk and part has remained the same.

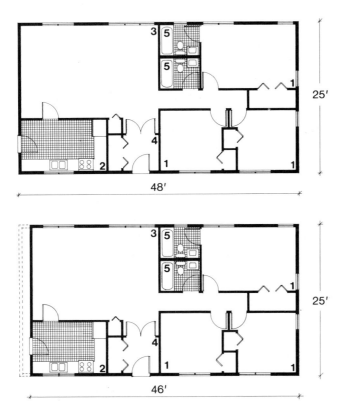

Figure 3-2. *Floor plans of two ranch houses, one of which has a shortened living/dining area and kitchen.*

1. Bedroom
2. Kitchen
3. Living/Dining Area
4. Entry
5. Bathroom

Which rooms you decide to shrink will depend on the uses you want to make of them. If a bedroom will be occupied only at night, you might prefer to shrink it rather than a living area. On the other hand, if you will use a desk in the bedroom during the day or evening, you might not be able to afford a reduction in the room's size. The lifestyle goals in your building program play a crucial role in guiding design decisions such as these.

One shrinkage technique that is proposed frequently is to reduce the height of the walls, thereby lowering the ceiling. This approach can save money as well as space by reducing the amount of material needed to construct the home's walls. In a typical development house, the floor-to-ceiling height is approximately eight feet. Some builders routinely drop ceilings to seven feet six inches, which was the floor-to-ceiling height favored by LeCorbusier in his residential work. Frank Lloyd Wright was renowned for designing extremely low ceiling clearances. In his residential masterpiece, Fallingwater, the ceiling height in some bedrooms is only six feet four inches.

The financial reward for such shrinkage is hard to calculate, because many building components such as plywood, precut wall studs, and gypsum boards are most cheaply and easily available in dimensions intended for eight-foot ceilings. If these products are used to create shorter walls, little actual savings in materials may result. Nevertheless, in a one-of-a-kind design—particularly one that you will be building yourself—the penalty for diverging from common construction practices is not great, so the strategy is often worthwhile.

Shrinking dimensions has been the approach taken by many developers in recent years. For example, they have squeezed inches from the rooms in homes that normally would have been 1,750 square feet, thereby getting them down to 1,550 square feet without requiring a change in house style and without reducing privacy in the homes. Unfortunately, if builders try to shrink a home too far, they have difficulty avoiding changes in the basic plan. Condensing rooms can only go so far before the size of some of the objects in them makes further contraction impossible.

We can define the limits of home shrinkage with a fair degree of precision. The federal government has influenced housing size through the formulation of Minimum Property Standards (MPS) for government-financed housing. (For more information on the MPS and other codes and standards, see Appendix 1.) While the MPS are by no means a definitive source of acceptable design criteria, they represent the preeminent national effort to articulate minimum size standards in housing, and as such they can serve as the basis for our calculations.

Until recently, the MPS included provisions that gave minimum acceptable dimensions for most individual rooms, including bedrooms, kitchens, dining rooms, and living rooms. Size standards also were prescribed for main storage spaces. However, no overall minimum dimensions were prescribed for whole houses. Moreover, the designer or builder was left to determine the necessary floor area for circulation (the corridors and connecting areas between or within rooms) and for other useful, but unspecified, spaces like entry vestibules, family rooms, dens, and auxiliary storage areas.

Based on the MPS, Table 3-1 shows the floor area of a house that contains three separate bedrooms and a distinct kitchen, living room, and dining room. Each room is shown at its smallest permissible size according to the MPS. For parts of the house not covered by the MPS, the table shows estimated minimum dimensions based on existing homes. For example, the table includes circulation space equal to 10 percent of the home's total floor area.

When all the various floor-area requirements are tabulated, Table 3-1 is a reasonable estimate of the smallest "acceptable" home that can be designed with a full complement of discrete rooms. For a three-bedroom home with separate living and dining rooms, this minimum size comes to 968 square feet. A three-bedroom home having a combined kitchen/dining room could be built in 902 square feet. A home with a living room/dining room combination would require approximately 890 square feet, and one with a living room/dining room/kitchen combination could be a mere 866 square feet.

Remember, this estimating procedure breaks down for nontraditional or alternative designs in which space is organized in the ways suggested later in this chapter. It is quite possible to develop house designs with smaller total areas than are indicated in Table 3-1, but you are probably not going to do it by shrinking the room. You will need to apply some of the other strategies for compact-home design.

Besides indicating how far you can go with shrinkage as a strategy, Table 3-1 indicates the need to evaluate trade-offs among amenities. For a three-bedroom house, the table suggests that you can save approximately 85 square feet (plus associated savings in circulation space and structure) if the house has a combined living room/dining room/kitchen rather than separate rooms for these functions. If you are clever in your design, the combined room might provide much of the privacy attainable in separate rooms, but not all. Are the square footage savings worth the loss of privacy? This is the kind of decision you will have to make many times when designing your small home.

| Table 3-1 | **Minimum Three-Bedroom House** | | |

Three-Bedroom House with Separate Rooms		Three Bedrooms with Combined Rooms	
	Minimum Square Feet		*Minimum Square Feet*
Living Room	170	With combined kitchen/dining room: Replace 70-square-foot kitchen and 95-square-foot dining room with 110-square-foot combined room.	
Dining Room	95		
Kitchen	70		
		Subtotal #1	745
		Subtotal #2	820
Bedrooms		Total Exterior Square	
total, three bedrooms	280	Footage	902
Bathroom*	35		
		With combined living room/dining room: Replace 170-square-foot living room and 95-square-foot dining room with 200-square-foot combined room.	
Storage*			
total bedroom closets	18		
coat closet	6		
general storage	55		
Laundry*	20	Subtotal #1	735
Misc. Required Area*	50	Subtotal #2	809
Subtotal #1	800	Total Exterior Square	
		Footage . . . . •. . . .	890
Circulation (corridors, halls, etc.)			
@ 10% of Subtotal #1 . .	80	With combined living room/dining room/kitchen: Replace 170-square-foot living room, 95-square-foot dining room, and 70-square-foot kitchen with 250-square-foot combined room.	
Subtotal #2	880		
Structure (exterior walls, columns, etc.)			
@ 10% of Subtotal #2 . .	88		
		Subtotal #1	715
Total Exterior Square		Subtotal #2	787
Footage	968	Total Exterior Square	
*Estimated		Footage	866

NOTE: Table 3-1 is based on traditional values from the Minimum Property Standards, values that are no longer enforced.

Photo 3-3. *No matter which strategy you use, the goal is to create living spaces that are comfortable and attractive. This open-plan living space clearly reaches that goal.*

Eliminate Space

Most traditional house designs were developed many generations ago. Since then, there have been changes in the way we live and, consequently, in the way we occupy our houses. For example, a formal living room or parlor with its overstuffed furniture and sense of decorum made sense in an era in which we drew clearer distinctions between visitors who were friends (and were allowed the run of the house) and mere acquaintances (who were dealt with formally). Today, for many families, the living room is a vestigial area that is used only sparingly.

It is nice to have a room in which you can display fine furniture and artifacts; a living room is also handy on those few occasions each year when a party or celebration of some sort is planned. But should you equip your new home with a living room just so you can receive such minor benefits? At today's average construction rates, homes cost approximately $50 per square foot to build. If your living room will be 16 feet wide by 22 feet long, or 352 square feet, it will cost $17,600 to build (352 square feet times $50). This is more than many entire homes cost just two or three decades ago.

You could reduce a living room's cost by shrinking its dimensions, but a better technique in many instances is to eliminate the room entirely. Indeed, many areas in typical American homes are good candidates for elimination. Consider basements and attics, for example. Too often, these areas are not put to any real use. Old stockpiles of *National Geographic* magazines are only so interesting, after all. If we cannot find better uses for basements and attics, maybe they should not exist. Historically, a major reason they were included in homes was to provide space for furnaces, boilers, and other mechanical equipment—a need that in many cases can no longer be justified, as we will see in Chapter 4. In some parts of the country where basements were once common, more and more homes now are being built with slab-on-grade foundations or crawlspaces to lower the homes' construction costs.

Dining rooms often are eliminated from contemporary homes. Eating then takes place in a combined room that serves the functions of both living room and dining room. Or you could go even further. The owners of the single-story, medium-size home shown in Figure 3-3 decided to do without a dining area of any kind. Not only does their home have no dining room, but it does not even have a location for formal dining. This solution would not suit everyone, but it met this family's needs.

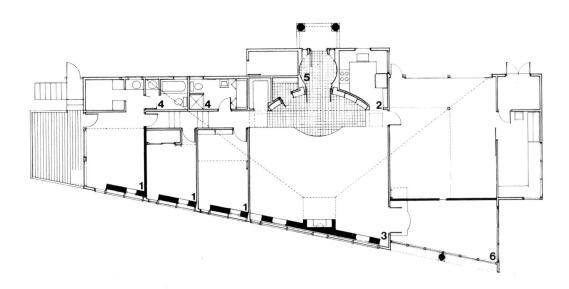

Figure 3-3. *This design dispenses with a separate area for eating. Dining space has been traded for a formal entry sequence and living room. (Design by Kelbaugh & Lee)*

1. Bedroom
2. Kitchen
3. Living Room
4. Bathroom
5. Entry
6. Solarium
7. Garage

Sometimes eliminating bedrooms can be sensible. For some families, a small home may only be a "starter" home—a first step toward what they hope will be grander accommodations. These families are apt to be young, with few if any children, and they may not require multiple bedrooms. Thus, a family that otherwise might have built a three-bedroom home might opt for two bedrooms. There is now a strong market for two-bedroom homes, so these families won't have trouble selling when they decide to move up to a larger home.

Besides eliminating whole rooms, we also can eliminate parts of rooms. One of the best approaches is to reduce circulation space: areas in which people move from one part of the house to another. If your home is conventionally designed, a corridor connects its individual rooms—it is a major circulation route within the home. What is a little more difficult to understand is that your home may also contain circulation space that has no obvious physical boundaries. A large combined living room/den, for instance, may contain two "zones": an entertainment zone oriented toward a television set and a quiet sitting zone oriented toward a fireplace. The area between these zones serves little purpose except to provide access from one zone to another.

Any compact design should attempt to keep such circulation spaces to an absolute minimum. This can be difficult to do, because these areas are hard to spot. Nevertheless, you should search for them as well as for any other elusive, wasted spaces. When designing a house, you can conduct this search by continually evaluating each part of the design, asking yourself the disarmingly simple question, "What kinds of activities will occur here?" If you conclude that any area lacks a clear function, eliminate it.

While hunting for wasted floor areas—horizontal space—don't forget that vertical wasted space should be eliminated as well. For example, space is often wasted under eaves, next to sloped walls, or in the upper reaches of attached greenhouses that have been contorted to hold solar collectors. Homes exist in three dimensions, and saving space calls for the ability to think in all three of them.

The idea of the "starter" home, mentioned earlier, suggests an exciting possibility for which the technique of elimination is ideally suited. You can design your home with expansion in mind: Eliminate rooms from the design now, but plan the house so that at some later time these rooms can be simply and efficiently added. If you are thoughtful about what rooms to eliminate and where these rooms should be located eventually, you can prepare for additions that will be both functional and beautiful.

It is not unusual to find early American homes with multiple additions that were appended over several generations. For instance, Mount Vernon, the birthplace of George Washington, grew in successive steps from a humble home to a stately mansion. A modern variation on this theme is embodied in several prefabricated building systems now being developed. They hold out the possibility that houses can expand as families grow and then shrink when the children leave home. For example, families could add "bedroom modules" to their homes as needed, then later detach

and resell these modules. Some analysts predict a thriving market for secondhand modules in the not-too-distant future.

Planning ahead for additions makes sense for other reasons besides the fluctuating size of a family. In some subdivisions, restrictive codes and ordinances can make constructing routine additions difficult. Getting a moderately large design approved and then building only part of it may be one strategy to counteract this situation. Check first to make sure this is a possibility in the location where you will be building.

There are some drawbacks to the technique of eliminating rooms now and adding them later. Sometimes there is a penalty paid in the inefficient use of space over the short term. An otherwise unnecessary corridor intended to lead to a future wing might creep into a design, for example, or circulation patterns in the starter home might become tortuous. Also, there's the danger that for the sake of economy, you will eliminate spaces that are essential, such as necessary storage space. Finally, there's the danger that your intentions or finances will take an unexpected turn, preventing you from building the contemplated additions. In this case, the "starter" home will be the final structure. If the layout of

Photo 3-4. *A home can start small and, through careful additions, grow to meet a family's changing needs. A case in point: Mount Vernon.*

the starter was less than optimal, you will have to live with its shortcomings as long as you reside there.

You should take great care in deciding what spaces are unnecessary. A space should not be eliminated just because it will not contain any objects, for example. On the contrary, empty space can be visually and psychologically important in a small home; it can make the difference between a feeling of confinement and a sense of comfort. So do not go willy-nilly through your design, eliminating space from rooms without first considering the damage you may be doing. After asking what activities will occur in an area, ask yourself an additional question: "What else will this area offer?" If it will contribute something valuable, such as a connection to the outdoors or needed breathing space, do your best to keep it.

Despite these cautionary notes, eliminating space can be a highly effective strategy. In a well-insulated solar home, for example, if you eliminate 20 square feet of floor area, you can reduce your construction costs by an amount equal to the fuel savings you would receive from operating a 60-square-foot solar heating system for 20 years. In temperate climates, the ratio is roughly three to one: Saving 1 square foot of floor area is equivalent to the financial benefits of 3 square feet of solar-collector area. Clearly, then, eliminating space can make great financial sense.

Combine Space

Since World War II, there has been a trend in architecture toward the use of the "open plan." In an open-plan house, separate rooms are combined into large, multipurpose floor areas. These combined rooms contain activity zones that are differentiated from each other not by partition walls but by the placement of furniture, changes in floor level, differences in lighting, or other space-defining elements (see the discussion of "implied rooms" in Chapter 5).

Open planning can mean transforming a living room and a den into a "great room" or amalgamating a kitchen and a dining room into a "family kitchen." Families who live in open-plan homes no longer expect various activities—eating, reading, watching television, and so forth—to occur in separate rooms. Why are we more willing than our forefathers to dispense with discrete, single-purpose rooms? Certainly, a less refined sense of social hierarchy and etiquette—and, therefore, a less strict requirement for privacy—is part of the answer. Few families now have servants who need separate facilities, nor do we treat our children as second-class citizens, isolating them in out-of-the-way rooms. Even more important, members of both sexes have become centrally involved in all aspects of family life. Parents are no longer content to be isolated in a remote workroom or kitchen, separated from the mainstream of the family's comings and goings.

In addition to these social factors, certain technical factors have contributed to the change. For example, it is no longer necessary to have fireplaces in every room: Heating equipment now can be located centrally, thus freeing the floor plan of the house. Structural advances also have played a part. The ready availability and low cost of long-spanning wood trusses have liberated the floor plans of many homes. With interior partitions no longer required structurally, walls between rooms can be removed.

The space-saving advantages of combining rooms can be great. When this strategy is used, the whole is equal to less than the sum of its parts: A combined room is smaller than the total size of the rooms it replaces. Yet reduced size does not cause a combined room to be cramped. Indeed, family members often can devote more space to an activity in a combined room than they could have in separate rooms. This is true because, generally speaking, one activity predominates over others at any given time. For example, during mealtime, eating is the predominant activity, so a combined living/dining room can be devoted entirely to this activity. Later, when the meal is over and the table is cleared, the entire room can be used for other activities, providing a sense of spaciousness that otherwise would have been impossible.

The disadvantages of combining rooms are equally obvious. One activity normally predominates over others—but not always. On occasion, various members of the family will want to perform different activities at the same time, and it can be difficult to simultaneously accommodate all the activities for which a combined room was intended. You can't have a meal in the dining area if other family members are using that space as part of the living area. In this sense, combined rooms can cause conflicts. The lack

a

b

Photo 3-5. *This prototype "New American Home" was designed and built for the National Council of the Housing Industry. a. Compact and affordable, its front facade is enlarged by "wing walls" that provide a car portal on one side and a privacy wall for the garden on the other side. b. The home has an open-plan first floor, with no full-height partition walls except around the bathroom. Note the high ceiling and exposed beams. (Design by Booth/Hansen & Associates)*

of privacy can also be annoying. Privacy, we should remember, includes not only visual privacy but also acoustical privacy ("Cut down the noise, I'm trying to hear the radio!"), olfactory privacy ("Did someone leave coffee grounds in the sink?"), and thermal

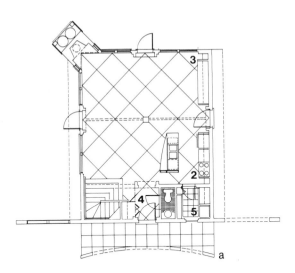

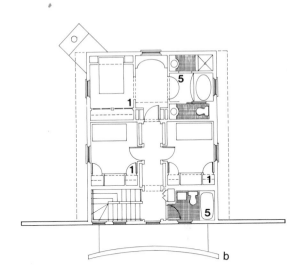

privacy ("Why did you pick the warmest day of the year to cook a roast?").

Another consideration is that an open plan generally provides less wall area against which to place furniture. This tends to reduce the amount of furniture you will need to furnish your home. Some may see this as a problem while others will applaud the savings.

The pros and cons of combined rooms are cleverly illustrated in a tongue-in-cheek proposal by architect Dan Scully. In his "Stayin' Alive" house (see Figure 3-5), specialized work areas are lined up along the sides of what amounts to a large live-in garage. The garage's multiuse room changes character as the inhabitants' activities change during the day. This design, though humorous, embodies a significant point. Like the traditional Japanese house discussed in Chapter 2, the "Stayin' Alive" house segregates those few activities for which a specific location is required—such as washing, waste removal, or cooking—and leaves the rest of the floor plan open, with the interior space organized by factors other than partition walls. In the "Stayin' Alive" house, the controlling factor is the automobile; in the Japanese house, it is the tatami mat.

Figure 3-4. *a. First floor of the New American Home. Note the open plan. Wing walls extend from the sides of the house. b. The second floor has three bedrooms and two baths. The master bedroom suite is organized around a short central corridor. (Courtesy of Booth/Hansen & Associates)*

1. Bedroom
2. Kitchen
3. Living/Dining Area
4. Entry
5. Bathroom

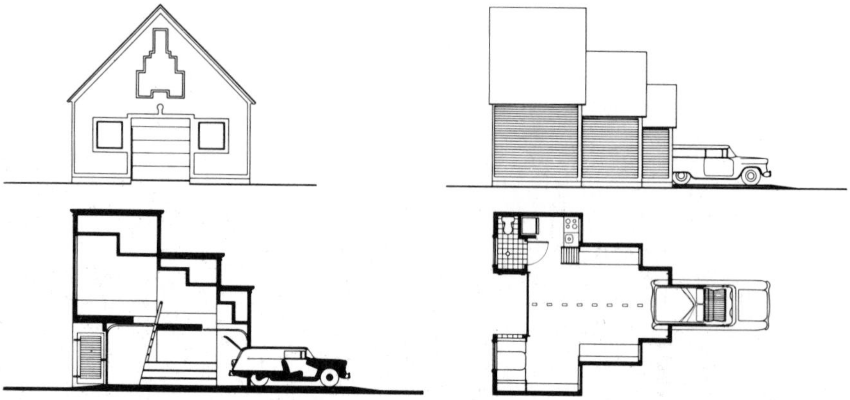

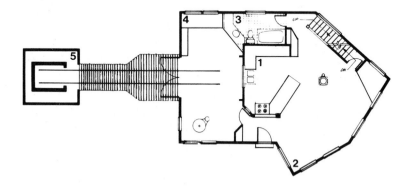

Figure 3-5. *Dan Scully's "Stayin' Alive" house, which the architect calls a "clapboard-covered pit stop." The car has a bed in its back; it plugs into the house and becomes a bedroom. (Design and rendering by Daniel V. Scully, Architect)*

Living and working environments can be combined to their mutual benefit. In the Glazebrook House, designed by architect Turner Brooks for a professional potter, the requirements of a working studio are combined with normal living areas in a single structure. Because of the combined bathrooms, storage areas, cleaning facilities, and circulation areas, little space is wasted. The result is a unique mix of particularized spaces and special details clothed in an almost traditional exterior.

Figure 3-6. *First floor of the Glazebrook House. Bedrooms are located upstairs. (Design by Turner Brooks)*

1. Kitchen
2. Living Area
3. Bathroom
4. Studio
5. Kiln

Combining activities can make sense not only spatially but thermally as well. In many climates, an attached solar greenhouse is an excellent choice for an entry vestibule. Plants can tolerate cooler temperatures than people—generally down to 40°F. This allows the greenhouse to be kept at lower temperatures than the

house. When the greenhouse's exterior door is opened, no warm air from the house is lost; only the cooler greenhouse air escapes, so less energy is wasted.

In some cases, a greenhouse can serve not only as an entry vestibule but also as a home's primary circulation path. In the Dekhan Home (see Photo 3-7 and Figure 3-7), the living room, dining room, kitchen, and bedrooms are all connected by a single greenhouse that performs triple duty: It is an entry vestibule, a corridor, and a growing facility. The greenhouse was not conceived as an after-the-fact addition to an otherwise completed house; rather, it was an essential element in the overall design.

Two rooms with identical functions can sometimes be combined effectively. Figure 3-8a shows two seemingly compact children's bedrooms, each measuring 7 feet 6 inches by 10 feet, for a floor area of 75 square feet per room or a combined total of 150 square feet. The rooms have beds (3 feet by 6 feet), closets (2 feet by 4 feet), bureaus (18 inches by 3 feet), and little else.

Photo 3-6. *The Glazebrook House epitomizes the concept of combining space: It is both a home and a ceramics studio. A track connects the home to a backyard kiln. (Design by Turner Brooks)*

Figure 3-7. *The Dekhan House with the roof removed to reveal the plan of the first floor. A sunspace connects the living room and kitchen to the bedrooms. (Design and rendering by Kelbaugh & Lee)*

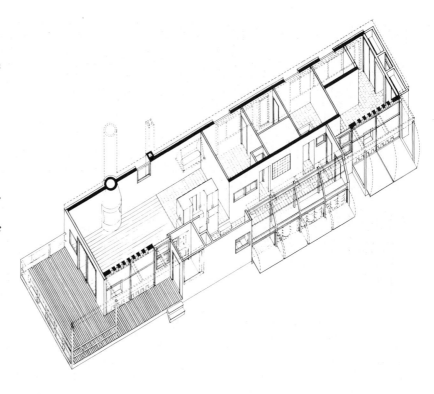

Figure 3-8. *Two bedrooms—each with a bed, closet, and dresser—can be combined. a. The separate bedrooms are 75 square feet each, for a total 150 square feet. b. The combined bedroom—having the same furniture—is smaller (130 square feet) but feels more spacious.*

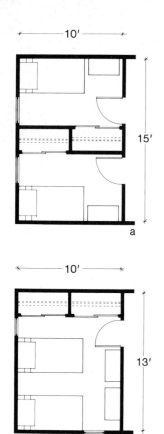

There is barely space between the furniture to move around and open the door.

When the two bedrooms are combined into a single room (see Figure 3-8b), the overall dimensions are 10 feet by 13 feet, for a total of 130 square feet—20 square feet less than the combined total for the two smaller bedrooms. At a construction cost of $50 per square foot, this represents a $1,000 savings (20 square feet multiplied by $50). The new combined bedroom has the same furnishings as the separate bedrooms: two beds, two closets, two bureaus, each the same size as before. Why, then, is the combined room smaller? The explanation is that we have eliminated underused square footage between pieces of furniture, thus making the area more space efficient. There is another benefit as well. The proportions of the combined room are friendlier. The single bedrooms would afford more privacy, but they also would feel closet-like:

a

b

Photo 3-7. *a. At this home, the greenhouse is an entry vestibule, a solar collector, an area for growing plants, and the home's primary circulation space. b. Virtually every room opens to the greenhouse. This is a view of the kitchen. (Design by Kelbaugh & Lee)*

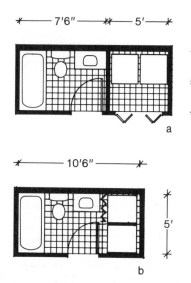

Figure 3-9. *Another example of combining space. a. A bathroom and a separate laundry area containing a washer and dryer have a total area of 62½ square feet. b. When the spaces are combined, the square footage drops to 52½.*

With standard 8-foot ceilings, they would be higher than they were wide. By comparison, the combined bedroom has a width of 10 feet, which would feel far more comfortable.

This example underscores the importance of minuscule space reductions. In the combined bedroom, it is obvious that unnecessary circulation areas were eliminated. But somewhat less obvious is the fact that an excess structural element also was eliminated: the wall between the separate bedrooms. By eliminating one wall, you can save approximately four inches of wall thickness. This doesn't seem like much, but every square inch helps. The accumulated total of such small savings can translate into large reductions in construction costs.

You should carefully create activity zones within combined rooms, encouraging activities to take place in specified locations. A recent survey by the National Association of Home Builders (NAHB) asked homeowners which of four kitchen/great room arrangements they preferred (see Figure 3-10). The arrangement shown in Figure 3-10a won hands down: It has a clear dining area and a clear kitchen area within a combined kitchen/great room. By contrast, note that Figures 3-10b and 3-10c show arrangements in which kitchens and dining areas are distinctly separated from each other, and Figure 3-10d shows an arrangement in which the two areas are totally open to each other. This result indicates that most people like combined rooms, but they also want these rooms to have clearly defined activity zones.

Figure 3-10. *Asked to select the kitchen/great room layout they prefer, 45 percent of the people surveyed chose visually open rooms with a divider (a), 24 percent preferred the rooms side by side with a full dividing wall (b), 22 percent opted for completely separate areas (c), and the remainder favored completely open kitchen/great room arrangements (d). (Source: National Association of Home Builders)*

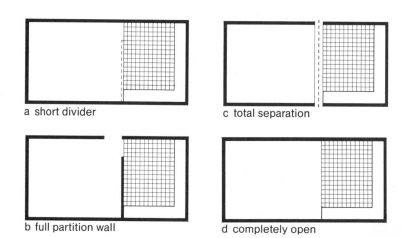

a short divider

c total separation

b full partition wall

d completely open

Photo 3-8. *This small room has been converted into a combination bedroom/studio by using a piece of custom-built furniture that includes sleeping, working, and storage space. (Design by Jennifer Clements & Robert Herman Associates)*

Some examples of combined rooms are particularly clever. In a San Francisco apartment, all the functions of living and working had to be incorporated into a single room. This was accomplished largely through the use of a single piece of furniture that includes a sleeping area, two desks, and storage areas (see Photo 3-8 and Figure 3-11). The desks receive light from a large bay window, and they buffer the bed from street noise while creating a small dressing area away from the window. We will return to the topic of multifunction furniture in Chapter 5.

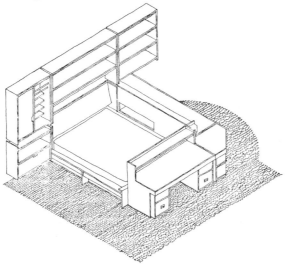

Figure 3-11. *The bed/desk/storage unit. The bed is enclosed on two sides, so it is buffered from street noise. (Design and rendering by Jennifer Clements & Robert Herman Associates)*

Find Space

What is "found" space? You may have trouble imagining yourself walking along a street, looking down, and finding space the same way you might find a quarter or a fountain pen. In a sense, however, this is precisely what found space is all about. You should "walk around" your design and look for space that can be used to better advantage.

Looking for found space is difficult, but the process can be highly rewarding. Found space is exciting: It is often unusually shaped and surprisingly positioned. It can be out in the open or hidden within the dimensions of a wall. It can be any size—maybe only a few inches wide and so subtle that it is beyond notice, or several yards wide and so obvious that it cannot be overlooked. In even the leanest design, you may discover pockets of wasted space, waiting to be rescued.

The best time to find space is before a house is built—then you can either eliminate it (strategy number two) or alter the design to make the found space productive. But you also can continue the search for found space after the walls are up and the roof is on. Indeed, even after you have moved in, you may still find usable areas that had escaped your notice previously. A few pages back, we spoke of eliminating attics and basements. This is often a good strategy for a home that is still being designed. But in an existing home, you can't very well eliminate areas that already have been built. So, instead, "find" these areas and turn them to good account. Consider attics, for example. In the past, most pitched roofs were constructed with individual wooden rafters framed up to a common ridge beam. The open attics that resulted generally were used for storage. Those of you who live in a home with such an attic know it is a mysterious place full of dusty memories and forgotten treasures. But it's a place with a future as well as a past. You may be able to construct entire rooms within it.

Newer attics tend to have less usable space, because today's builders frequently use roof trusses: The attics beneath such roofs are webs of slender truss members. Still, although trusses limit an attic's utility as found space, they do not abolish it altogether. Space often can be found between trusses for skylights or "roof monitors" that increase the spaciousness of the room below, or space can be found at the eaves for solar water heaters. Small storage areas also can be fashioned between roof trusses. However, in today's homes, roof insulation generally is located in the ceiling cavities formed by the bottom chords of the trusses. This means the attic will be chilly in the winter and warm in the summer—suitable only for storing items that can accept wide temperature fluctuations without damage.

If you decide not to eliminate the attic from the home you're designing, consider making the attic large enough for later use: In effect, you could intentionally build found space into your design. The Triple A House in Chapter 7 is specifically designed to allow future expansion into the attic. When it is first built, a Triple A functions as a one-story, one-bedroom starter home. However, an ample, wide-open attic is left unfinished, to be completed as the family grows. A wide variety of options is available for finishing the attic: Zero-, one-, two-, and three-bedroom schemes are all possible. The trick in this sort of expandable home is to make the design work both before and after the home is expanded.

Another place to look for found space is in the vertical dimension of the rooms on the main floors; this means looking up and down. In most homes, the floor-to-ceiling height is the same throughout the house. Usually, a house has a single ceiling height because this simplifies construction. But if you think about it, why should a narrow corridor, a sprawling living room, and a bedroom closet all have ceilings of the same height?

Is there a corridor in your home whose height is excessive, given its narrow width? Perhaps the topmost region of this corridor can be converted to storage space. Is the space under and over your bed put to good use? Perhaps a platform bed with roll-out drawers is the answer. Or consider whether storage is a possibility above the bed—perhaps you don't really need an eight-foot ceiling above a surface on which you are always horizontal. Do the cabinets in your kitchen reach all the way to the ceiling? If not, maybe some extra storage area could be created above them. The opportunities for finding unused space—and turning it to good use—are endless.

Stair landings—particularly those on the top floor of a multi-story house—often use space inefficiently. Don't forget to take advantage of the "dead space" above stairwells by building out over flights of stairs (making sure you leave adequate headroom,

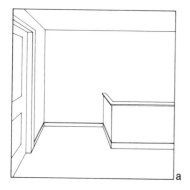

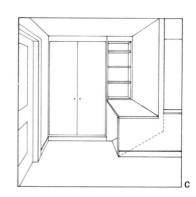

Figure 3-12. *Once adequate headroom has been provided, the unused space above a flight of stairs can be put to good use. For example, stair landings can be transformed from an unused corridor (a) to closet and shelf space (b) or to closet/desk/bookshelf space (c).*

Photo 3-9. *An example of making good use of found space: "The world's strongest spice rack" has been formed into the concrete Trombe wall at architect Douglas Kelbaugh's home.*

of course). Figure 3-12 shows several options for converting the found space at stair landings into living or storage areas.

Found space often can be discovered inside partition walls or between the ceiling of one story and the floor of the next story. In a low room, for instance, removing the ceiling material to expose the ceiling beams can make the room feel more spacious. Even very small patches of found space should be rescued. In a kitchen, a spice rack might be carved out of the space between wall studs. This location is perfect for such a purpose, because spice jars are small and should be kept as handy as possible for the harried chef. A little extra construction work, opening the area between the studs, is justified to provide storage exactly where it is required. The same approach can be taken to create a spice rack within the dimension of a poured-in-place concrete Trombe wall (see Photo 3-9).

Perhaps you can find space for built-in appliances or other electrical devices. For example, recessed light fixtures have become quite popular as space savers, particularly in homes that make use of lower-than-standard ceiling heights. A recessed light can eliminate space-consuming table lamps or hanging fixtures. However, you pay a price in lost flexibility—it is difficult to relocate recessed fixtures once they are installed, so take care to position them in the most effective locations. You also need to take special care to minimize heat loss through recessed fixtures. A light buried in a ceiling is, in effect, a hole in the ceiling—a hole through which indoor heat will try to escape.

Much of this section has focused on using found space for storage. The reason is that providing sufficient storage can be a real problem in a compact home where the total amount of space is minimized. Found space can alleviate the problem, especially if you match storage needs with space availability, storing flat things in flat spaces, tall things in tall spaces, and so on. You can even store clear things in clear spaces, in which case your found space can be right out in the open. For example, in a tight kitchen where cabinet space is at a premium, transparent glassware can be hung in front of a kitchen window, allowing sunlight to penetrate and brighten the room. The trade-off here is between a clear view and extra storage.

Don't go overboard in an attempt to cram storage into every empty cubic foot in the house. As we have already noted, sometimes the best use for space is no use at all. By leaving some spaces open, you can prevent the house from being too cramped. An

Photo 3-10. *A window can double as storage space. If you hang transparent items in front of the window, light can still pass through. (Design by Bruce Gordon, Shelter Associates)*

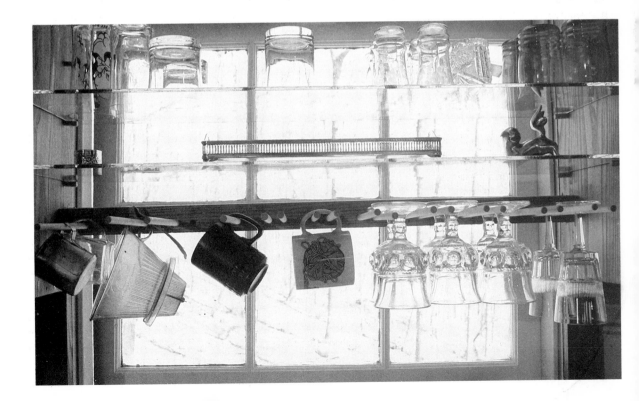

Photo 3-11. *A steel floor grate (visible to the right of the hanging plant) lets light filter down from the upstairs windows, increasing the sense of spaciousness on the first floor. (Design by John Randolph Design + Construction)*

easy application of this idea is opening up an enclosed stairwell to admit light from above.

You also can look for found space outside. For example, outdoor storage sheds can free interior rooms for more important uses (see Photo 3-12). Roofs can be used to support mechanical equipment such as flat-plate solar collectors or the exterior units of a split heat pump. Similarly, large-diameter woodstove flues can be snaked outside the home to free floor area on upper stories. True, waste heat from such a flue will no longer help to warm the home, but compact homes generally have lower heating requirements, so this should not be a problem.

Why, you may wonder, don't homebuilders generally make more efficient use of space in the homes they erect? The answer is that a considerable amount of labor may be required to piece the gypsum board, run the wiring, insulate the perimeter, and otherwise "finish off" hard-to-get-at areas. For some people (particularly

Photo 3-12. *Outdoor storage structures save indoor space. Here, a shed built into a fence has a roof sloped to receive a future solar water heater. (Design by Douglas Kelbaugh)*

builders who are not the homeowners-to-be), the effort is not worth the relatively small amount of useful space that results. But in a modest mansion, finding and using such space is an opportunity that should not be overlooked.

Extend Space

Why do even the most friendly, petless neighbors build fences around their yards? There are, of course, many explanations, but one of the most likely is that the neighbors are responding to a basic impulse to stake out their domains. By constructing fences, they enclose their yards, gardens, and porches, creating "exterior rooms." These rooms are as much a part of their homes as the kitchens or the master bedrooms are. Thus, fences allow us to extend the boundaries of our homes without making the homes physically larger.

You can extend your home by a variety of means. One of the most familiar is the construction of an actual, spatial extension, such as the fence in the example above or a dormer that enlarges an attic. Somewhat less obvious is the technique of visual extension, whereby views of distant scenes relieve the severity of tight rooms. For instance, a picture window that allows views into the landscape beyond can make the wall of a living room "dissolve" so that the room feels larger.

Physical Extensions

So much of this book is about removing square feet from houses, you might get the impression that compressing space is always a good idea. Actually, however, adding modest amounts of square footage (or even square "inchage") to your rooms can pay big dividends if these additions are precisely located. Additions need not be large; they can be as small as a window greenhouse; they can even be purely symbolic, such as an entry gateway or a manicured garden orchard. Adding modestly to an otherwise compact house can provide welcome visual relief and excitement.

For many reasons, it makes good sense to keep your home's "footprint"—that is, the foundation area—to a minimum. But sometimes the compact shape that rises out of a tight foundation is too restrictive. By cantilevering a bay window, attaching an entry porch, or creating a breakfast alcove, you can extend one of your rooms without enlarging the foundation of the entire house. A simple addition like a double-bay window in a breakfast alcove can feel like an entire new room, when in fact it is only a modest extension on the edge of an existing room.

(continued on page 76)

a

b

Photo 3-13. *a. This home was constructed in the corner of an old barn foundation: The remnants of the foundation extend the home's boundaries into the landscape.*
b. Large windows provide a view of the old foundation and the trees beyond. (Design by Bohlin Powell Larkin Cywinski)

Photo 3-14. *A corner bay window constructed of stock window units transforms a kitchen wall into a nook for dining. The chair rail trim turns the corner and becomes a backrest for window seats. (Design by John Randolph Design + Construction)*

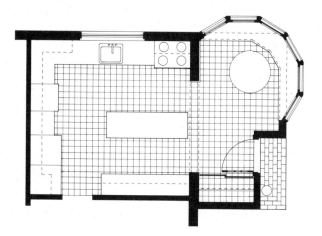

Figure 3-13. *The bay-window dining alcove is conveniently located beside the kitchen.*

Photo 3-15. *Architect Stephen Sparn added this 100-square-foot solar greenhouse to a 900-square-foot home. This minor addition greatly enhanced the home's attractiveness and comfort. Also note the outdoor-living features (patio, deck) that effectively extend the home's usable space beyond the exterior walls.*

You should not take this principle too far in cold climates. Too much exposed exterior surface can make a home's heating bills go up. Nevertheless, high insulation standards and good construction practices can compensate for many thermal sins. Besides, the goal of saving energy should not dictate all your design decisions; providing for the other needs listed in your building program is equally important.

Enclosed additions are just one type of physical extension to consider. Roof decks, porches, and even sleeping balconies are good methods of adding living space outside the home's main structure. As a young architecture student, I was surprised to discover the endless outdoor living possibilities in a housing project my classmates and I were designing for Ahmadabad, India. Limited to a stingy 250 square feet per house—for families of seven—we quickly learned the advantages of using roofs, gardens, and decks to expand cramped living quarters.

Even more subtle are house extensions in which fragments of the structure reach out and claim usable space that is neither in nor on the house. An entry gateway can reach out as a welcoming hand in the landscape. A garden trellis can provide a cool, sheltering

Photo 3-16. *A welcoming entryway connected to the garage makes this long, narrow manufactured home seem larger. The home actually has just 924 square feet of living space, including three bedrooms and two baths.*

retreat for relaxation and recreation. By giving spatial definition to a volume of exterior space, you take possession of it and enlarge its apparent size. Almost everyone agrees, for example, that landscaping a yard makes it feel bigger. What is not so well understood is that by effectively enlarging the yard in this way, you make the house itself seem larger. Even an extremely modest manufactured house (see Photo 3-16) takes on a much greater presence when a ceremonial entrance gate is added beside the garage. The gate creates the wall of an outside room where a party may be held, a dinner barbecued, laundry dried, or a body sunbathed. It is clearly "of" the house without being in it.

By comparison, the front yards of typical suburban developments leak to the streets: They are almost always blank no-man's lands between the public streets and the private homes; they do not invite use. Landscaping elements—lines of trees, hedges, changes in level, entry gates—are vital ingredients for differentiating the public from the private realm, ensuring that outside space will be used actively.

The importance of outside space in making the modest mansion more livable is generally understood by architects. Today, many of the most creative site-planning ideas in new developments are aimed at salvaging adequate amounts of outdoor space for the home while allowing lot size to shrink. Smaller lots can mean more affordable homes. Among other solutions, zero-lot-line housing—in which homes stand on the property line at one side of the property to open up a reasonably sized yard at the other side—is becoming increasingly popular.

Visual Extensions

Imagine making a phone call in a telephone booth that is wrapped in aluminum siding from top to bottom. It would feel claustrophobic; you would suddenly notice how small the phone booth really is. But when you occupy a regulation glass-walled booth on a street corner, you are hardly aware of its narrow dimensions. You feel as though you were still outside, participating in the passing scene. You are comfortable inside a very small space.

For the same reason, the placement and size of windows is crucial in home design. You should consider windows to be visual relief valves for compact quarters. If a glazed area is large enough,

Photo 3-17. *Large windows dissolve the barrier of a home's exterior wall: Note how the ceiling plane continues from the interior to the exterior, providing visual extension into the space outdoors. (Design by Leslie Armstrong)*

the wall in which it is set tends to disappear. For example, in a master bedroom (see Photo 3-17), a generous band of windows can frame a view of the natural landscape: The wall of the bedroom is, in effect, extended to the line of trees.

Different windows have different primary functions. Some provide views, others provide light, ventilation, heat, or simple visual relief in an otherwise unbroken wall surface. Yet from the exterior, these windows might all appear the same. You should learn to distinguish the advantages of various window placements. A window designed to provide general illumination is best placed high on a wall, for example, while a window designed to give a view of the outdoors should be placed at eye level.

Consider using unusual window shapes and locations to increase the effectiveness of each window. Can a window serve more than one function at once? Absolutely. In fact, the more the better. Do not be content to let your windows work only as solar collectors or light sources—make them contribute spatially to your rooms as well. Each element in a small-home design should be ambidextrous, performing several tasks at once.

In the most exciting houses, windows and doors invariably are special events. For example, a large sliding glass door can provide easy access to an exterior deck. Nature is drawn in and people are invited out as the glass nullifies the boundary between inside and outside. Indoor functions—dining, recreation, even sleeping—easily drift over to the outside. It all seems so effortless. For the residents, indeed it should be effortless. But for the designer, the job is demanding. Careful detailing of the door edges is required to reinforce the illusion of transparency. No reveals, bulkheads, or jambs should interfere, calling attention to the existence of the wall. Further, the planes in the room should draw the eye to—and through—the glass. For example, the room's floorboards might run at right angles to the glass door, so the grooves between the boards point toward the door, directing attention toward the outdoors. If the deck boards outside run in the same direction, the effect will be reinforced: The floor and deck will become, in effect, a single surface, extending the interior of the house to the exterior.

A window does not have to give a view of the landscape to be effective. It does not even have to be set in a wall. A skylight that allows natural light to enter but provides no view of forests or flowers is still quite valuable. Daylight, with its daily and seasonal variations, relieves the closeness of small spaces. The clouds become the ceiling. By allowing light to pierce a home in unexpected places, we expand the visual perimeter of the home. Similarly, a clerestory over a stairway leads you upward; a skylight over a counter extends the apparent size of a small kitchen; a shaft of daylight makes a loft come alive or gives visual warmth to a bathroom.

We will return to the important subject of window placement in both Chapters 4 and 5.

Photo 3-18. *a. A senior citizens' development has a centrally located community building that serves as a neighborhood gathering place and an apartment for visitors. b. Each home has a greenhouse, Trombe wall, and skylight. (Design by Kelbaugh & Lee)*

a

b

Share Space

As our homes get smaller, we can learn a great deal by investigating communities where homes have been compact for a long time. Throughout much of Europe, a tradition of smaller homes has generated creative responses to compact living, responses that often are based on a strategy of sharing facilities. Travelers soon realize that even the smallest village in France or Italy has a guest house to accommodate the visitors of town citizens whose own homes are too compact to include a guest room. Similarly, public restaurants and bars in the same villages serve as shared living rooms for parties and celebrations of all sorts. Necessity has fostered spatial cooperation. The whole fabric and organization of the community is affected by house size.

The concept of the single-family detached home is so deeply ingrained in the American psyche that only a few tentative steps have been made toward providing shared facilities in this country. Most suburban and rural Americans live in homes that are spread fairly far apart and therefore are not easily adapted to sharing space. There is a trend in new housing, however, toward attached housing developments and planned unit developments (PUDs), a trend that suggests new possibilities. You may be able to incorporate some of these possibilities in your own planning, particularly if you design a home for more than one family or if your home will be part of a community in which other residents are amenable to the concept of shared facilities.

In a PUD, homeowners share ownership of certain property in cooperative or condominium arrangements. Often, the most important shared resource is outdoor space, which is reserved for common use and might include recreational facilities like a swimming pool or tennis court. Some attached housing developments or PUDs even have dining rooms or party rooms for hire. In other cases, a simple community building may house sufficient space to hold "block" parties or other affairs. This process frequently allows higher-density—and, presumably, more affordable—housing than would be possible if the building lots were individually owned and no facilities were held in common.

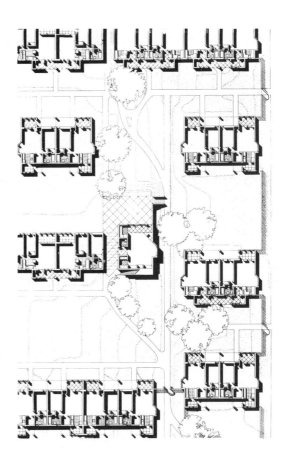

Figure 3-14. *Portion of the site plan for the senior citizens' community. The community building anchors the center of the site, alongside a walkway that links the various clusters of houses. (Design and rendering by Kelbaugh & Lee)*

Shared outdoor space in the form of community gardens has become quite popular in some urban areas of the country. Public land—or unoccupied private land—is carved up into small plots for use by neighborhood residents who otherwise have no opportunity to cultivate a garden. Often, shared responsibility for compost piles, water sources, and security helps create a sense of community among the gardeners. The result is fresh vegetables, a rejuvenated urban landscape, new friends, and neighborly activity that makes tight urban homes more acceptable.

Most of the smallest new housing being constructed in this country, particularly on the East and West coasts, is taking the form of condominiums where dwelling units are constructed in either high-rise or walk-up multifamily buildings. In California, particularly, 500- to 600-square-foot studio homes and one-bedroom homes are gaining popularity as the cost of larger housing skyrockets. These homes share structural elements with their neighbors: party walls, floors, ceilings, or entrance ways. The square-foot construction cost of the homes is commensurately lower.

In the future, new technologies may encourage additional forms of sharing. For some locations, neighborhood power plants already make sense, and in the future we may see groups of homes agree to share local cogeneration plants (which provide heat as well as electricity) or banks of photovoltaic cells (which generate electricity directly from sunlight). Thus, compact homes will be able to become even more compact, as mechanical systems are moved from the homes to community facilities.

While some of these changes may seem remote, certain shared facilities already have become institutionalized around the country. Have you noticed the number of miniwarehouses that are mushrooming on sites close to major suburbs across the country? As our homes get smaller, providing less storage space, entrepreneurs have responded with these community storage facilities, approximately 6,000 of which now exist across the country.

Admittedly, most of the miniwarehouses that have been built to date are eyesores. Still, they could serve as useful prototypes, inspiring other—and, we would hope, more attractive—shared outbuildings. For example, two or more families that are planning to build adjacent compact homes could agree to construct shared garages, storage sheds, or gardening sheds. This would permit a reduction in both the size and cost of their homes. A two-car garage shared by two families can be more compact and cheaper to build than a pair of one-car, one-family garages. And the potential savings grow significantly as the shared facilities expand to accommodate more and more families. A community parking facility can be appreciably cheaper, on a family-by-family basis, than a series of individual or small shared garages.

Besides facilities, the residents of many attached homes share something more intangible: a common idiom or means of expression. In many housing developments, efforts are consciously made to create an image of greater size by designing two or more dwelling units to look like one large dwelling. Each home is altered slightly to contribute to an overall image for the building group. Because of this image, each home can be more compact than otherwise might have been acceptable. After all, house size often is selected not only because of a practical need, but also because of the desire to express an acceptable status within the community.

At this time, it is difficult to say how fully Americans will accept the strategy of sharing space or what forms this sharing will take. But because it is the least examined housing strategy in our society, sharing offers the most fertile field for exploration and development.

Chapter 4

CONSTRUCTING THE COMPACT HOME

The skills, knowledge, and techniques required to build a modest mansion are not much different from those required for any high-quality residential construction. What *is* different is that the builder of a compact home should be willing to expend labor to save inches. We need to reevaluate construction practices from the special perspective of space-saving design. Decisions about design sometimes dictate the construction systems we choose, and, conversely, construction decisions can influence the design of a home. This chapter will help you choose the structural systems and components to use in a modest mansion. Along the way, we will discuss design questions that are linked intimately to construction decisions.

One *caveat:* In their zeal to save space, some designers forget that the real goal is high-quality housing. Do not make a room or a clearance too small for comfort; there are minimum dimensions below which you should go only with great caution. To get a sense of these limits, you should refer to Appendix 2, which gives size and clearance standards based both on codes and on common practice. The standards are offered as yardsticks against which to measure a compact-home design. There is no need to conform slavishly to these standards (unless local codes or your

Photo 4-1. *The space under a low roof need not go unused. Here, varied storage compartments have been crafted along a short wall. (Design by Bohlin Powell Larkin Cywinski)*

mortgage lender requires it), but if your design is very much out of line with the standards, you may want to think twice before proceeding. Changing a design while it is still on paper is much easier than changing a house after it is built.

Dimensions

How large is a 1,200-square-foot house? This may seem like an easy question, but the answer can be tricky. There is no universal agreement about how to interpret dimensions. If you give two individuals the same house plan—particularly one that is a little complicated—and ask them each to calculate the square footage of the house, you are apt to get two very different answers. It works in reverse, as well. Ask two people to design a 1,200-square-foot house, and you will be shocked at the discrepancy between the sizes of the designs that result. Should square footage be calculated by measuring exterior or interior dimensions?

How do you account for sleeping lofts, overhead storage areas, basements, or outside decks and patios? These and similar ambiguities make a puzzle out of the seemingly simple matter of house size.

Square footage figures are not very important in themselves. After all, how many people know the precise measurements of the houses or apartments they occupy? But calculating square footage can be productive—it is useful for estimating costs and appraising values, as long as consistent methods are used when the calculations are performed.

Realtors, architects, and builders usually calculate the overall size of a home according to its exterior dimensions, which are measured at the outside surface of the studs in the exterior walls. Thus, a two-story home with a 40-foot by 25-foot floor plan (as measured along the exterior walls) would be called a 2,000-square-foot home: 1,000 square feet on each of the two floors.

The convention for measuring the size of individual rooms is different. When a Realtor shows you the floor plans of a house, the size of each room usually is indicated by its interior dimensions. If you were to add up the area of all the rooms based on these dimensions, you would see that the sum is smaller than the advertised size of the entire house. No deception is (necessarily) involved: Room sizes normally are given in terms of interior dimensions, which are inevitably less than exterior dimensions.

A reasonable rule of thumb is that the combined floor area of all the rooms in a house (interior dimensions) will equal about 80 percent of the total gross area of the house (exterior dimensions). This means that approximately 20 percent of the gross size of the house is taken up by structural elements (such as walls, columns, and flues) and by circulation areas (such as corridors, entry vestibules, and stairs). The exact percentage will vary by a small margin, depending on the house style you are considering. When designing a house, you should generally try to keep a high ratio of usable space to overall house size.

To clarify how this works, consider Figure 4-1. A small three-bedroom ranch house with a rectangular floor plan has 1,200 square feet measured by exterior dimensions (25 feet by 48 feet). However, when you subtract the area occupied by the exterior walls (73 square feet), the interior partition walls (35 square feet), and the circulation space (130 square feet), you are

Figure 4-1. *The interior walls and the circulation space consume 20 percent of the space in this house. The double-crosshatched areas represent obvious circulation space. The single-crosshatched area represents space that often is used for circulation but that may not be recognized as such.*

1. Bedroom
2. Kitchen
3. Living/Dining Area
4. Entry
5. Bathroom

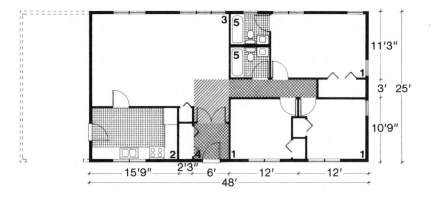

left with 962 square feet of floor area. In this case, the 80 percent rule of thumb works exactly.

Compounding the difficulties involved in calculating the size of a home is the fact that there is no universal agreement about accounting for in-between spaces like sleeping lofts, attached garages, and porches. These spaces are some of the most exciting and cost-effective solutions to making small homes seem bigger. Should they be included in square footage estimates? Often they are not. But don't deceive yourself. If you are planning one of these areas for your home, be sure to include its construction costs in your budget even if you don't count its area when calculating the home's floor space. For example, some reference books say that for purposes of cost estimating, unfinished garages should be calculated "at half square footage"—that is, you should treat them as if they were only half as big as they will really be. Thus, if you estimate that your home will cost $50 per square foot to build, and if your garage will contain 200 square feet, you can estimate the cost of the garage by cutting its square footage in half, then multiplying this by $50 to get the result: $5,000 (100 square feet multiplied by $50).

Related rules of thumb are that uncovered porches or decks should be rated at one-quarter their real size and unfinished basements at half their size. If anything, rules of this kind may be a bit optimistic, and it is better to increase your cost estimates by a slight margin.

Photo 4-2. *Lofts and other "unconventional" spaces should be included when estimating the construction costs of a home. (Design by Douglas Kelbaugh; furniture by Alan Smith)*

The Cost Penalty of Small Size

It is unfortunate but true that, all else being equal, costs per square foot usually go up as the size of a home comes down. The reason is straightforward: In many instances, the contractors who work on a compact home need to spend as much time getting things ready as they would if they were working on a larger home. The charge for this "setup time" must be allocated to the smaller number of square feet in the compact home, so the cost per square foot rises even though the total cost of the home is probably far less than the total cost of a larger home.

How much do costs per square foot go up in a compact home? Generalizations are difficult to make, given the enormous variety of house types and local economic conditions. But we can make certain observations. Construction industry publications such as *Means Square Foot Costs* (see our bibliography) estimate the costs per square foot of different housing types in different locations. A study of these sources suggests that the cost penalty for decreasing a home's size from 2,000 square feet to 1,200 square feet is approximately 20 percent per square foot, assuming the smaller home is as well built as the larger home would have been and assuming the construction work is done by professionals. Thus, if a 2,000-square-foot home was estimated to cost $50 per square foot, a 1,200-square-foot home of comparable quality should cost about $60 per square foot. Overall, then, if the 2,000-square-foot home would have cost $100,000 to build (2,000 square feet times $50), the 1,200-square-foot home should cost $72,000 (1,200 square feet times $60).

For a home of 1,000 square feet, the rule of thumb is a penalty of about 30 percent compared to the cost of the comparable 2,000-square-foot home. Armed with this information, you can make a rough estimate of your construction costs. Locate a 2,000-square-foot home of the quality you seek in the area where you are planning to build. Based on the square-foot cost of this larger home, you will be able to estimate the cost of your modest mansion.

Choosing a Foundation

When you have chosen a design and estimated the cost, you will be ready to make some construction decisions. A good place to start is at the bottom.

Selecting the type of foundation for your home is one of the numerous construction decisions that is virtually indistinguishable from a design decision. Depending on the region of the country in which you live, you are apt to be more familiar with

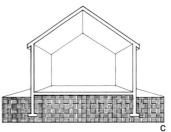

Photo 4-3. *Full basements often go unused. To cut costs, a crawlspace or slab-on-grade foundation can be selected instead.*

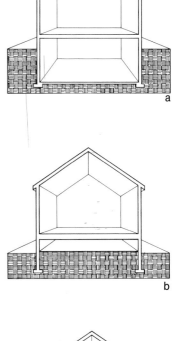

Figure 4-2. *Foundation types: a. Full basement, b. crawlspace, c. slab on grade.*

full basements, slab-on-grade foundations, or crawlspace foundations. Each of these has advantages and disadvantages for the compact home. When you choose a foundation, you commit yourself to that foundation's special characteristics, which have profound implications for the design of the rest of your home.

The full basement is the most expensive of the three alternatives, but it provides the greatest amount of usable space. In regions in which full basements are common, constructing one normally costs about $5 to $10 more per square foot than a slab-on-grade foundation. This additional cost may be justified if you will make good use of the basement. Otherwise, consider a slab on grade or a crawlspace.

Slab-on-grade construction is increasingly popular. Until recently, slab foundations were widespread in the South and Southwest, but they were rare in northern parts of the country. Today, however, more and more new homes throughout the United States are being built with these relatively low-cost foundations. A word of caution: Give careful thought to the placement of plumbing lines, electrical conduits, and heating ducts. In slab-on-grade construction, these systems usually are placed inside channels buried in the concrete slab. Moving them is very difficult after the slab has been poured, so make sure you put them where you want them the first time around.

Crawlspaces often are found in regions where high water tables are common or where sloped sites make slab-on-grade foundations too cumbersome and expensive. Many seasonal structures such as vacation homes are designed with crawlspaces that have cement-block walls; thus, no concrete pour is required. Perhaps the best use for a crawlspace is as exterior storage for lawn furniture, fencing, and other items that will not be damaged by exposure to temperature and humidity fluctuations.

Minimizing the Footprint

The perimeter of a building's foundation where it meets the ground is called the building's "footprint." There are several good reasons why you should try to keep your home's footprint as small as possible.

In the first place, minimizing the footprint will cut down on the cost of the foundation, allowing you to preserve your financial resources for better uses elsewhere in the home. Even more important, a needlessly large footprint almost inevitably leads to a needlessly large house. Partly, this is a simple matter of structural necessity. The footprint establishes a house's minimum exterior dimensions: The house must be at least large enough to cover the foundation on which it rests. But human psychology also enters the equation. If you start your design with an unrestrained footprint, you are less likely to make the hard decisions needed to save space elsewhere in the design. Beginning your diet by sneaking a cookie before breakfast does not bode well for the rest of the day.

While the footprint establishes the home's minimum dimensions, it does not impose maximum limits. Your home is not restricted to the floor area of the footprint: Parts of the home can be cantilevered over the foundation to provide more space where it is required. Bay windows, turrets, and decks are but a few of the design elements that can be cantilevered in this way. Thus, a small footprint need not lead to a cramped home.

In a two-story house, the optimal size of the second floor often does not match the optimal size of the first floor. For example, it is often desirable to group all the bedrooms on one floor and all the "public" rooms on a different floor. When two floors require different square footages, there is a tendency to build a foundation that will accommodate the larger floor, then to add space on the smaller floor until it is the same size. Resist this temptation. Look to other strategies—such as cantilevering the second story over the first story—to keep your design compact.

Picking Up Inches

Having chosen a compact footprint, your next task is to maximize the amount of usable space in your home. Picking up inches is crucial in this effort. Consider the following example. What is the usable square footage in a rectangular two-story house that is 20 feet by 30 feet in plan (exterior dimensions)? Using the size conventions outlined earlier, we get a total of 1,200 square feet. But we know that the usable interior floor space will be less. Let's assume that the nominal thickness of the exterior walls is six inches, which is common for today's well-insulated homes. We also will assume that there are 150 linear feet of interior partition walls and that each of these walls is nominally four inches thick. With these assumptions, it is easy to calculate that the walls consume more than 12 percent of the overall floor space (150 square feet), reducing the net floor space to 1,050 square feet.

Is there anything that can be done about this? Let's change some of our assumptions. The house's exterior walls will now be nominally four inches thick (as we will explain, this can be done without greatly reducing insulation values). Also, we will assume that the design is altered to an open plan, thus eliminating 50 linear feet of interior partition walls. When you recalculate the net floor area after making these changes, the total is now 1,100 square feet. We have saved 50 square feet compared to the original design. This is the spatial equivalent of a good-size bathroom or a large entry vestibule, and we gained it by literally shaving inches from the walls.

The following sections look at the types of walls, ceilings, floors, and roofs that are appropriate in a compact home. Among other considerations, we will explore opportunities for saving inches in several of these construction systems.

Exterior Walls

No element of residential construction causes more debate today than exterior-wall design. Historically, the walls of most American wood-frame houses have been constructed with 2×4 studs placed 16 inches "on center" (that is, the distance from the center of one stud to the center of the next stud is 16 inches).

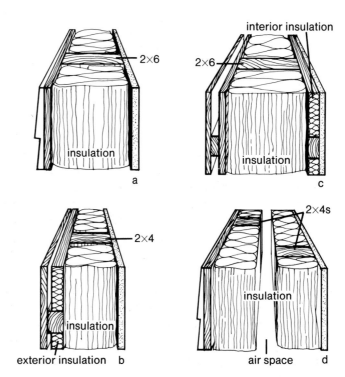

Figure 4-3. *Types of exterior walls:*
a. Conventional 2 × 6 wall.
b. 2 × 4 wall with exterior
insulation. c. 2 × 6 wall with interior
insulation. d. "Envelope" wall built
with 2 × 4 studs.

Today, however, concerns about energy efficiency, prefabrication, and durability are leading to the development of new wall systems, many of which result in much thicker exterior walls—up to 12 inches thick for wood-framed walls in some superinsulated houses. This extra thickness creates deep wall cavities that can be filled with insulation.

Although their long-term performance has not been confirmed in extended field tests, several alternatives to the standard 2×4 stud wall have gained wide acceptance. They include (1) walls made with 2×6 studs placed 24 inches on center; (2) 2×4 walls covered by exterior insulation; (3) 2×6 walls sheathed on the interior with rigid insulation; and (4) "envelope" walls comprising a sandwich of insulated walls that enclose an air space.

Masonry wall systems also are changing. The exterior masonry walls of one- and two-story homes are usually built with six- or eight-inch-wide concrete blocks. Insulating such massive walls on their exterior surfaces helps control indoor temperatures: The walls soak up indoor heat when a house is too warm and then release this stored heat into the house when indoor temperatures drop. Many builders are experimenting with exterior insulation systems protected by weatherproof finishes such as stucco or fiberglass-reinforced cementitious coatings.

The various wall systems we've mentioned have different thicknesses and different insulating values—and, of course, different costs. Which one is right for the modest mansion? A compact home can ill afford to relinquish interior space, so you might conclude that thin walls would be best, because these take up the least space. But, as we indicated in Chapter 1, when the size of a home is reduced, the ratio of wall area to floor area increases. This means exterior walls are more significant sources of heat loss and heat gain in compact homes than in larger homes. These considerations might lead you to conclude that modest mansions should have extra-thick walls to accommodate extra-plentiful insulation.

Clearly, some sort of compromise is needed. Systems that place continuous sheets of impermeable insulation over the exterior surfaces of relatively thin walls have the advantage of not taking up much of the home's usable square footage. Yet they can yield high R-values because the exterior insulation compensates for the relatively small amount of insulation between the studs. These systems also have a potential disadvantage: They eventually may cause water condensation problems in the wall cavities unless the interior of the house is carefully sealed with a continuous vapor barrier. Still, for homes in which the quality of construction can be monitored carefully, thin walls with exterior insulation seem advisable.

One more subject related to exterior walls: When planning your home's walls, you should consider how people will pass through those walls. How will people enter and leave the house? I usually recommend inclusion of an entry vestibule in a home designed for a cold climate, even though the vestibule will take up floor area. In such a climate, a small house without an airtight vestibule is an example of penny-wise but pound-foolish design. If a vestibule decreases the infiltration of cold air into the house by an average of just one-tenth of an air change per hour over the heating season—a very real possibility—it will save about the same amount of energy as you could save by increasing the exterior wall insulation from R-20 to R-30.

Interior Walls

The first question to ask yourself about the interior walls in any design is why they are placed where they are. Among other possibilities, a wall may provide structural support, visual privacy, or acoustical separation. Go back to basics: Examine each wall, considering whether the house could do without it. If a particular wall's main purpose is to give structural support, perhaps you could eliminate the wall and substitute a beam—a wall occupies floor space, but a beam does not. If a wall's purpose is to provide visual privacy, perhaps a retractable curtain or Roman shade could serve your needs just as well. Each wall you eliminate represents a gain in net floor space.

In most homes, the interior walls are constructed with the same 2×4 lumber used for the exterior walls. If an interior wall helps support the weight of the house, it must be built with lumber sufficiently large to prevent structural failure. However, most partitions between rooms support only themselves—the house would stand perfectly well without them. In these cases, 2×4 lumber is structurally unnecessary; builders often use it simply because the 2×4s are already on the construction site.

Today, some builders use 2×3 lumber for interior walls. Not everyone feels comfortable with this, because 2×3 partitions are more susceptible to warpage and feel less "stiff" than 2×4 walls. Structurally, however, 2×3 partitions generally are quite adequate. In any event, a compact home's interior walls rarely run for many feet without some sort of bracing. If you are concerned about the stability of a 2×3 partition, just be sure to brace it with buttressing elements such as beams or adjoining walls.

Contrary to some people's belief, 2×3 walls do not necessarily allow more noise to travel from room to room. Acoustically, they are really no worse than 2×4 walls. Sound isolation is achieved primarily by placing massive materials in the walls and by sealing off holes. Most of the mass in a normal wall is contained in the gypsum board attached to the wood framing. The thickness of the gypsum board, and the size of openings in the wall, will have far more influence on sound isolation than the size of the studs will. (We will discuss sound isolation further in Chapter 5.)

Besides the use of unnecessarily large lumber, another reason walls sometimes take up too much space is that they are framed out to achieve smooth surfaces and "clean" lines. For example, many modern fireplaces are prefabricated units made of sheet metal. Homeowners often decide to enclose the flue of a prefabricated fireplace in a framed-out wall, attempting to make the flue look more like a traditional chimney. Sometimes the entire wall is made thick enough to receive both the fireplace and its flue. A substantial amount of space is thus wasted. The design instinct behind this approach may be reasonable, but in a modest mansion, it is a luxury you may decide to forgo.

The thickness of a wall is only one of its dimensions. We need to consider the appropriate height for each wall as well. You may decide to make some walls shorter than the conventional eight feet. In a multistory design, for example, the distance from a lower floor to the floor above can be crucial, because it dictates the height and length of the stairway. Changing from eight-foot walls to seven-foot six-inch walls can result in the need for one less tread and riser. This, in turn, can create more flexibility in stair placement and design.

Shorter walls have other benefits as well. A seven-foot six-inch wall height can simplify construction, because workmen can more readily reach the tops of the walls for framing and finishing work. In addition, shorter walls tend to increase apparent room width (because the ratio of horizontal-to-vertical dimensions is greater), and they increase the structural capacity of the studs (the studs become shorter columns capable of carrying greater loads without buckling). The increased stiffness of short walls is particularly beneficial if the spacing between studs has been increased,

Photo 4-4. *A combination of short and tall walls contributes to the unusual shape of this child's bedroom, making the space more interesting. (Design by Leslie Armstrong, Design Coalition)*

because such an increase entails a reduction in the number of studs and a consequent reduction in wall strength.

A customized home, built with studs that are individually cut on the site, can have more varied wall heights than mass-produced development homes built with precut studs. Don't forget that this means you can incorporate some extra-high walls as well as some short walls. A variety of wall heights adds architectural excitement. While low walls can reduce the profile of a home and lend coziness to its interior, tall walls and high ceilings in one or two special places can impart airiness and elegance to a tight home. One caution: Extra-high walls can create a closet-like feeling if the ratio of wall height to floor area becomes too extreme. A rule of thumb is that a passive room (one in which you primarily sit or lie) should not have walls that are higher than the room's greatest length or width. So, for example, a 10-foot by 12-foot room should not have a ceiling that is higher than 12 feet. If the room is a transitional space, however, such as an entry vestibule, or a ceremonial space, such as a central hall, this rule does not apply, and you may want a very high, dramatic ceiling.

Ceilings and Floors

The structure of a ceiling is usually hidden behind gypsum board or some other surface. What we often do not see, therefore, is the network of wooden spanning members, called joists, that are the main components of the ceiling and that, in a multistory home, support the floor above. These joists are nominally 2 inches wide, and 6, 8, 10, or 12 inches deep. The depth you select depends on the distance the joists must span between supports, how much deflection (springiness) you are willing to accept in the floor supported by the joists, and how far apart the joists are spaced. Occasionally, joists are 12 inches on center; more commonly, they are 16 inches on center; and sometimes they are as much as 24 inches on center. Any of these spacings allows the even placement of 4-foot-wide gypsum ceiling boards and plywood flooring materials.

Wood-spanning tables, printed in several of the reference books cited in our bibliography, give the appropriate depth for joists used in various situations. For example, if joists are spaced 16 inches on center, and if a typical grade of framing lumber is used, then a span of 14 feet requires joists made of 2×10 lumber. You can use shallower joists (2×8s, for example) if you reduce the distance between the joists. This strategy can help you fit a sleeping loft into your design or carve new space out of an existing area in which lack of headroom is a problem. By reducing the amount of vertical space taken up by the joists, you increase the amount of usable space in the home. But shallower, more frequently spaced joists tend to make a springier floor, so be sure to verify the amount of deflection indicated in the wood-spanning tables.

Another way to reduce joist depth is to select lumber of a higher grade. Framing lumber is available in several grades: The higher the grade, the greater the strength. If you are willing to pay a premium price, you can purchase high-quality lumber for those special cases in which minimizing structural depth is very important.

Joists usually are supported from below by a load-bearing wall or by a beam (see Figure 4-4a). If the beam is in the middle of a room, you naturally must ensure adequate headroom under the beam. One way to do this without paying a space penalty is to raise the beam to the same height as the joists, then hang the joists from the beam using steel straps called "joist hangers" (see Figure 4-4b).

Sometimes the ceiling structure can be left exposed. This often entails eliminating joists and using beams in their place. Photo 4-5 shows such a "beam-and-deck" ceiling. In such installations, beams are spaced up to four feet apart and nominally two-inch-thick tongue-and-groove wood decking spans the distance between the beams. While the beams are deeper than joists, they nevertheless add to the feeling of spaciousness in the room because the space between the beams becomes part of the room's volume. This technique can be quite effective. However, caution should be used if acoustic privacy is an issue: Sounds may pass through the decking to the rooms above. To prevent this, sound-attenuating board and carpet can be laid over the decking.

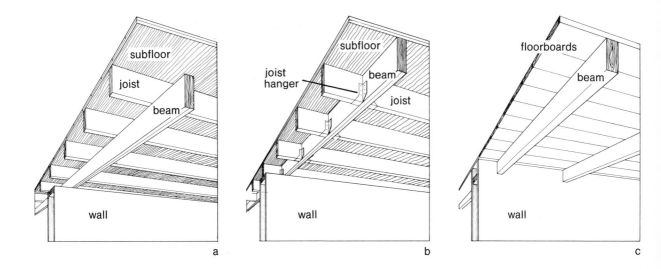

a   b   c

Figure 4-4. *Three methods of supporting a floor. a. Floor joists sit atop beams. b. Floor joists are hung from beams using joist hangers. c. Floorboards are supported by closely spaced exposed beams.*

A variation of the exposed-beam technique is shown in Photo 4-6. Here a ceiling framed with joists spaced approximately 16 inches on center has been converted into a series of small coves through the use of corrugated plastic and lengths of ordinary rain gutter. The small dining alcove in which this ceiling is located benefits from the extra volume scooped into the room.

A recent innovation in floor structures is the use of trusses instead of joists. Introduced only in 1970, floor trusses have become enormously popular—they already are used in approximately two-thirds of all development houses. They consist of lengths of 2×4 lumber gang-nailed together with metal plates at the intersections. Floor trusses often are deeper than joists, so they have limited value for a modest mansion. However, in a two-story home built with slab-on-grade construction, trusses under the second floor might provide space in which to weave ductwork and conduits.

Photo 4-5. *A beam-and-deck ceiling: Wood decking spans large exposed beams. The decking serves as the ceiling of the rooms shown, and it is the floor of the rooms on the upper story. (Design by John Randolph Design + Construction)*

Photo 4-6. *The ceiling of this dining alcove is a series of small coves. The glass doors on the cabinets let light enter the alcove from the adjacent kitchen. (Design by Howard Katz)*

Roofs

In most areas of the United States, roofs are the single greatest source of architectural expression for single-family homes. There are flat, shed, gabled, saltbox, hipped, mansarded, gambrelled, and other forms of roofs (see Figure 4-5). They can have eaves, rakes, skylights, overhangs, dormers, clerestories, or cornices. They can be slightly sloped or heavily sloped. Most development homes have roof pitches of 3-, 4-, 5-, or 6-in-12. This means that for every 12 feet of horizontal run, the roof rises 3, 4, 5, or 6 feet vertically.

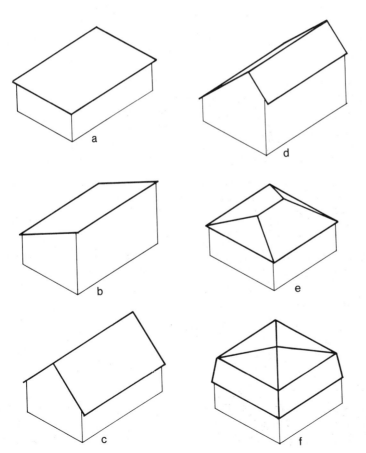
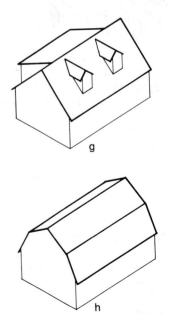

Figure 4-5. *Common roof types: a. Flat, b. shed, c. gabled, d. saltbox, e. hipped, f. mansarded, g. dormered, h. gambrelled.*

If a roof is pitched at a 3- or 4-in-12 slope, and if it has no dormers or other protrusions, you usually can conclude that it is supported by trusses. While residential roof trusses have been available only since 1952, they can be found in nearly 95 percent of today's site-built houses. Trusses have made roof construction less expensive, but unfortunately they prevent use of the attic for large-scale storage or expansion, as we noted in Chapter 3.

Several basic types of roof trusses are available. The "Fink" or common "W" truss is the most widely used. The arrangement of its web members is structurally efficient and allows good access through the center portion for service runs. The "Howe" truss also is quite efficient structurally, but the arrangement of its web members tends to interfere with attic access during construction. Fink or Howe trusses with 2 × 4 top and bottom chords (that is, 2 × 4 top and bottom framing members) are normally adequate for houses up to 26 or 28 feet wide; 2 × 6 top and bottom chords are required for greater spans.

Variations on the basic truss forms allow greater spatial freedom for the small-home designer. Most lumberyards now can provide scissor trusses, for example. In these, the bottom chord is not flat but takes an inverted "V" shape. This allows the room below to have a sloped ceiling, thereby increasing room volume. Scissor trusses cost only slightly more than standard trusses.

Besides the use of trusses, another approach in roof design is to construct a steeply pitched roof using large framing lumber. Although more costly, this technique keeps the attic free of truss web members, and it creates maximum attic headroom, thus permitting future expansion into the attic. Basically, some additional building expense is incurred to provide space where relatively inexpensive rooms can be built. A tangential benefit is that the resulting steep roof improves the profile of the house. A shallow-pitched roof can make a home look mass-produced and commonplace.

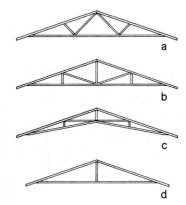

Figure 4-6. *Roof trusses: a. Fink, b. Howe, c. scissors, d. king post.*

Sloped Ceilings

By imparting additional space to an otherwise small room, a sloped ceiling can create a surprising sense of spaciousness. Even if you live in a region where flat roofs predominate, you

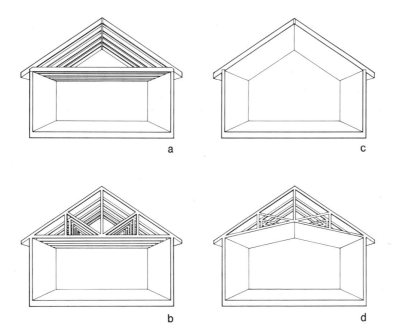

Figure 4-7. *Some roof-construction techniques: a. Roof rafters and floor joists form an open attic. b. Roof trusses leave little usable attic space. c. Roof rafters without floor joists create a large living space. d. Scissor trusses create added spatial interest in the living space.*

should consider the advantages of overhead slopes. Absolutely flat roofs are not desirable, because they can lead to standing water and eventual leaks. For this reason, most so-called flat roofs actually have at least a slight slope for water drainage. (The minimum recommended pitch is 1/4 inch per linear foot.) Why not take advantage of this necessity by providing a more perceptible roof pitch that can be experienced in, and add interest to, the room below?

One problem with conventional sloped ceilings (those built without trusses) is that providing proper ventilation can be difficult (see Figure 4-8). The depth of the rafters used in a sloped ceiling is often insufficient to provide adequate space both for insulation and for ventilation over the insulation. Ventilation is required to ensure that any water vapor passing through the ceiling's vapor barrier will not cool down, condense, and soak the insulation, thereby reducing the insulation's effectiveness and possibly causing rot in the wood framing. One solution is to place

Figure 4-8. *Ordinary construction can prevent ventilation in a sloped ceiling.*

furring strips above the rafters to provide additional space for air to circulate above the insulation. Another solution is to use shallower batt insulation and include a layer of rigid insulation below the rafters. By reducing the depth of the batts, you provide ventilation space; the rigid insulation compensates for the reduced R-value of the batts.

Components

While foundations, walls, floors, ceilings, and roofs are the major assemblies from which a house is fashioned, combining them in a desirable pattern is not the whole story of house design. In fact, the components that are incorporated into these assemblies—the windows, doors, stairs, dormers, trim, and so forth—are arguably more important in giving a house its unique character.

Windows

Windows are critical in the design of any house. They are the "eyes" of the house, and—along with the doors—they are important clues to the scale of the structure. When designing a small house, we must make sure the windows are selected, sized, and placed so they make sense both inside and out.

Large windows often can be effective in small homes, relieving restricted dimensions by providing a view of the landscape beyond. But there are also times when small windows become the proper choice. Probably the most difficult task for the novice house designer is to locate windows properly, so they enhance the interior of a room while also giving the exterior of the house a pleasing and coordinated appearance. How can something that fits the scale of an 8-foot-wide room be sized properly for a 30-foot-wide house facade? Frequently, the answer is that modestly sized windows can be arranged so they fit into a discernible exterior pattern: The individual windows suit the scale of particular rooms, while the overall pattern is appropriate to the house's facade.

There are many different types of windows, each having its own virtues and drawbacks when used in a modest mansion (see Figure 4-9). Double-hung windows are the most traditional.

Photo 4-7. *Small windows are combined in large patterns on the exterior of this New England home. The windows thus suit the scale of the home's rooms while the patterns suit the home's facade. (Design by Venturi, Rauch and Scott Brown)*

They date from the 18th century, when large panes of glass were impossible to produce and hardware was at a premium: Multiple small panes of glass were fitted together by means of structural mullions, then two sashes were placed in a tracked frame that allowed the sashes to be raised or lowered.

Today, double-hung windows are produced in a wide range of standard sizes by a host of manufacturers. Multipane sashes have become rare, however, because sophisticated technology has made large panes of glass easy and inexpensive to produce. As a result, most major manufacturers no longer produce double-hung windows with multiple panes. Instead, they offer fake, plastic mullion grids that snap onto the surface of large panes to simulate traditional small-pane windows.

Two limitations of double-hung windows should be noted. Only half of the glazed area of each window can be opened for ventilation at any one time. A two-foot-high double-hung win-

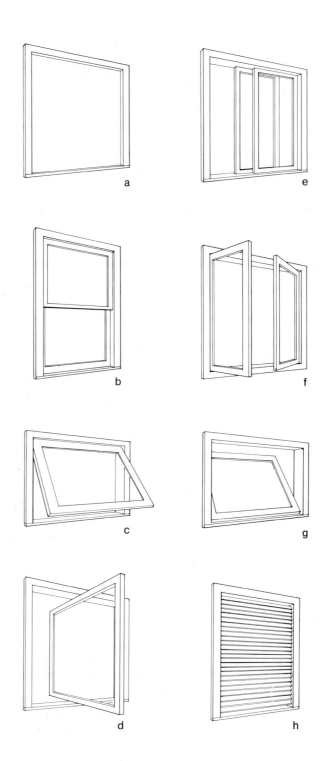

Figure 4-9. *Window types:*
a. Fixed, b. double-hung, c. awning,
d. pivoting, e. sliding, f. casement,
g. hopper, h. jalousie.

dow would offer only a one-foot-high ventilation area, for example: quite restricted. As a result, very small double-hung windows are rare. Also, double-hung windows generally have vertical configurations, because of their operating characteristics. This limits their applicability in situations for which horizontal openings are needed.

Awning windows are hinged at the top to pivot outward. Their entire glazed area can be opened for ventilation; also, they shed rain, which means they can be left open during hot weather. They generally seal more tightly than double-hung windows, thus cutting down on air infiltration and unwanted heat loss or heat gain. They come in a wide variety of shapes and sizes. Some people are leery of the cranks or levers required to operate them, and it is undeniable that awning windows are more complicated mechanically than double-hung windows.

Casement windows pivot from the side. They are available in a wide range of sizes, and they provide a full aperture for ventilation. One drawback is that they must be closed in the rain; another is that they have essentially the same hardware as awning windows. Casement windows usually are available in vertical shapes, although it is relatively easy to group several of them together to form a horizontal band of windows.

In general, you should decide on a single predominant window type—though not at all one size—for your home. The small home is too humble to speak several architectural languages at the same time. The best window type for your design usually will be suggested by the architectural style to which you are most clearly referring. A Colonial design might call for double-hung windows, for example, while a contemporary scheme might want awning or casement windows.

Further suggestions about windows are given in Chapter 5.

Doors

Doors are necessary inconveniences. Exterior doors are required to close out the weather and intruders; interior doors are required for visual and acoustical privacy. But doors sometimes can wreak havoc in the small home. The problem is not the doors themselves but the clearances they require when they swing open. The more doors a home has, the more floor space their swings eat up.

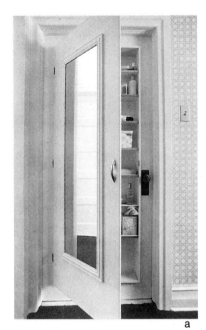

a   b

Photo 4-8. *Even the space inside a door can be put to good use. a. This door has shelves hidden behind the hinged mirror. b. Pantry doors often can be fitted with shelving, also.*

Among other penalties, this can make it difficult to locate the entrances to several rooms close to one another.

Most residential doors are two to three feet wide. The narrowest doors usually are reserved for closets or small powder rooms, while the widest ones are invariably ceremonial doors such as the front door. Most hinged doors require a quarter-circle of clearance to function properly. The radius of the circle is the width of the door: Thus, a two-foot-wide door needs a quarter-circle having a two-foot radius, or a total floor area of slightly more than three square feet. The swing of a three-foot-wide door consumes a bit more than seven square feet.

One way to prevent a door's swing from being totally wasted is to use the door for storage. A common practice is to store ties or shoes on closet doors. In some instances, it is even possible to graft cabinets or shelving onto doors (see Photo 4-8). There are limits to the number of doors you can treat in this way, however, so wherever possible you should install doors that require less space to open, such as sliding doors or bi-folding doors.

Another issue to resolve is whether your swinging doors should open in or out. The front doors of most homes swing

inward, whereas the entry doors of commercial buildings typically swing outward to make it easier for people to exit during
emergencies. You could follow the commercial pattern, moving a
door's swing outside so it will not take up interior floor space.
The swing would then be less welcoming and it would take up
space on the porch, but this may be a trade-off you would be
willing to accept. In interior rooms, you should arrange the doors
so their swings won't invade circulation space, impeding indoor
traffic. This may mean hanging a door so it swings out of a room
rather than into it or so its hinges are on the right rather than on
the left.

Stairways

When a house has more than one story, the stairway often
becomes the most important organizing feature, determining the
precise locations of the rooms. There are as many different kinds
of stairways and stairway locations as there are designers and
builders. Despite this diversity, however, we can cite some general
principles.

The vast array of stairways can be broken down into three
broad categories: (1) single-run stairways, which go from one level
to another without turns or landings; (2) spiral stairways, which
wind back on themselves to make the best use of space (although
usually circular in plan, they can have square plans, such as the
side-winding stairs in the Trinity house described in Chapter 2);
and (3) return stairways, which start up in one direction, reach a
landing, turn, and continue upward.

Which kind of stairway is the most space efficient? A spiral
stairway with 3-foot-long treads consumes about 30 square feet
of floor space. In a house with 8-foot-high ceilings, a single-run
stairway with 3-foot-long treads normally consumes 36 square
feet, and it may create spaces above and below the stairway that
are hard to use to their fullest. A return stairway with 3-foot-long
treads and a 3-foot-wide landing (the landing should normally be
at least as wide as the tread is long) usually consumes 54 square
feet of floor space. Like the single-run stairway, the return stairway may create spaces above and below that are difficult to use for
anything other than storage.

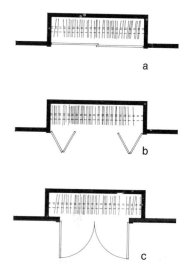

Figure 4-10. *Compared to conventional hinged doors, alternative door
types require less floor space to open.
Used in a closet, for example, sliding
doors (a) require no floor space,
folding doors (b) require a slight
amount of space, and double doors
(c) require some space but allow the
installation of shelves or cabinets on
the doors.*

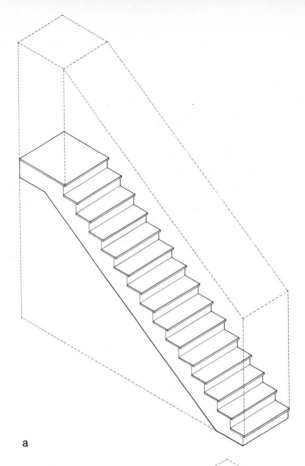

Figure 4-11. *Stairway types:*
a. Single-run stairs, b. spiral stairs,
c. return stairs.

a

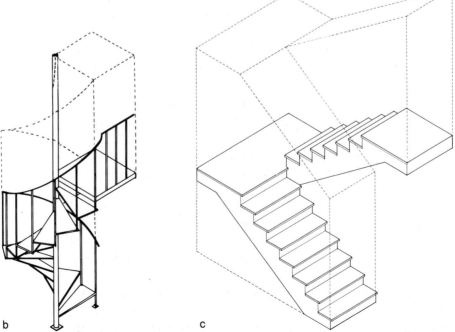

b

c

This analysis does not mean everyone should select spiral stairways for their small homes. There are many reasons why the other stairway types are superior in particular circumstances. For example, spiral stairways often do not meet code requirements. Moreover, they make furniture moving difficult—try moving a large bed or divan up a spiral stairway sometime. Even if you're not lugging a heavy load, spiral stairways can be uncomfortable to maneuver on: Ascending one is a bit like climbing a giant corkscrew. For all these reasons, I cannot imagine making a spiral stairway the primary path from one floor to another in a home I designed for myself.

Nevertheless, spiral stairways are well suited to certain applications. I know a house, for example, where a spiral stairway provides access to a loft above a small bedroom. Any other type of stairway would have eaten too much of the bedroom's limited area. The loft in question is a very private place, a nest reserved for adults, so the slight inconvenience of the stairway is acceptable—even welcome—in this case.

How wide should a stairway be? In Trinity houses, the stairways are often just 20 inches wide, while in today's development homes, they are routinely built 36 inches wide. Frequently, the minimum width is determined by the dimension required to move furniture. However, you may be able to provide alternative furniture-moving options so you can let the stairway narrow down to the width of a single individual. Some houses are equipped with hoists, for example, allowing furniture to be lifted to the upper stories without using stairs.

Other important dimensions in stairway design are the riser-to-tread ratio, the width of the stair treads, and the height of the stair risers.

• The riser-to-tread ratio determines how steep the stairway is. A riser is the vertical piece of wood that rises from the back of a tread and connects to the underside of the next tread. A well-known rule of thumb for interior stairs is that the depth of a tread (the distance from the front to the back of the tread) added to the height of a riser should equal 17 to 18 inches. This rule reflects the dimensions that most individuals find comfortable when climbing stairways.

• The width of each tread is very important in itself and is based on the average length of the human foot. For indoor stairways, nine inches is generally the safest minimum width.

Every tread in a stairway—ideally, every tread in all the stairways in the home—should be the same width.

• Riser height is similarly constrained—it must not exceed the distance that people can lift their feet comfortably. The maximum height for each riser in an indoor stairway is generally eight and a quarter inches. Every riser should be the same height.

Note that different building codes specify different stairway requirements; you should check the codes in your area. (See Appendix 2 for further information about interior and exterior stairway risers, treads, and clearances.)

Even if no codes apply in your area, you should think carefully before straying from standard stairway dimensions. A stairway that deviates just slightly from the norm can be quite dangerous. For example, an apparently conventional stairway that is slightly steeper than average may inspire false confidence in uninitiated climbers, leading to accidents. If a stairway will be used by visitors, you almost certainly should keep it well within conventional limits. But if you do decide to deviate from convention, then you should deviate by a wide margin so that anyone approaching the stairs will immediately notice the difference and therefore exercise caution when climbing or descending.

Dormers and Bays

Most house designs start with relatively simple building forms: Rectangular solids capped with wedge-shaped roofs are placed on rectangular foundations. Cubes, domes, or pyramids sneak in from time to time, but—for the most part—the array of shapes is restricted. Usually what distinguishes one house from the next, and gives each its own special character, are the protrusions added to the elemental shapes. In the modest mansion, mini-additions such as dormers and bay windows are wonderful opportunities to create interest while adding to the usable space in a room. But because they complicate construction and raise construction costs, it is important to locate them carefully.

The dormer is technically defined as any structure protruding from a sloping roof; it usually contains a window or ventilating louver. Dormers are often used to provide headroom in upper-floor areas that otherwise would be too low to stand in.

a

b

Photo 4-9. a. The large dormer on the south side of this home admits plenty of sunlight and warmth. The adjacent solar panels heat the home's water. b. The interior view shows light from the dormer flooding both floors of the home. The spiral stairway, open railings, and wicker furniture contribute to the open, airy feeling. (Design by Bohlin Powell Larkin Cywinski)

They also provide light and air, further increasing the habitability of the spaces in which they are installed. A dormer can sit entirely on the roof, or its front wall can share the plane of the house's front wall. Considerable variety is possible: A dormer can be quite large or quite small—it can encompass an entire room or define a zone for just one person.

The bay window is a protrusion from the wall of a house. It usually is faceted with glazing on several sides, but it can be a simple rectangular shape. It can be cantilevered structurally from an existing wall or supported by its own foundation; it can be purchased as a prefabricated unit or built on-site. Whatever its structure, a bay window adds extra volume—and a delightful sense of space—to a small room.

Dormers and bays must be insulated carefully to prevent thermal leaks. A considerable portion of a dormer or bay is composed of framing lumber. These wood members are poor insulators, readily conducting heat. If possible, provide an exterior sheathing of insulation around the structure to block excessive heat flow.

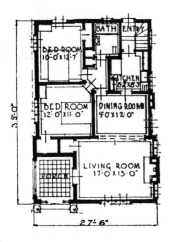

Figure 4-12. *An example of a small house plan from the Architects' Small House Service Bureau. (Source: Architects' Small House Service Bureau)*

Corridors

Surprisingly, the use of corridors is a relatively recent event in the history of architecture. When Louis XIV built his splendid 17th-century palace, Versailles, the bedrooms were enfilade—linked directly from one to the next—without benefit of corridors for privacy. The modern tourist at Versailles is struck by the difference in social mores that must have existed for this arrangement to have been acceptable even in this most opulent edifice.

A small-house design of the 1920s depicts a variation on the theme of corridorlessness (see Figure 4-12). In this scheme, a tiny foyer connects the bedrooms to each other and to the rest of the home. The kitchen, dining room, and living room are telescoped together, with each room still preserving a separate identity. The design foreshadows the open-plan houses being built today.

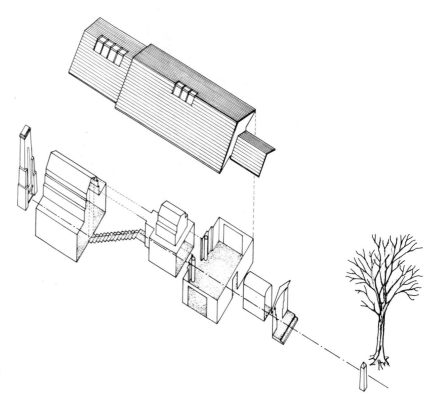

Figure 4-13. *Exploded drawing of the Wilkes House. The central corridor begins at the front door, runs through the dining room and kitchen, becomes a stairway, descends to the living room, and ends at an obelisk-shaped fireplace. (Design and rendering by Kevin Wilkes)*

Photo 4-10. *The Wilkes House is a conventional ranch house whose interior was completely gutted and redesigned. The exterior appearance also was altered, although the basic form was left intact. (Design by Kevin Wilkes)*

A more recent design takes a different tack completely. The Wilkes House is designed around a dramatic central corridor—conceived as a processional path—that leads to a living room culminating in a two-story obelisk-shaped fireplace (see Figure 4-13). Almost every room in the house is bisected by the corridor. However, because the corridor is an integral zone in each room, there is little wasted space. And the long view from the front door across the dining room, through the kitchen, and down to the living room gives a sense of grandeur to a house that is actually just average size.

You generally should try to eliminate corridors from a modest mansion: The less circulation space a home contains, the more compact it can become. But if a corridor creeps into your design, how wide should it be? Corridor widths vary from less than three feet to a bit more than four feet. The appropriate width depends largely on the corridor's length—a long corridor needs ample width to avoid a tunnel-like feeling. But because your corridor will be short (if exists at all), this is unlikely to be a problem. So minimum widths as well as minimum lengths should be the rule.

Trim and Finishes

When you select exterior finishing materials and detailing for the modest mansion, there are several distinctly different attitudes you can take. One is to subtly modify local finishes to connect the small home with larger nearby homes in a particular local style. The small home then will fit comfortably into the neighborhood, and it may actually borrow a sense of large size from the neighboring homes.

The importance of details as a clue to size cannot be overemphasized. For example, when builders attach shutters to Colonial-style homes, they have at least two intentions. First, they hope people will equate the traditional Colonial image with quality craftsmanship. Perhaps more realistically, they also hope the shutters will add a sense of scale to the homes by providing elements that relate to human experience. We can imagine using our hands to open and close the shutters even if—as is so often the case today—they are screwed open permanently. Shutters thus provide a clue to the size of a home: We all know, more or less, the size of a shutter, and we can use this information to gauge the size of the rest of the home.

Most manufacturers of building components understand the significance of human scale in residential construction, and they design their products accordingly. For instance, vinyl siding almost always is embossed with a fake wood texture. Similarly, plywood siding often is textured to approximate the appearance of board-and-batten wood siding. Indeed, efforts to give scale and familiarity to new building materials are the rule rather than the exception.

An entirely different approach to finishing the modest mansion is to eliminate traditional (or traditional-looking) materials and details, thereby minimizing the amount of size information that you provide to anyone looking at the house. What does this accomplish? It abstracts the form of the house, altering our perception of the house from a size to an idea. The house then becomes a three-dimensional sculpture: People are encouraged to focus on the house's shape and on the idea represented by that shape rather than on the size.

Photo 4-11. *Shutters, shingles, and other familiar elements give clues about scale. If a home provides no such clues, people often perceive it as being smaller than it actually is. (Design by Turner Brooks)*

Small homes lend themselves to being treated like sculptures. Caution is in order, however. A lack of size information will frequently make a structure seem smaller, not larger. So you should abstract the form of your house only with great care, making sure that you are achieving the effect you intend.

Heating the Home

How should you heat a modest mansion? Heating systems—like other forms of household mechanical equipment—are often bulky. For example, a typical oil furnace with a rated heat output of 100,000 Btu's per hour is about 36 cubic feet in volume. Moreover, the furnace should stand out in the open, permitting access on all sides so ductwork can be attached, maintenance can be performed, and sufficient ventilation can be provided. The machine takes up a significant amount of floor space, in other words—and the oil tank that accompanies it requires another substantial slice of space. In many small houses—especially those with slab foundations—these space requirements cannot be met.

A related dilemma is that most conventional central heating systems produce more heat than a modest mansion needs. A well-insulated small home may require 15,000 to 20,000 Btu's per hour, for example, whereas the minimum output of most oil or gas furnaces is roughly 50,000 Btu's per hour. Buying such a furnace can give you unnecessary expenses in two ways. You will be paying for heating capacity you don't need, and you will probably wind up buying extra heating fuel each year because a seriously oversized furnace will cycle on and off frequently, wasting fuel. The high efficiencies advertised for modern furnaces can be achieved only when a system is properly sized.

As a result of these problems, the owners of many new small homes are turning to alternative heating systems such as the following.

New Oil and Gas Systems

Kerosene and gas minifurnaces are now available with rated heat outputs of 10,000 to 30,000 Btu's per hour. They can be installed within a home's habitable rooms and are admirably compatible with the heating needs of the modest mansion. Some of these units are direct-venting appliances that expel their combustion gases via a snorkel-like tube extending through one of the house's walls. This procedure completely isolates the combustion process from the living areas, so indoor air stays healthful. Each unit can be controlled like a standard heating system, with a thermostat mounted on a wall some distance from the unit. Models are available in an assortment of shapes, including baseboard units that are suitable for bathrooms or kitchens or for placement under picture windows.

A huge market for unvented portable space heaters has developed over the last few years, primarily to provide supplemental heat. These units typically burn kerosene or natural gas, and one or two of them often can produce enough heat for a small home. Generally, however, they should not be selected as primary

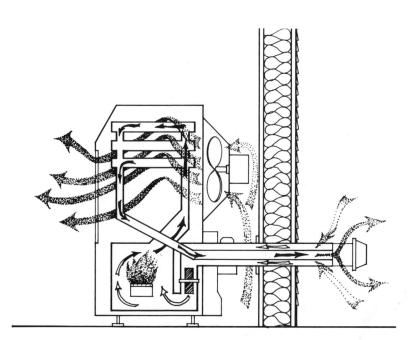

Figure 4-14. *Direct-venting heaters help keep indoor air clean: All the combustion products are vented outside the house. The modest heat output of these units can suffice for energy-efficient compact homes.*

heating sources because of their inconvenience and the concerns they raise about safety, air quality, and insurance.

Woodstoves

An airtight woodstove is a realistic central-heating option in a region with an abundant wood supply. Numerous brands are available with rated heat outputs of 10,000 to 20,000 Btu's per hour. Since about half the heat emanating from a woodstove is delivered by direct radiation from the stove's heated metal surfaces, as much of the house as possible should be able to "see" the stove directly in order to receive this radiant heat. A compact, open floor plan is ideal for this: No part of the house is very far from the stove, and most parts are in a direct line of sight to the stove. Indeed, many designers of small homes in northern climates make the location of the woodstove a primary design consideration.

For safety reasons, a woodstove should be located at least three feet from any wooden materials, so why not use the stove as a space-defining element? A woodstove can visually separate a kitchen area from a living area, for example. This places the stove on the edge of two areas rather than in the center of either—thus, it can heat two rooms directly. If a woodstove cannot be located where its heat will reach most of the house, you can employ small fans—with or without ductwork—to move heated air from the stove to remote locations in the house.

Fireplaces are less efficient than woodstoves, but they have undeniable appeal. Should you select a prefabricated fireplace or a site-built one? Prefabricated metal fireplaces often occupy less space than site-built fireplaces, but this is only one issue to consider. The appearance and symbolic value of a fireplace also must be considered. Few sights evoke a more intense feeling of comfort and hominess than a fire in a traditional masonry fireplace.

Should a chimney be placed inside or outside the house? An indoor chimney can provide heat for the house, but it takes up space. An outdoor chimney can provide interest to the house's exterior, but it will experience more rapid creosote build-up, because outdoor air will cool its walls, encouraging creosote to condense from the smoke rising through the flue.

a

Photo 4-12. *a. A woodstove is situated where it can provide heat throughout the open-plan space in the McLane House. The woodstove also separates the kitchen from the dining and living spaces. b. The exterior of the house combines familiar elements in a wholly original form. (Design by Turner Brooks)*

b

Solar Heating Systems

Several special considerations apply to the use of solar heating systems in compact homes. For instance, many active-solar water-heating systems require dual hot-water tanks. In some compact homes, space for these tanks may be unavailable.

On the positive side, the heating requirements of many small homes are ideally matched to the heat output of modestly sized solar systems. In particular, passive-solar space-heating systems are excellent options. They can be grouped in three classifications: direct-gain, indirect-gain, and isolated-gain systems (see Figure 4-15). Some direct-gain systems are as simple as large south-facing window areas placed near thermal-storage materials—such as masonry walls or floors—that soak up the warmth received from the sun. These materials then release the heat into the house at night or during the next cloudy day.

Many people think the trick to designing a successful passive-solar heating system is to cram as many feet of south-facing glazing as possible into a design. But in fact, the real trick is to provide sufficient thermal-storage materials. A rule of thumb is that you need about one cubic foot of masonry thermal storage for each square foot of solar glazing. Usually, you run out of places to conveniently locate masonry well before you run out of south building facade on which to place more glazing.

A small home with a slab-on-grade foundation has a built-in solution to this problem: The slab itself can serve as thermal storage. For such a system to operate best, the slab should be left exposed to the incoming sunlight, or it can be covered with thermally conductive material like ceramic tile or thin vinyl asbestos tile. Be sure not to cover the slab with a carpet or large rug that will inhibit the flow of heat into and out of the slab. Rigid insulating boards should be installed around the foundation walls so the heat gathered by the slab will not escape from the slab's perimeter. If the home will be built in an area with low winter temperatures or moist soil, you should also consider placing insulation boards under the slab. The best tactic is to place them under the entire slab, but you should at least place them under the perimeter, extending in a minimum distance of two feet all the way around.

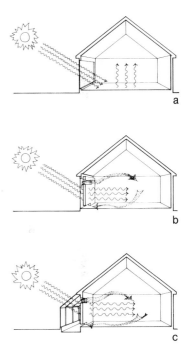

Figure 4-15. *Types of passive-solar space heating: a. Direct gain (the sun shines directly into the home; heat is stored in a concrete floor or other thermal mass). b. Indirect gain (in this case, a Trombe wall: Heat is stored in the wall during the day and released into the home at night). c. Isolated gain (in this case, a solar greenhouse: Heat is collected and stored in the greenhouse, then sent into the home as needed).*

Another passive-solar application is the Trombe wall. This indirect-gain system is a massive wall composed of thick masonry located directly behind an expanse of south-facing glazing. In

Photo 4-13. *Solar greenhouses can add excitement to a small home. Here, metal fins that provide passive solar water heating break up the light. The door in the far wall leads to a sauna. (Design by Kelbaugh & Lee)*

effect, the wall is a huge solar collector that runs "thermal interference" for the home: Heat is gathered by the masonry while the sun is up, then it is released into the home when the sun is down. The thickness of the wall can be a distinct penalty: a 30-foot-long, 12-inch-thick Trombe wall displaces 30 square feet of floor area. Despite this, a Trombe wall can be an excellent choice in some circumstances. It can provide thermal storage for heat from a woodstove, for example, or it can act as an acoustical and visual barrier between the home and a busy street.

Depending on how it is attached to your home, a solar greenhouse can be an indirect-gain or an isolated-gain passive system. Besides providing warmth, it can contribute spatial and visual appeal to a home that otherwise might be nondescript. It also can function as an entry vestibule to cut the amount of cold air that infiltrates the home. Permanent, weatherproof greenhouses are expensive, however, and it is easy to overestimate the amount of heat you will receive from one. The prospect of having a greenhouse—a warm, sunny hideaway where you can bask on cold winter days—is so alluring that many people lose objectivity on the subject. Carefully calculate the true Btu output of any heating system before putting your money down.

Superinsulation

By superinsulating a 1,000-square-foot home, you may be able to lower its heating requirements to just 6,000 Btu's per hour in a temperate climate. This is approximately equal to the waste heat a family of four gives off while using a standard array of household appliances and, perhaps, baking some cookies. The point is that a superinsulated small home may be able to get by without any heating system at all. Of course, banks and code officials may demand the inclusion of a heating system anyway, but this does not mean you will have to turn the system on. Numerous families who live in superinsulated homes report that they have never fired up their heaters.

To superinsulate a home in a cold climate, you might insulate the floors to between R-20 and R-30; the walls to between R-30 and R-50; and the roof to between R-40 and R-60. This is two or even three times as much insulation as is normally installed in many new homes in northern states. Of course, additional insulation costs additional money, but you may recoup the expense if you can get by without using a heating system.

One problem for compact homes is that superinsulation generally calls for extra-thick walls into which all that extra insulation can be stuffed. Another potential problem is that superinsulated houses typically have minimal window area, to reduce window heat losses. We have mentioned the value of relatively thin walls and large windows in small homes. Both of these considerations may lead you to back away from strict application of superinsulation principles. You might opt for somewhat thinner walls (and lower insulation values) than you originally intended, and you might install fairly extensive windows in at least some rooms. Such compromises should not seriously damage your home's energy efficiency, however, because—as we indicated in Chapter 1—the small size of a modest mansion is itself an energy-saving feature. Thus, reducing your home's dimensions may offset any energy penalties that otherwise would result from these compromises.

Electric Heat

All-electric space-heating systems have been around in various forms for some time. The arguments for and against them are numerous. Proponents point to the cleanliness of electricity, which creates no pollution at the home; the prospect of national energy independence if we generate electricity through nuclear power or by burning coal; and the potential for room-by-room temperature control—each room of a home can be equipped with its own thermostat, so you heat only the rooms that are being occupied. On the other side, critics emphasize the high cost of electricity in most localities; the potential safety problems, especially those related to nuclear power; and pollution at the power plants, particularly those that burn coal.

Clearly, electric heat is controversial. Nevertheless, many electric heating systems are both space efficient and flexible, making them realistic candidates for use in compact homes. Particularly if a home is well insulated, the amount of electricity needed for heat should be small.

There are basically three types of electrical space-heating systems in widespread use: resistance baseboards, radiant panels, and heat pumps. A baseboard unit large enough to heat an average ten-foot by ten-foot bedroom generally only needs to be three inches by six inches in cross section and six feet long: It takes only about one and a half square feet of floor space.

In a radiant panel system, electrical energy heats an interior surface of a room, such as a ceiling or floor. This surface provides heat in two ways: Room air is heated by contact with the warmed surface, and the occupants of the room receive radiant heat directly from the surface. Because the system is buried inside the heated surface, it has almost no impact on the available living space in the house.

A heat pump uses electrical energy to run a compressor that "pumps" heat into the home from the outside air or from some other heat source, such as a subterranean aquifer. (A refrigerant gas inside the heat pump finds heat in air that, to us, feels quite cold. The pump is able to convert this "heat" to temperatures high enough to warm a home.) In the summer, the system can be run in reverse to cool the home, much like an air conditioner. A single heat pump usually can handle a home's entire heating and cooling load. One drawback is that a heat pump is controlled by a central thermostat: you cannot place separate thermostats in various rooms. However, this is largely offset by the fact that heat pumps have very high energy-efficiency ratings.

Many residential heat pumps are "split" systems having part of the unit located in the house and part outside. The interior portion is generally about three feet deep, three feet tall, and four feet wide. It is flexible in its orientation and placement and can be hidden in closets or attic spaces as long as access for maintenance is provided.

Cooling the Home

A modest mansion often will prove easy—and inexpensive—to cool. In many climates, the job can be handled either by natural ventilation or by whole-house fans.

Most rooms in a compact home are likely to have ample window area to promote natural cross-ventilation. Often, this may be adequate to cool the house without requiring any mechanical cooling system. Otherwise, forced ventilation can be employed as a viable alternative to air conditioning, particularly on summer days when heat and humidity are less than maximum. Whole-house fans can provide such ventilation at very low cost.

A whole-house fan is a large fan recessed in a ceiling near the center of the house: It pulls heated air from the house, venting it through the attic, while cooler air enters the house through ground-floor or basement windows. The fan should be sized to create rapid air changes throughout the house. A rule of thumb is to try to achieve 30 to 60 air changes per hour. Thus, in a 1,200-square-foot house with an average ceiling height of eight feet, a total of 9,600 cubic feet of air must be drawn through the house every one or two minutes. This would require a 5,000-cfm (cubic feet per minute) fan having 24-inch-diameter blades. A piece of equipment this size could easily be located in an attic or other central ceiling space. Larger houses would require considerably larger fans, perhaps too large. In this sense, using whole-house fans is a technique that seems uniquely suited to small homes.

Plumbing and Electrical Systems

Sometimes the modest mansion will strain the ingenuity of even the most dedicated plumber or electrician. By eliminating space from our designs, we may eliminate the chases and cavities that usually hide plumbing lines and electrical conduits. This can create numerous challenges. For example, open plans and exposed beam-and-deck ceilings can make the job of concealing second-story plumbing much more difficult. One solution is to accept the exposed plumbing as an element in your design.

Concealing stacks can be a particular problem. In most homes, a "vent stack" must be connected to each water closet to remove fumes and to supply sufficient air for the plumbing system to operate properly. These stacks are typically several inches in diameter and must extend vertically through the building to the outside. In large houses, stacks often are buried inside partition walls, but concealing them in an open-plan modest mansion can be difficult. You might box them in, send them up the outside surfaces of exterior walls, or simply leave them exposed.

Photo 4-14. *Plumbing can be left exposed as part of the home's interior design. (Design by Kelbaugh & Lee)*

Water-supply lines are apt to be less problematic, for they need be only about one-half inch in diameter and can be more flexibly located. You should be able to conceal them by routing them through partitions, storage areas, floor channels, or ceiling cavities. Or, at the least, you can route them to places where they can be left exposed without being obtrusive.

The use of instantaneous point-of-use water heaters can be wise in some small houses. These heaters do not have bulky tanks to hold preheated water. Instead, they heat water the moment it is required. They are compact enough to be squeezed into even the smallest bathrooms and kitchens.

In a superinsulated small house, on the other hand, a regular water heater can be advantageous: It can provide the house's space heating if water from the heater is pumped through hydronic baseboard radiators. If you try this system, be sure to oversize the baseboard units, because the water from a water heater is cooler (130° to 140°F) than the water for which most baseboard systems are engineered (190° to 200°F).

When planning your electrical system, keep an eye on the future. The emerging information society is witnessing the invention of an awesome array of devices for listening, viewing, and "interfacing" from within the home. The finely crafted small home should be capable of plugging into whatever new technologies come along. In the past, if you needed a new, remotely located electrical outlet, you just snaked a wire through a basement ceiling or ripped open an interior partition wall. But what do you do if your home has no basement and the only wall nearby is an exterior wall with a vapor barrier that you do not want to breach? One answer is to use "energized" exterior wall systems, such as those commonly used in Sweden today: An electrical conduit is permanently located in a channel on the interior side of a vapor barrier in the exterior walls.

Chapter 5

COMPLETING THE COMPACT HOME

Whether you will design your own modest mansion or live in a compact home designed by someone else, there are many interior-planning principles you can employ to make compact living more gracious. While some of these principles are as simple as selecting appropriate colors of paint, others require considerable planning and ingenuity—they deal with such important issues as light control, sound isolation, and storage.

Most houses are not unique: They are variations on time-tested floor plans. But all human beings are unique, and they need to express their individuality. Often, the interior of a home is the product of this need, saying a great deal about the aspirations and lifestyles of the occupants. Therefore, the first rule when planning the interior of your home—whether a modest mansion or a sprawling estate—is to be true to your own tastes and preferences. Applying the principles explained in this chapter will not necessarily lead to any specific solution or style. Your challenge is to apply the principles in a personal way. This may seem like a tall order, but don't be overwhelmed. Some of the suggestions we will discuss are integral to the design process; others are less pressing matters that can be phased in after the home is built.

One dilemma is that contemporary style, reinforced through prodigious advertising campaigns, has such a strong influence on our tastes that we often have difficulty distinguishing genuine design principles from mere fashion. Can we, in fact, identify interior-planning principles that have special applicability to the compact home? The answer is yes—there are rules of thumb that hold for most people. Even if your tastes differ from the norm, you will benefit from understanding these rules. They will either apply directly to your situation, or they will serve as a basis for your own variations.

Spatial Strategies

Provide Storage

Clutter can make a house seem smaller than it really is. The only reliable antidote to clutter is a sufficient amount of usable storage space. "Usable" is the key word here. In too many instances, houses have plenty of storage space, but because this space is not well located or organized, it does not get used.

Several storage rules apply to the modest mansion:

1. Store things in the room where they are needed. This is an obvious but often overlooked concept. Do not limit storage to closets. As we indicated in Chapter 3, storage space can be located almost anywhere—overhead, within walls, or ankle-high. For example, most doors are six feet eight inches high, while most ceilings are eight feet high. This leaves a zone of 16 inches above the doors, perfect for all sorts of storage. Or consider the slice of space on which kitchen base-cabinets sit. Why not add a drawer in this "toe" space? Once you train your eye to look for such storage opportunities, you will begin finding them in even the tightest rooms.

Some rooms, particularly the kitchen, call for precise storage schemes. You should organize your kitchen into a sink area, range area, refrigerator area, and—if you have the space—food-preparation area. To the greatest extent possible, the items used in each area should be stored in that area or immediately adjacent to it. Thus, a hanging rack for pots and pans should be located within reaching distance of the stove. Similarly, dishware, glassware, and silverware should be stored within reach of the sink or dishwasher.

2. Store, do not pile. If returning an item to its proper place is too much trouble, you will not do it. Storage works best when there are many individual compartments or shelves rather than just a few large ones. This facilitates getting an item into

Photo 5-1. *This compact kitchen is carefully planned. Among other features, note that cookware is stored above the wall cabinets and window; cabinets have glass fronts; there are built-in shelves and ample counter space. (Design by Leslie Armstrong, Armstrong Childs Lang Associates)*

or out of its assigned space with a minimum of rearranging. The use of many small storage spaces is particularly suited to the small home, where large closets are hard to provide but small alcoves can be carved throughout the home.

3. Determine the height at which something should be stored by the frequency with which it is used. Store frequently used items between knee-level and eye-level, or roughly between two and five feet above the ground. Put seldom-used items on higher and lower shelves. Be honest with yourself about which items should be in "active" storage and which should be in "dead"

Photo 5-2. *The dog can attest to the value of using even the space below stair treads. Pets can nap there—or, on a more practical note, you can use it for storage. (Design by Jersey Devil)*

storage. Just because you are fond of something, don't assume it deserves a prime location in one of your active-storage areas. Remove all dead-storage items from the two- to five-foot zone, then look up or down for less accessible storage space.

There are two basic types of storage compartments: open and closed. Examples of open storage include shelves without doors (or with glass doors that allow a view inside) and hanging storage arrangements such as racks. In the modest mansion, it is best to use open storage whenever possible, because this augments the apparent size of the room: We see the room as extending to the rear wall of an open-storage compartment rather than ending at the front of the compartment. But open storage only works if you are neat. Most people want more storage space not because they lack places to neatly store their possessions but because they want the luxury of being messy. This is a luxury you may need to give up in a compact home.

Bathrooms, garages, and attics are good locations for additional storage. We generally do not spend much time in these areas, so we can accept a tight fit in them. If an attic is too small for living space, rods still can be suspended between the rafters, forming storage racks. Likewise, storage space can be found in the upper reaches of garages or above water closets, where headroom is not required. Chapter 6 offers some additional thoughts on where to find storage space in existing homes.

Provide Sound Isolation

Privacy is a cherished commodity in a compact home. If you create a truly private retreat—a private bedroom, study alcove, or den—small-home living will be far more enjoyable. But what does "truly private" mean? For Americans, privacy is incomplete unless we feel confident that our conversations are not being overheard. Other cultures have different standards. In Japan, for example, visual privacy is carefully assured with a variety of enclosures and paper screens. But acoustical privacy is not expected: Paper is a poor sound barrier.

The size of most American homes assures a certain degree of acoustical privacy, because the rooms are spread some distance apart: You generally can get away from the family's din by retreating to a remote room and closing the door. But in the modest mansion, rooms are apt to be close to one another or even completely open. How, then, can privacy be achieved?

Sound is a form of energy. When our eardrums are activated by it, they send an impulse to our brains that we interpret as "hearing" the sound. The perception of sound is logarithmic; this means it takes ten times as much energy for a sound to seem twice as loud. Conversely, a tenfold reduction in sound energy is required for a sound to seem half as loud. In practical terms, then, we must make a very large reduction in the amount of sound energy passing through a wall if we are to reduce even slightly the amount of sound we hear through that wall.

In Chapter 4, we discussed two of the simplest methods of reducing sound transmission through walls: sealing holes and adding mass. Sealing holes involves no space penalty—a well-sealed wall can be just as thin as a porous wall. But adding mass can make a wall substantially thicker. For example, a partition wall built of concrete blocks filled with sand will shut out sounds, but it will take up more floor space than a wall built with 2 × 4s or

2×3s, and it will be more expensive. You should create thick masonry partitions only when a high degree of acoustical privacy is truly required. Otherwise, consider using multiple layers of gypsum board on ordinary wood-frame walls. This will increase the massiveness of these walls while consuming only slightly more space than single layers of gypsum board.

One way to reduce the number of sound-blocking walls you will need is to surround a room requiring acoustical privacy with closets and other spaces that normally will be quiet. If the room does not share any walls with rooms in which noise will be made, it will not require massive walls.

Some people try to block sounds by placing acoustical materials on partition walls, but this does little good. Such materials primarily affect "reverberation time," the length of time a sound takes to die out. In other words, acoustical materials affect the sound quality within a room, but they do little to reduce the passage of sound *between* rooms. A room packed with acoustical materials will feel muffled, but the total amount of sound entering the room will be unaffected—you will still hear it.

Just how important is acoustical privacy? To put the question in context, let's close this discussion by heeding the words of a philosopher who had practical experience with compact-home living. In *Walden*, Henry David Thoreau humorously complained about his famous retreat:

> One inconvenience I sometimes experienced in so small a house, was the difficulty of getting to a sufficient distance from my guest when we began to utter the big thoughts in big words. You want room for your thoughts to get sailing trim and run a course or two before they make their port. The bullet of your thought must have overcome its lateral and ricochet motion and fallen into its last and steady course before it reaches the ear of the hearer, else it may plough out again through the side of his head.

If you, like Thoreau, go in for weighty conversations, take note. When such dangerously big words and thoughts are being slung about, it is more important than ever to have the sanctuary of a quiet room.

Control Light Sources

Anyone who has pulled back a window curtain to admit the rays of the early-morning sun understands the special quality that light can give a room. And brilliant light is not the only illumination that inspires us, for the glow from a dying fireplace ember—a mere fraction of a footcandle of light energy—can affect us just as deeply.

Light is one of the most expressive tools available to the small-home designer, because it comes in so many forms. It can be natural or artificial, constant or changing, diffuse or direct, directional or nondirectional. The amount of light striking a surface, the color of the light, the degree of contrast within a field of view—all these factors can be manipulated by the clever designer. The effects of this manipulation can be great, yet the cost can be pleasingly low.

Natural light is any form of illumination whose ultimate source is the sun. We experience it primarily in two ways, either as direct light—such as a shaft of morning sunlight entering an east window—or as diffuse light—such as the even, reflected light that enters a north-facing window. Direct light is brighter, warmer in color, and more dramatic, while diffuse light is bluer, more constant, and less directional.

In either form, natural light is a welcome addition to almost any room in the compact home. It serves many functions. The dynamic quality of natural light has the psychological effect of expanding the boundaries of a small room. The variability of the light connects us to the vast natural cycles—the diurnal and seasonal migration of the sun across the sky. In a modest mansion, enough window area can easily be included to give adequate general illumination throughout the house.

Direct sunlight is perhaps the most desirable light of all. Besides contributing to a sense of interior spaciousness, it can focus our attention on objects or surfaces of special interest. Direct sunlight has the added advantage of providing heat when used in passive-solar applications such as those discussed in Chapter 4.

The natural lighting received in each room depends on window placement. A rule of thumb is that a bank of windows will light a zone that is twice as deep as the windows are high. Thus, a bank of windows whose head is 7 feet above the floor will

Photo 5-3. *Clerestory windows can provide natural light to make a small space feel larger, as in this bathroom. (Design by Kelbaugh & Lee)*

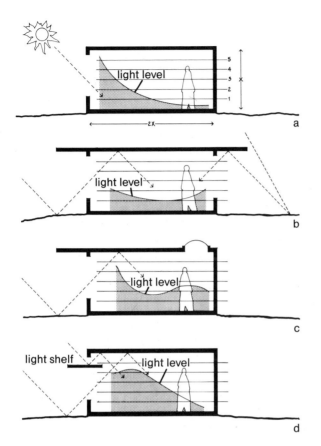

Figure 5-1. *Four daylighting situations: a. A window on one wall creates strong light at one side of the room, dim light at the other. b. Windows on opposite walls create relatively uniform light levels. c. A skylight can raise the light level in an otherwise dim area. d. A "light shelf" (a horizontal plane with a reflective surface) sends light further into a room.*

provide sufficient ambient lighting for a room up to 14 feet deep. If the room is deeper than this, artificial lighting will be required in the portion of the room farthest from the windows. Skylights and clerestories, the highest "windows" of all, are extremely effective for brightening up rooms.

Windows not only permit light to enter a room; most of them also allow the room's occupants to see out. The view from a window in a small house is a particular concern. As we discussed in Chapter 3, a window can increase apparent room size by allowing a view into the distance: The eye perceives the landscape as an extension of the room. A window need not be large to serve this function, if it is properly located. For example, the portal windows of an airplane, while quite small, often are positioned

Photo 5-4. *Glass blocks let in light without sacrificing privacy. They can be effective in a small bathroom, for example. (Design by Kelbaugh & Lee)*

precisely to allow views from the seats, thus relieving the claustrophobia that otherwise might afflict some passengers. Similarly, in traditional Zen, a restricted view through a small opening to a dramatic hidden landscape is used to relieve the spiritual intensity of Zen ritual.

Sometimes there may be conflicting demands on the limited exterior wall area in a small room. A desire to place furniture against a wall may compete with window location, for example. A partial solution is to place some windows high enough to free wall space for furniture below. However, if the windows get too high, we can no longer see out. Some view windows should be positioned for people who are standing and others should be at the proper level for people who are seated.

Occasionally, windows are intended to bring in light while excluding views altogether. Certain glazing materials such as glass block and fiberglass-reinforced polyester plastics transmit light without being truly transparent. They let through almost as much light as clear glass does, but they diffuse the light, scattering it in many directions. If privacy is important, such as in a bathroom or in an urban setting, this type of glazing may be advantageous. Think carefully before using such glazing as the only source of light in a room, however. The glowing surfaces that result can be unsettling—they contradict our normal experience by providing light without any accompanying visual information. We are accustomed to seeing through windows to gauge the weather or time of day; when our expectations are not met, we become uneasy.

Light can be used to affect our sense of a room's size. We expect rooms to be lit in a conventional way—by ceiling fixtures and normal windows. Hidden light sources, such as remote clerestory windows or back-lit partitions, have a mysterious quality that can make determining true room size difficult. In a modest mansion, this quality can be used to suggest there are unexplored realms in the house.

You should make judicious use of artificial light to supplement natural lighting. Sources of artificial light can be placed almost anywhere in a room, and this flexibility makes all kinds of effects possible. Artificial light even can be used to mimic natural light in its direction and color. For example, "complete-spectrum" light bulbs, placed in fixtures high on a wall, can mimic the light received from a high window. The changing moods of natural

Photo 5-5. *Light from an unseen source draws your eye upward and suggests realms as yet unexplored. In a compact home, this has the effect of psychologically enlarging a small space. (Design by Leslie Armstrong)*

light are not copied easily, however, so to this extent the illusion will be incomplete.

During the daytime, at least, you normally should use artificial light only to define activity areas and use natural lighting for ambient or general illumination. Thus, windows or skylights could provide most of the light in a room, while lamps could provide focused "task" lighting on a tabletop where work is to be performed.

When using artificial light for ambient illumination at night, you should illuminate the rooms indirectly by focusing the fixtures at surfaces that reflect the light back to the room. White, off-white, and other pale surfaces are best for this. The same principle holds when employing natural-light sources. Windows placed near the corners of rooms permit light to wash adjacent wall surfaces. The walls themselves become, in effect, natural-light fixtures that send light deep into the room, thereby decreasing glare from bright windows. Deep reveals in thick masonry walls serve this function also: Sunlight passing through the windows in the reveals is reflected off the sides of the reveals and is dispersed throughout the room.

How to control and manipulate light is a vast subject—far too complex to fully summarize here. A discussion of artificial light fixtures (such as suspended, recessed, and track fixtures) and bulbs (such as incandescent, fluorescent, and halogen) could fill a book, yet it would still leave much unsaid. You needn't undertake an elaborate study of illumination technology, however. Instead, cultivate a sensitivity to the effects of light. Examine the rooms in your present home and in your friends' homes, noting which make good use of natural as well as artificial light. Analyze the factors that contribute to the success of these rooms: The placement of windows, their orientation, the types and locations of light fixtures, the colors of walls and ceilings. Before long, you'll learn what sorts of lighting patterns suit you best, a lesson that will prove invaluable when you plan your new home.

Furnishing Strategies

Create "Implied Rooms"

Suppose that one day you wake to find that you have been given a warehouse in which to live. The warehouse, it turns out, is

a large open loft with a high ceiling. You want to move in as soon as possible, so you begin to bring over a few possessions to spruce up the place. You bring a bed, of course, and then maybe a large potted plant to stand at the side of the bed next to a chest of drawers that you have already placed nearby. Before long, you decide you want a little privacy, so you place a screen at the foot of the bed to separate it from the rest of the loft.

This kind of nesting impulse is so natural you are unlikely to stop and consider what design principle you are employing. You are creating an "implied" room, a space that is defined by something other than solid, opaque walls and ceilings. As soon as you

Photo 5-6. *This stairway changes dimensions to define space for a dining table. The columns and lowered ceiling also help establish the implied dining area. (Design by Terry Vaughan)*

placed the screen next to the bed, you created an implied room by marking a visually private zone.

The purpose of implied rooms is to create human-scale activity settings. When eating, sleeping, bathing, or reading, we instinctively feel most comfortable if we are sheltered in some fashion. The zones we create serve to intensify and focus the task at hand—while reading, we are not as apt to notice the table being cleared in the same room if we are seated in a niche formed by low partitions, for example.

In a compact home where privacy comes at a premium, implied rooms can provide at least partial privacy. They need not be complicated affairs. A well-known example is the canopied bed. In hot climates, the bed's gauze curtains allow ventilation while they prevent flying insects from invading. In cold climates, heavy curtains around the bed create a warm haven in a cool room. In both cases, the bed becomes a room within a larger room, not simply a piece of furniture.

A more contemporary example of a bed and its implied room is shown in Photo 5-7. Operable jalousie windows surround a bed that sits within a loft apartment. The jalousie win-

Photo 5-7. *a. Jalousie windows section off a portion of the living space in this home, creating a small bedroom. b. When the jalousies are open, the bedroom is part of the main space; when they are closed, the bedroom is private. (Design by Bray/Schaible)*

a

dows provide visual privacy when they are closed, because the windowpanes are a milky translucent glass. When the windows are open, the "bedroom" effectively disappears. This highlights one of the potential advantages of implied rooms: They can be designed to come and go.

Homeowners often create implied rooms after a house has been built, by carefully positioning roll shades, potted plants, or other space-defining items. Creating the "rooms" thus becomes a sort of impromptu, after-the-fact alteration of the house's layout. But implied rooms also can be integral to the original design of a house. In the northern California house shown in Photo 5-8, the roof and exterior walls are conceived as a simple hut-like enclosure, setting the stage for two large "aediculae" that dominate the house's interior. The boundaries of each of these implied rooms are established by four large columns that support an interior pyramidal "roof" above which the house's real roof hovers independently. There are no enclosed rooms in this house at all.

Whenever possible, implied rooms should reinforce natural behavior patterns. For example, behavioral scientists have determined that there are preferred distances for human conversation.

b

Photo 5-8. *Implied rooms are created in this California home by canopies supported by tall wooden columns. a. Note how the canopies are independent of the roof structure. b. The home's exterior has large sliding doors that, when opened, expose the home's windows. (Design by Charles Moore, Architect)*

Based on the carrying capacity of the human voice and the need to retain eye contact during intimate discussion, a circle of roughly ten feet in diameter is the limit for private conversation. If you are outside this range, voices must be raised, and a different, more public kind of communication takes place. This explains why the traditional arrangement of a sofa or couch with flanking chairs is so popular: It encourages conversation by providing sufficient proximity in an implied conversation area.

There are other natural patterns that can be reinforced by implied rooms. A stove or fireplace creates its own heated district. Consider changing floor finish, lighting level, or ceiling height to coincide with and emphasize this thermal "room." Likewise, a south-facing window providing bright sunlight can serve as the focus for an arrangement of seats or houseplants, creating an implied solarium. The possibilities are limitless. In fact, implied rooms can overlap—a part of the "thermal room" around the stove can also be part of the "solarium" by the window.

The opportunity for exterior implied rooms should not be overlooked. What is more delightful than a simple vine-covered trellis or a garden gazebo? Such areas offer relief from the summer sun while permitting view and sound. Our sense of smell should also be embellished—a "room" of fragrances from herbs and flowers can be entered through a gate in an evergreen wall, for example.

Select the Right Furniture and Accessories

Most people cart their furniture with them through life. Good new furniture or distinctive antiques are expensive, and mediocre used furniture is worth very little on the open market. The result is that furniture is not readily replaced—people actually change their addresses more readily than they change their furniture. You may not want to purchase a complete new set of furniture for your modest mansion, but do not be locked into existing furniture groupings. Indeed, the dimensions and layout of a modest mansion may force you to rethink your furniture preferences.

There are some fairly well established rules for selecting and arranging furniture, appliances, and accessories for small rooms. Some of them are:

1. Do not put too many pieces in a small room. It can make the room feel crowded—ready to burst at the seams. Excessive furniture calls attention to room size, making a small room seem smaller still.

2. Do not be afraid to use a few large pieces in a small room. One or two large pieces will alleviate the tendency of a small room to feel dollhouse-like. Generally, you should include furnishings and accessories of varied sizes. Some designers suggest using at least three sizes of furniture in each room—small, medium, and large—to provide different scales of visual reference.

3. Do not place furniture or appliances where they will obstruct passage through a room either visually or physically. According to one researcher, Edward Hall, "If Americans are asked to compare two identical rooms, the one that permits the greater variety of free movement will usually be experienced as larger." Admittedly, this rule is culturally biased; but we are the product of our culture, and in most cases we need to respect the culture's dictates. Japanese families tend to place furniture in the center of a room, leaving its perimeter clear for circulation. North Americans, by contrast, tend to leave the center of the room open, placing furniture along the walls.

4. Ask furniture to do double duty. When you think about it, most furniture gets off pretty easy. Why not ask it to do more? A dining table can double as a desk or kitchen counter, for example, or a hinged table can fold up to close a kitchen pass-through when it is not in use (see Photo 5-9). Partial-height bookcases or cabinets might become dividing elements between zones in living/dining room combinations. You could sneak additional storage under beds or tables (see Photo 5-10), or you could emulate the ingenuity of the early American furniture craftsmen who created the handsome chair-table shown in Photo 5-11. When the tabletop is down, it rests solidly on the handrail of the chair; when the tabletop is rotated up, it creates the back for a sturdy—if perhaps a little uncomfortable-looking—chair.

Many different furniture styles can fit comfortably in a compact home, but they need to be considered individually. Some traditional furniture styles, such as those created with wicker or rattan, consist of skeletal elements. Certain styles of modern furniture also have thin structural dimensions: Mies Van der Rohe's classic Barcelona Chair and popular designs by architects

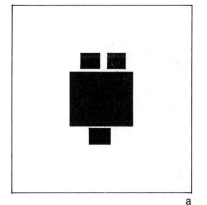

a

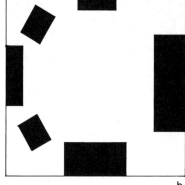

b

Figure 5-2. *Different cultures have different attitudes about organizing space. Japanese tend to place furniture in the center of a room (a) while Americans tend to place it around the perimeter (b).*

a

b

Photo 5-9. *a. A kitchen pass-through is closed off when this table is lowered. b. The legs of the table become shelves when the table is raised.*

Marcel Breuer and Alvar Aalto immediately come to mind. Their light skeletal forms allow us to see more of the room.

Massive furniture styles—such as heavily upholstered Victorian, overstuffed Art Deco, and recent Post-Modern furniture—occupy more space. They make a stronger presence in the room and block the visual flow of space. You probably will want to use fewer of these large, bulky pieces.

Furniture can include transparent materials. Glass cabinetry, for example, can be both practical and aesthetically pleasing. Of course, glass detailing brings with it a special responsibility for safety. Be sure to use safety glass—which can mean either tempered or laminated glass—where inadvertent shattering would be dangerous. Several plastic glazing materials such as lexan, acrylics, and polycarbonates offer transparency while also providing shatter resistance. However, some of these products experience considerable deflection when heavily loaded, so they would be inappropriate for horizontal or sloped installations.

Appliances are getting smaller and smaller, a real boon for the modest mansion. While technology can do little to reduce the size of a chair required to accommodate a typical posterior, it has done wonders in reducing the size of other household items. Whereas the typical television set of 1950 was 20 percent picture screen and 80 percent controls and cabinet, today's compact models are the reverse. The sizes of stereo decks, video recorders, home computers, and AM/FM radios are similarly shrinking—portability has become the rule. One result is that the concept of a fixed "home entertainment center"—so recently conceived—is already anachronistic. A fixed location for television viewing, in particular, is a needless luxury in the modest mansion. Perhaps future archaeologists will be able to date ruins from the mid-20th century by the existence of television rooms.

Fold It or Move It

In most households, certain activities such as eating and sleeping take place only at scheduled times, yet the rooms are continuously set for these activities. Beds are always lazily stretched out in bedrooms, waiting to be used, and dining tables seem to collect junk mail and empty lunch boxes while waiting for mealtime. Why not devise some method to move furniture out of the way when it is not on call? The size of your furniture need not be a

Photo 5-10. *Two double-duty dining tables. a. A table with storage space below. b. A foldable, portable table with storage space and built-in cooking surface, sink, and miniature refrigerator. (Designs by Michael Jantzen)*

Photo 5-11. *An early example of double-duty furniture: A New England chair/table from the last quarter of the 17th century. The back of the chair folds down to form a table surface. (The Metropolitan Museum of Art, Gift of Mrs. Russell Sage, 1909)*

major obstacle. With the use of wheels, castors, hinges, or pulleys, you can do amazing things.

Think about beds. If you can get them out of the way, the floor space they consume can serve other functions during the day. Roll-up mattresses were common in the small homes of the 17th and 18th centuries: When the occupants woke up, they put on their clothes, then rolled up their beds and put them away. More recently, the Murphy bed (invented in 1901) mastered the trick of folding up into wall cavities. During the last decade or two, Murphy beds seemed doomed to extinction, but today they are making a strong comeback. William K. Murphy, son of the original inventor, attributes his company's renewed sales to smaller home sizes and an increased awareness of the benefits of multiuse

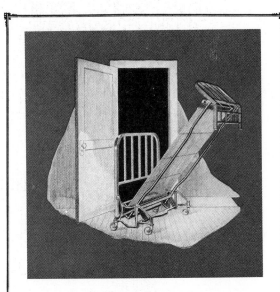

The Murphy In-A-Dor (Roller Type) Bed
A Portable Convenient Bed

HOMES already built do not need expensive alterations to enjoy the convenience of Murphy Concealed Beds. The Murphy Portable (Roller Type) Bed can be concealed in either a narrow deep closet or a wide shallow one and practically every home has closet space of the right size. With one of these beds the arrival of unexpected guests never cause the embarrassing position of being without an extra bedroom. Just roll the Murphy Portable Roller Bed out of its closet into any **convenient** room and take care of guests at any time. It is constructed to give solid comfort and, like all Murphy Beds, has a world-wide reputation for its practicability, durability and appearance because it's a Murphy Product. Substantial, good-looking Rubber Tired Castors are used on all Murphy Portable Beds.

Figure 5-3. *Another type of movable bed: This one—shown in an early Murphy catalog—can be positioned vertically and wheeled into a closet for daytime storage. (Courtesy of Murphy Door Bed Company)*

space. Guest bedrooms have been eliminated from many new homes, so Murphy beds have been installed in some of these homes to accommodate visitors. The Murphy bed—or its func-

a

b

Photo 5-12. *a. A Murphy bed has been fashioned into a temple-like pavilion. Mirrors on the doors increase the apparent size of the small living space. b. At bedtime, the doors are opened and the bed is lowered. (Design by Richard Oliver, Architect. Photo by Keith Meyer/ New York Times)*

tional equivalent—solves the problem of the folded mattresses and frequently uncomfortable sleeping geometries of convertible couches, because it folds up flat. If your modest mansion doesn't include a wall into which such a bed could fold, you might consider a cable-and-pulley arrangement to hoist a bed off the floor during the daytime, storing it neatly in a ceiling cavity.

The advantages of moving large objects out of the way is obvious. But don't overlook the benefits of moving small items, also. In the compact bathroom shown in Photo 5-13, there seems to be no mirror provided for use at the sink. This is an illusion,

Photo 5-13. *a. This small bathroom feels spacious because of the large window. b. When a mirror is needed, the picture on the wall swings out: The mirror is attached to its rear surface. (Design by Bruce Gordon, Shelter Associates)*

a   b

however. When it is needed, the mirror can be found behind the picture on the wall—the picture frame is hinged, and the mirror is attached to its rear surface. By swinging the picture out from the wall, you bring the mirror into position above the sink. Thus, the mirror is analogous to a Murphy bed, folding up when not in use, swinging out when it is needed.

Modern technology has provided other ways to move—or stack, or abolish—household objects that otherwise would be in your way. For instance, stackable washer-dryer combinations are now widely available. When you stack these appliances, you cut the amount of floor space they require by 50 percent. These and other movable, stackable items are ideal for the modest mansion.

Finishing Strategies

Manipulate Color, Pattern, and Shape

I have a two-year-old niece with a limited vocabulary who, nevertheless, has mastered colors. In fact, she requests her meals by color rather than by food name. She will ask for "brown and red," by which she means a hamburger with ketchup, or for an "orange," by which she means a carrot. The point is that color is one of the most important characteristics of an object or surface. It elicits an instant response, and it makes a deeper impression than shape or form. When we want to emphasize the significance of an object, we rely mainly on color identification: So stop signs and fire trucks are invariably red and school buses are always yellow.

It should not be surprising, then, that color affects our perception of the apparent size and position of objects. While there are many theories about precisely how we perceive color and light, most researchers agree that "warm" colors, such as red and yellow, are perceived as "advancing" toward the observer. Conversely, "cool" colors, such as blue and green, appear to "recede" from the observer. In addition, most researchers agree that pure colors appear to advance more than do grayed colors. Pastels, neutrals, and light colors such as beige, taupe, and gray are considered receding colors.

The consequences of color selection for the surfaces of small rooms can be pronounced. Advancing colors make the walls of a room appear closer to us than they really are. A room whose walls are painted red, for example, tends to feel small. Conversely, a room whose walls are painted light blue tends to feel spacious. For this reason, you should avoid painting a small room with intense primary colors unless you are intentionally seeking a sense of proximity and enclosure. You probably have noticed that many fast-food restaurants are decorated in garish, warm, intense colors. This coloring is certain to produce a restless, active mood—precisely the effect desired, because the restaurant owners want you to eat and get out. In a compact home, by comparison, your design goals are quite different—you usually want to create a calm, restful space with receding walls. To achieve this, your color palette should emphasize light blues, light grays, and similar shades. Do not forget that these colors can be applied to ceilings as well as walls. Perhaps a light blue can be used on a ceiling to suggest the sky.

Using the same color on adjacent planes can be effective. For example, when the walls and ceiling of a room are the same color, the room's apparent dimensions expand: The surfaces appear to blend and become continuous. For this reason, some designers favor monochromatic schemes in small rooms to simplify the visual landscape. As a side benefit, these schemes make it hard for the eye to discern irregularities in planes, such as those caused by imprecise plastering work. This can be a boon in an age when first-class workmanship is discouragingly rare. However, remember that color accents are necessary in monochromatic interiors. We expect visual clues to the size and distance of objects; if we eliminate all such clues, we run the risk of creating boring and unstimulating environments.

An extremely sophisticated technique is the use of color to create "trompe l'oeil" effects. Trompe l'oeil, literally "fool the eye," is a style of painting in which objects are depicted with photographically realistic detail. This technique gives a flat surface a sense of depth by illustrating scenes that seem to extend beyond the surface. So, for example, doorless walls can be painted so they seem to have entrances leading into lush gardens, and closed cabinets can be transformed into open cupboards full of foodstuffs. The trompe l'oeil tradition is an old and effective one,

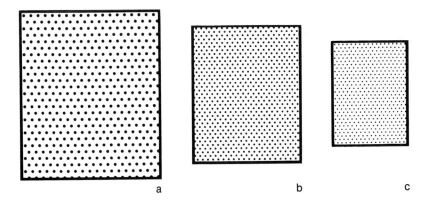

a   b   c

dating back to the Renaissance and the first use of perspective drawing. In the Renaissance and late Baroque periods, designers frequently manipulated false perspectives and multiple vanishing points to create illusions of grand spaces in compact surroundings. Unfortunately, such techniques require considerable virtuosity, so they probably are not appropriate for the average homeowner.

Related to the selection of color is the choice of pattern and texture. Particular patterns and textures create particular perceptions of distance. For example, we perceive surfaces with large grid lines or large dot matrices as being closer than surfaces with finer grids or matrices. In Figure 5-4, the dots in figure "a" appear large and close, while the dots in figure "c" seem to be in the background.

We sometimes hear the expression that a pattern is too "busy." This usually refers to a surface on which mixed spatial messages are being transmitted. If some patterns on a surface advance while others on the same surface recede, our brains are unable to make a coherent, comfortable interpretation of the whole. When color and pattern are overlapped, the perceptual effects can become even more pronounced.

Use Mirrors

A well-known trick is to use strategically placed mirrors or other reflective surfaces to increase the apparent size of small rooms. How often have you entered a small restaurant and wondered

Figure 5-4. *The patterns chosen for wall coverings and other furnishings can significantly affect our perception of space. Patterns of large elements typically feel closer than patterns of small elements.*

if the tables you see across the way were real or merely reflections of those nearby? If the lights are low and the ambience is right, the illusion can be very effective.

When the image we see in a mirror is familiar, such as our own faces, we automatically realize we are really seeing a reflection. If, on the other hand, the image is not recognizable, we have no immediate way of knowing whether it is a reflection. We are easily fooled into believing we are looking at a scene beyond the wall on which the mirror is mounted.

A problem with the use of too many mirrors is that multiple reflections can create psychological discomfort. In the mirror-house at the carnival, this disorienting effect can be a source of fun. But in the home environment, too many mirrors can cause unpleasant visual chaos.

Photo 5-14. *A surface of mirrors extending from floor to ceiling and from wall to wall dissolves the corners of the room, making it difficult to determine actual room size. (Design by Anderson-Wheelwright Associates)*

To create a successful illusion of depth, a mirror should encompass an entire surface, covering a wall from corner to corner and from floor to ceiling. In this way, the mirror will reflect the edges of the room continuously, emphasizing the effect of perspective lines receding into the distance. A mirror that occupies only a part of a wall will be "read" as a mirror, for the wall upon which it is hung will serve as a reference, allowing us to judge the boundaries of the room.

There are several traditional mirror locations. Homes usually have large bathroom or dressing-room mirrors, and often they have substantial entry-hall mirrors as well. Consider whether you can enlarge any of these mirrors to cover an entire wall. Some people prefer to marbelize or in some other way provide a tone to the surface of a mirror. However, this emphasizes the surface of the mirror, spoiling the illusion of depth that would have been created by a clear mirror.

Analyze Trim and Finish Decisions

In any residential construction project, installing trim is an important final step. Trim serves two very important functions. First, by covering joints between materials—such as between gypsum wallboard and the wood jamb of a window—it hides construction errors and discrepancies. As long as workers know a trim piece will be installed at a given place, they can work more quickly, without needing to cut each piece of material with painstaking precision. Second, trim is one of the chief decorative opportunities in a home. Because it is nonstructural, it can be configured in all sorts of unique shapes. As a result, most identifiable architectural styles have their own characteristic trims.

Interior molding trim is usually found around doors, windows, and other wall openings; at the bottom of walls; and—in older homes, particularly—at the top of walls. There are numerous other types of moldings, as well, such as wainscoting (a facing applied to the lower portion of a wall), moldings around bookcases or mantles, and chair rails that protect walls against scrapes from chair backs. Moldings can tie a home together decoratively, unifying an otherwise disparate collection of rooms.

In rooms with very high ceilings, a trim course sometimes is added at normal ceiling height to mimic the trim that once was common at the top of walls. This technique has the effect of reducing the apparent height of the room: The eye interprets the trim as the effective height of the ceiling. The illusion can be reinforced by changing wall color above the molding and by lighting the room to increase the contrast between the top and the bottom of the room.

Oversized trim should be avoided in compact homes. By calling too much attention to itself, trim can give a room a cluttered appearance. Also, trims such as high-contrast wainscoting or a bulky chair rail can reduce the apparent size of a room by visually chopping it in half. The solution generally is to deemphasize trim by using it only where absolutely necessary. For the same reason, some designers prefer to paint the trim the same color as the walls. In any event, all trim used in a compact home should be simple. This does not mean it has to be standard or boring, but it should probably not be wide or intricately sculpted.

Eliminating trim altogether requires careful attention to detail and excellent workmanship, but it can lead to a dramatically clean appearance. In so-called "zero detailing," gypsum wallboard is butted up to an "L" bead that stops short of the jambs and heads around doors and windows. This creates indented joints so the doors and windows are emphasized by recessed shadows rather than by protruding moldings. A more modern appearance results, but the home does not feel stripped down or unfinished, because the hand of the craftsman can be felt in the precision required to make the joints even.

Besides selecting trims, you must select finish materials for your home. In the vast majority of new homes today, gypsum board is the predominant wall-finish material, with tile reserved for walls in bathrooms and an occasional kitchen. Floor finishes exhibit more variety: Carpet, vinyl tile, ceramic tile, and wood flooring are all reasonably common. Each of these finishes works well in a modest mansion. As with trim, however, you should aim for clarity and simple detailing.

A surefire means of increasing apparent room size is to extend the interior finishes to the exterior, creating a visual continuity between indoors and outdoors. For example, the tiles on a den floor can be carried out through a floor-length window or glass door to an adjacent patio. In a similar way, the beams in a

Photo 5-15. *A cleanly detailed banquette coupled with an oversized window provides a compact yet comfortable place to eat in the corner of a kitchen. (Design by Kelbaugh & Lee)*

post-and-beam ceiling can be continued outside to form a trellis for vines or to support awnings that shade an outdoor deck.

In striving for these effects, precise detailing is extremely important. For example, a tiled patio should be at the same level as the interior floor that is covered with the same tiles: Even a single step down from inside to outside can ruin the illusion of continuity. Yet, in some locations, such a step is necessary to guard against snow build-up or flooding. In these situations, you might do best to extend a wall or ceiling finish to the outside. For example, a stone fireplace wall can continue outside to become a garden retaining wall or to mark the boundary for a patio.

Photo 5-16. *Stenciling adds a festive decoration that is well suited to a compact home. (Design by Tom and Kristen Beeby)*

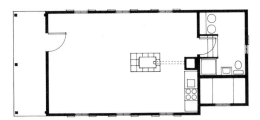

Figure 5-5. *The stenciling shown in Photo 5-16 was done in a unique modest mansion: a one-room school-house converted into a compact home. (Design by Tom and Kristen Beeby)*

One decorative finish that is particularly suited to the compact home is stenciling. Painted stencils can give a wall a festive and three-dimensional appearance without requiring the raised moldings or ornate trim that, for the reasons we have discussed, may be too obtrusive. And stenciling is an accessible technique—with a little patience, most homeowners can achieve spectacular results.

The greatest danger associated with stencils is the danger implicit in all the strategies discussed in this chapter: You must take care not to impose extraneous materials or details that conflict with, rather than complement, the home's basic design. People are generally more likely to remember the furnishings than a home's layout or design. But the architecture of a home—the proportions of the rooms, how the various rooms relate to each other, where light is permitted in, and so forth—creates the home's true character. Furnishings play a distinctly secondary role, even though they are more immediately visible. Therefore, the key to planning your home's interior is to identify the good qualities inherent in its design and then to use spatial, furnishing, and finishing strategies to emphasize these qualities.

Chapter 6

IMPROVING YOUR PRESENT HOME

Although, according to recent statistics, the average American moves every five years, there are a great many families who stay put. For these people, building a new home is not an option. Still, the principles of space efficiency can be important to them. There are many ways an existing home can be streamlined for compact living, regardless of its size. This chapter describes some of these techniques.

The statistics about our "mobile" society are actually a bit misleading. Bear in mind that the "average American" is a statistical construct, an abstraction based on the population as a whole, including people who rent apartments, people who travel from job to job, and other migratory types. Homeowners—people who have made a substantial commitment to a particular home in a particular community—move far less frequently than the average American, and the tendency of homeowners to stay where they are has increased during recent years. In 1977, American homeowners could be expected to stay in their homes 7.5 years. By 1982, this figure had increased to 11 years, largely as a result of high interest rates that discouraged people from making nonessential moves.

Experts generally agree that the trend for families to stay in their homes longer cannot continue indefinitely; but they also say it is unlikely that we will see a return to high turnover rates in homeownership any time soon. The result is that more people are

Photo 6-1. *Many families are remodeling their existing homes to create additional rooms or to close off unused rooms. Either way, most homes can be made more space efficient.*

staying put, and this situation will probably continue for the foreseeable future. Americans, therefore, are giving more thought to how to modify their current homes to take care of changing family needs.

Some stationary families are growing larger as infants arrive on the scene or grandparents move in to enjoy their retirement years. These families often are confronted with the problem of how to carve new rooms out of a fixed amount of existing space. On the other hand, many families are getting smaller as children leave the nest. These families find their homes becoming too large; often, they can benefit by cutting off and storing away underused rooms. Surprisingly, these two very different strategies— carving out rooms and cutting off rooms—can have the same effect. If executed properly, they can result in space-efficient homes that are both more comfortable to occupy and less expensive to maintain. Thus, families in both circumstances can benefit from reevaluating the spatial arrangements in their homes.

If you plan to stay in your present home, this may be a good time to adapt it for compact living. About 25 percent of America's houses were built before 1939, so they are approaching or are past their 50th birthdays. In many cases, major components of these houses need to be repaired. Siding, roofs, plumbing, or electrical systems need replacement. Sometimes the basic house structure itself needs repairs. If, like so many Americans, you are preparing to undertake major repairs on your house, you should take advantage of the opportunity to make the house more space efficient at the same time.

Carving Out Space

The size of a house does not determine whether the house is compact. More accurately, the controlling factor is how densely the house is occupied. As more people move in, the number of square feet of living space available to each individual is reduced, and space efficiency becomes an increasingly important consideration.

Of the two principle circumstances that lead to larger families and greater density, the arrival of children is usually the easiest to "handle." To a great extent, a child's arrival can be anticipated, and indeed most young families consider whether a house can accommodate children when they begin their search for housing. More difficult to anticipate is the arrival of grandparents or other relatives who come for extended—or even permanent—stays. Providing for the comfort of an elderly relative can be a particularly difficult demand in a compact home.

Earlier, we alluded to the fact that the average age of the American population is rising. In 1982, there were approximately 23 million Americans over the age of 65, and it is estimated that by the end of the century the number of elderly will have increased to 30 million. More and more resources are being spent on nursing homes and other housing facilities for senior citizens, but there is also a growing need for senior-citizens' housing within private residences. Unfortunately, not many private homes have adequate provisions for the elderly or the handicapped. Lack of privacy, adequate bathroom facilities, and handicap access can make caring for an elderly family member a trial for the entire family.

To visualize the magnitude of the handicap-access problem, consider the apparently simple problem of providing a ramp that will allow a handicapped individual to get from ground level to a 3-foot-high front porch. Access ramps should not be sloped at more than an 8.33 percent incline (they should not rise more than 1 foot for each 12 feet of horizontal run). This means a 3-foot-high ramp must be 36 feet long. An 8- or 9-foot rise from one floor to another would require a ramp 100 feet long. Obviously, this is impossible. Alternatives such as individual elevators become necessary.

Making provisions for a senior citizen in an existing home can be a challenge even if he or she is not handicapped. For example, the easiest way to provide space for an elderly relative may be to use an existing bedroom. But this may not be the best solution. Most elderly individuals seek a mix of privacy and community—they want to be able to choose when to mix with the family and when to be alone. Unfortunately, most existing bedroom clusters are not arranged with this consideration in mind. A bedroom originally intended for a child may not afford much—or any—privacy; it may be immediately adjacent to other bedrooms, for instance. A somewhat more remote location is usually preferable for a senior citizen's bedroom, and a private bathroom may also be needed.

Sometimes when an elderly relative arrives, the phasing works nicely—a child is leaving home at about the same time the relative appears. Even if the child's former bedroom is inappropriate for the relative, at least the total number of residents in the home does not increase, so working out suitable sleeping arrangements is comparatively easy. But more typically, no one is moving out when the new occupant arrives, so the problem becomes how to add a bedroom and bathroom to a home that already seems to be full. At first, this may appear to be a daunting task, but the truth is that most homes have underused space that can be converted into the needed rooms.

Finding Bedrooms

When you reconnoiter your home, looking for space that can become an extra bedroom, keep the following points in mind:

1. Learn from your existing house plan. Most plans have an underlying design logic. Rooms may be clustered together (see Figure 7-6), strung out linearly (see Figure 7-22), or stacked vertically (see Figure 7-24). At the same time, houses are invariably organized into a "private zone" containing sleeping quarters and a "public zone" containing living quarters (see Figure 6-1). As you search for new bedroom locations, consider how these rooms will relate to existing room patterns. In general, alterations that reinforce an existing pattern will prove the most successful. Whenever possible, use renovation projects to clarify the organization of your home, not to confuse it.

Figure 6-1. *Homes are usually designed so that "private" areas such as bedrooms are separated from "public" areas such as living rooms and dining areas. In the three layouts shown here, the private areas are shaded and the public areas are unshaded.*

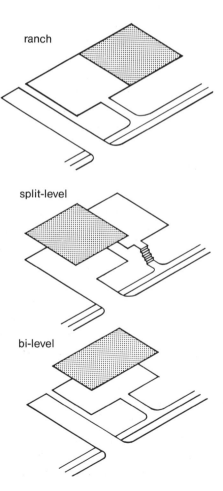

ranch

split-level

bi-level

There are some pattern disruptions you should definitely avoid. Do not create a bedroom that can be reached only by walking through private areas, such as other bedrooms. Try to avoid putting bedroom doors where they will open directly into public rooms, such as living rooms or dens, thus compromising privacy. Whenever possible, it is best to have a bedroom door open into a hallway or vestibule that can serve as a buffer zone between public and private space.

2. Incorporate any new room within the "environmental envelope," the area of the home that is heated or cooled for the comfort of the occupants. Of course, it is easiest if you can place the new bedroom in a part of the house where the basic requirements for habitability have been met already so no new insulation, waterproofing membranes, vapor barriers, or air-infiltration barriers will be required. However, often this is not possible: You may find it necessary to place a room in an un-air-conditioned and uninsulated part of the house, such as a basement or attic. In these cases, you will need to extend the environmental envelope to include the new room. Do the job thoroughly. For example, be sure not to leave gaps between new vapor barriers and existing ones. Structural degradation can occur at the joints of new and old construction if the details are not handled properly.

3. Respect structural integrity. Most homes are structurally very forgiving; they generally are built with a considerable margin of safety, so they usually can take a fair amount of abuse before they rebel. Anyone who has seen large holes cut through floor joists to make way for plumbing and wiring can easily understand that this must be true. But do not take the structural needs of your home lightly. Even though alterations in your home's structural bearing system (load-bearing walls, beams, posts, and rafters) may not result in an immediate structural failure, they may lead to all sorts of problems over the long run: Walls, floors, or ceilings may slowly sag or shift.

Bear in mind that not all walls function equally, even if they are built from the same lumber and are finished with the same materials. Some transmit roof and floor loads down to the foundation, while others carry only their own weight. Be sure to find out which kind of wall you are dealing with before you make any alterations, and remember that even non-load-bearing walls can have hidden plumbing and wiring that should not be breached. Before you remove any walls, check with a knowledgeable professional.

4. Conform to codes. Most codes stipulate that the habitable floor area of a new bedroom cannot be less than 70 square feet. Generally, no horizontal dimension can be less than 7 feet, and there are often limits on ceiling heights as well.

Often, the light and ventilation provisions of a building code are the most difficult to meet. Most codes require not less than 10 square feet of window area in each bedroom, and they further stipulate that the window area must equal at least one-tenth of the floor area. Therefore, in a minimal bedroom of 70 square feet, 10 square feet of exterior window would be required, one-half of which must be openable. If you want to carve a bedroom out of a windowless area of the home, this provision may be especially troublesome. Some people resort to creative plan-labeling—calling a bedroom a den or family room, for example—in order to get code approval. Before adopting this strategy, however, remember that the primary reason for building codes is to assure minimum standards. Are you really willing to settle for less?

In some localities, the extent of your home-improvement project will determine which codes and standards you must obey. If you are doing work on an old house that does not conform to current building codes, check to be sure that you will not be forced to bring the whole house—not just the improved area—up to existing codes. Some jurisdictions require that if the improvement is estimated to cost more than 50 percent of the cost of an equivalent new house, you must bring the whole house up to code specifications.

Further code information is included in the appendixes.

Where to Look

Attics

If you have an attic tall enough to stand in, this is a good place to start looking for extra bedroom space. The possibility for view, light, and air often makes an attic bedroom desirable. Located above it all, the attic is a naturally private haven. What's more, improved building components such as skylights and new insulation systems can make attics more hospitable than they were in the past.

If you are extremely fortunate, your attic will be partially or wholly insulated already. But if not, adding insulation should prove relatively simple, because the studs and rafters in most attics are exposed, leaving wide-open cavities waiting to receive insulation. Be sure to include an unbroken vapor barrier and provisions for ventilating the exterior side of the insulation. You will also need to tighten up the attic with caulk and weatherstripping, because the exterior surfaces of most attics contain numerous gaps that let the wind in—either the original builders saw no need to make the attics tight, or the attics have loosened up over time.

The biggest problem in many attic conversions is providing access. Few homes have stairways leading to their attics. If your

Photo 6-2. *Leaving the collar ties exposed increases the volume in this attic room. Multiple storage and work spaces have been fitted into the far wall. (Design by Bohlin Powell Larkin Cywinski)*

Photo 6-3. *A dormer can dramatically increase the usable space in an attic. The work and expense involved are small compared to the benefits.*

attic is 9 feet above the top floor in your home (a typical distance), a straight stair run leading to the attic would need to be about 13 feet long. Finding space for a stairway of this size may be all but impossible. A spiral stairway may be the only viable option in some cases.

The problem of access has another implication. The attic is not an ideal location for a senior citizen's bedroom—many elderly individuals find climbing stairs to be both difficult and dangerous. So if you are seeking room for an elderly relative in your home, perhaps you can give him or her one of the home's existing bedrooms and let a younger family member have the new attic bedroom.

Lack of headroom can be another problem. You may be able to stand erect in the middle of the attic, but headroom usually declines rapidly as you move away from the center because of the slope of the roof. Building a dormer is the traditional solution to this problem, and it is an excellent one. A dormer creates additional headroom, and it also provides one or more additional windows, thus contributing light and ventilation.

If a dormer is inappropriate for your attic, providing light and air can become the third obstacle to the creation of an attic bedroom. Windows can be added with relative ease in the gable walls at the ends of many attics. But providing windows in attic rooms that are located under hipped roofs or in the center of an attic can be more difficult. It is only in the last ten years that reliable, operable skylights, suitable for placement in steeply sloped surfaces, have become economical. The best of these roof-windows have built-in curtains or screens for shading, which can be essential to prevent overheating. High temperatures are a particular concern in rooms having skylights—sunlight can pour in unrelentingly.

Any new insulation you install in the attic's roof and walls should help ameliorate the extreme temperatures usually asso-

Figure 6-2. *Dormers provide ceiling clearance at the eaves of attics, increasing the amount of attic living space. The dashed line shows the profile of a full two-story house. An attic with dormers (solid lines) is far more compact.*

ciated with an attic. But almost certainly you will still need to provide mechanical heating and cooling. You may be able to extend your home's central heating and cooling systems to cover the additional load caused by the new attic room; many residential heating and cooling systems are oversized. Otherwise, you can install auxiliary systems of the sort described in the section of Chapter 4 called "Heating the Home."

Finally, a crucial matter: Check to be sure the attic floor joists can support the weight of a full floor load without undue deflection. In most older houses, this should not be a problem, because attic floors were frequently designed to allow the construction of attic rooms. Tables of acceptable spans for joists of varying sizes are available in most of the basic house-building texts listed in the bibliography at the end of this book. At worst, you may need to add some new joists to beef up the structural capability of the attic floor, particularly under any new partition walls you plan to install.

Basements

"Basement" is a term applied to a wide variety of actual conditions. A basement can be fully underground, only partially buried, or even entirely aboveground. This wide range of conditions affects the suitability of various basements for habitation; some basements are excellent candidates for a new bedroom while others present serious problems.

After a peak in the 1950s and 1960s, the popularity of basement conversions has waned. Evidently the difficulties involved in such conversions have taken their toll. The need for waterproofing and damp-proofing tops the list of problems, followed by the need to insulate the basement and the need to install additional doors or windows.

Your basement must be free of water leaks before you proceed with any renovation work, so be sure to address this issue first. Frequently, water pooling against a foundation wall is the culprit: The water works its way through the wall and into the basement. As a first step to correct this, be sure roof runoff is spouted away from the house for at least five feet. Also, if your yard slopes toward the house, create a swale (a shallow depression in the yard) to direct groundwater away from the foundation. If these steps do not keep your basement dry, more drastic remedies may be in order. Sometimes it may be necessary to dig a trench and install a drain line outside the footer at the base of the foundation wall to collect excess water and channel it away from the house.

Unless you live in an arid region, another step that often is required is treating the outside surfaces of the basement walls with a waterproofing compound or membrane. In many existing houses, the basement walls were not treated in this way, or the treatment was done poorly. Putting a membrane on the walls now is possible, but it is a substantial undertaking that involves excavating to expose the entire surface of each wall. Interior paints and sealers are available to impede the flow of water through walls, and some of them are pretty good as secondary lines of defense. But you should not rely on them to do the entire job of keeping water out of your basement. So if you have serious water problems, you may face the prospect of a major dig all around the perimeter of your foundation, both to install drain lines and to treat the exterior surfaces of the walls.

Besides drying your basement, you will need to address the issue of insulating your new rooms. Basement walls are best insulated on the outside, down to three feet below grade. You can install exterior insulation if you are excavating outside the basement walls to solve water problems. Otherwise, insulation can be placed on the inside of the walls. Rigid insulation can be installed between furring strips, or you can put fiberglass batt insulation in the cavities of new wood-frame walls. Build these walls with their studs pressing against the interior surfaces of the basement's masonry walls. Before erecting the wood walls, coat the interior surfaces of the masonry walls with a damp-proofing sealer.

One cautionary note about basement insulation: In regions of deep frost, insulating a basement can be dangerous, unless the soil outside the basement is well drained. If insulation prevents heat from passing through the foundation walls into the soil, water in the soil could freeze, expand, and push in the walls. This potential danger reinforces the importance of solving any water problems in or around the basement before proceeding to other work.

Most basement floors are slabs of exposed concrete, cold to the touch and potentially a serious avenue of heat loss. Generally, a basement room requires floor insulation if it is to be used as a bedroom. To provide such insulation, wooden "sleepers" (such as 1 × 3s or 2 × 4s) are laid on the slab—which should first be damp-proofed—and the insulation is placed between the sleepers. A plywood subfloor is then nailed on, and a carpet or wooden finished floor is placed on top. Thus, you wind up with an insulated wood floor above the basement's uninsulated masonry floor.

By insulating the walls and floor of the new basement room, you are constructing a self-contained, insulated "capsule" within the basement—a capsule that, like an attic room, will need to be heated. In some instances, heat can be provided by existing equipment (a furnace located in the basement may have enough excess capacity to heat the new room, for example). The alternative is to use heaters of the type discussed in Chapter 4.

Some basement conversions will require the addition of windows or doors to meet code requirements for adequate light, ventilation, and fire egress (see Appendix 2). And even if your basement already meets the code minimums, you may want to provide extra window areas to create a more hospitable living environment. For example, the codes usually do not stipulate that windows must provide distant views, but such views are certainly desirable. In England—where there is a long tradition of

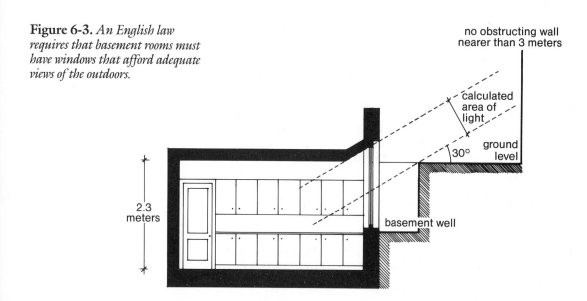

Figure 6-3. *An English law requires that basement rooms must have windows that afford adequate views of the outdoors.*

ensuring adequate daylighting through the enforcement of building codes and legislation—a law passed in 1963 mandates that a basement bedroom should have windows equal to at least 10 percent of the floor area and that these windows should be positioned where anyone within 30 degrees of them and up to three meters away (about ten feet) will have an unobstructed view to the outdoors (see Figure 6-3). Most United States residential building codes treat all windows equally, regardless of whether they provide an unobstructed view.

Garages

Most existing garages were designed at a time when the large gas guzzler was the vehicle of choice. A typical 1968 Cadillac, for example, measured a bit over 19 feet long and 6 feet 8 inches wide. Today, cars have become shorter and narrower: The 1984 Honda Civic is 12 feet 6 inches by 5 feet 4 inches. The upshot is that old garages tend to be bigger than necessary for today's cars, so the unused space in these garages can be put to other uses. Typically, single-car garages in the early 1970s were built up to 22 feet long and 12 feet wide. It is entirely possible to renovate a garage of this size to accommodate a bedroom measuring 12 feet by 7 feet 6 inches and still have enough space left over to park a 1984 Civic.

A garage bedroom will probably be located at the rear of the garage, and—if the garage is attached to the house—it may use an existing doorway as the entrance into the house proper. But in most cases, a new door will have to be installed so you will have separate doors for the bedroom and for the remaining car-storage area. The requirement for a new door need not be a drawback, however. One of the big advantages to garage conversions is that the new bedroom can have its own private entrance—a particularly important detail for teenagers or the independent elderly.

The floor of an attached garage is usually at least one step lower than the floor of the house itself, to keep potentially noxious automotive spills from leaking into the house. It is good to raise the floor of a garage bedroom by putting down sleepers of the type we discussed for basements. You should do this whether or not the garage is physically connected to the house. It will protect the bedroom from spills; it will provide space for floor

Photo 6-4. *Garage conversions are popular. A home's usable living space is increased by renovating the garage as a bedroom, living room, den, or other area.*

insulation; and—in attached garages—it will bring the floor level of the bedroom even with the rest of the house.

Make sure the garage is well ventilated, and thoroughly seal the wall between the bedroom and the car-storage area to prevent fumes from infiltrating the bedroom. Tighten the bedroom's other walls to shut out the weather, then insulate all of the bedroom's walls and its ceiling. In an attached garage, you may be able to heat the bedroom by extending the home's central heating system. Usually, however, you will need to install separate heating and cooling equipment.

If your garage is not large enough to divide into separate bedroom and car-storage areas, then consider turning the entire garage into a new room or set of rooms. This is one of the most popular renovation projects in some areas of the country. You'll have to park your car outdoors, but exchanging car space for people space can be a good trade.

Closets

Sometimes an extra bathroom can solve a space shortage just as well as another bedroom. There are many homes in which a den or study could serve as extra sleeping quarters if adequate bathroom facilities were easily accessible. Find a convenient location to insert a bathroom near such a den, and the den can readily be converted into a bedroom. But where can you find space for this new bathroom?

A walk-in closet is an ideally sized space for conversion into a compact two-fixture bathroom (see Figure 6-4). Moreover, such closets frequently are located in a home's "service core," which comprises bathrooms, additional closets, and other support spaces— the part of the house that already contains plumbing lines and vent stacks. Thus, in this location, it is relatively easy to hook up a new bathroom.

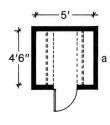

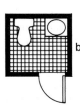

Figure 6-4. *A walk-in closet (a) may be converted into a two-fixture bathroom (b).*

New Space

Occasionally, finding adequate space within the house for an extra bedroom is virtually impossible. You may be stuck, for example, if the house has no basement or attic, and if none of the existing rooms can be divided or converted from its present use

a

b

Photo 6-5. *a. An existing porch can be enclosed, creating a new dining area so the old dining room is freed for a different function. b. Careful detailing—skylight, built-in spice rack, single-pane sashes at eye level and multiple panes above—gives the new dining area a feeling of generosity. (Design by Tony Atkin, Architect)*

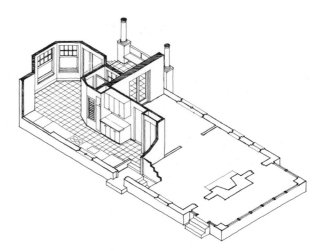

Figure 6-5. *This isometric drawing shows the new kitchen/dining area.*

into a bedroom. You then may have no option but to add some new space to the house to accommodate the bedroom. It is still possible, however, to make use of some existing structural elements of the house or garage to lower your costs. One popular solution is a second-story addition on a garage. This works best when your garage has a flat roof that can become the floor of the new second-story bedroom. But if the garage has a high-peaked roof, you may be able to fit a bedroom in the area under this roof, particularly if you add a dormer to the side of the roof.

Another popular project is the conversion of a partially enclosed porch into a fully weatherized room. This new room can sometimes be a bedroom, but often—to keep the house properly zoned between public and private space—it may more appropriately be another room such as a den or family room. The old den or family room then may be converted into the new bedroom.

One of the big advantages of conversions like these is that no new foundation work is apt to be required. However, before you undertake your project, check the condition of the structure onto which you will be building. Garages and porches are likely to be more exposed to the elements than the other areas of the house. They may require additional floor or wall reinforcement—or even foundation repairs—before they can carry new loads.

Cutting Off Space

We have been dealing with the question of finding space for an extra family member. Let's turn now to the opposite situation: closing off space in a house that has become too large either because the family has gotten smaller or because the family's needs have changed for other reasons.

The high cost of heating unoccupied rooms has led many cold-climate homeowners to examine how much space they really need. Some have decided to cut off and "store" rooms they no longer need on a regular basis. Perhaps one or more children have moved away, leaving empty bedrooms behind. Or perhaps the family simply has realized that its home contains more rooms than it ever actually needed—more rooms than it cares to keep heating, in any event.

If done properly, placing items in long-term storage can be a big job. A wool sweater, for example, needs to be cleaned, packed with camphor, and kept in a cool place. Similarly, rooms headed for storage must be properly prepared for their hibernation. This is not always as easy as it may sound. Unlike ships, designed and built with watertight compartments that can be isolated during emergencies, most houses are conceived and built as organic wholes, analogous to the human body. There is a central nervous system—the heating, plumbing, and electrical equipment—and an outer skin—the continuous insulating envelope. To store a

Photo 6-6. *A space can be closed off permanently, or it can be closed and opened daily. This is not a converted garage: The large insulated door was installed between a dining area and an attached greenhouse. a. During the day, the door is raised, so the greenhouse becomes part of the home's living space. b. At night, the door is lowered. (Design by Daniel V. Scully, Architect)*

a

b

room properly to realize real energy savings, the room must first be removed from the life-support systems of the house.

What this means in practical terms is that the room being stored should be separated from the home's heating, ventilating, and air-conditioning (HVAC) systems. With some systems, such as forced-air furnaces and ducts, this is a relatively easy task, because the ducts usually are equipped with manual dampers in each room to control the quantity of airflow. Closing one or two dampers will curtail the flow of heat to the stored room.

Other HVAC systems may be harder to zone. A hydronic system, such as a baseboard system that relies on hot water to temper the air temperatures in a room, needs to be equipped with a bypass valve at the boundary of the room that is to be stored. When closed, the valve will prevent water from flowing through the baseboard units in this room. If such a valve is already in place, isolating the room is as easy as turning a knob. But installing a valve usually entails additional plumbing work: You must add pipe that will reroute the water to the baseboard units in another room.

Whatever HVAC system you have, the essential point is that the stored room must be zoned off from the rest of the house. Once this has been done, the next step is to ensure that the room does not rob hot or cold air from rooms that are still being occupied. To reduce air infiltration, care should be taken to seal doors leading to the room. Among other benefits, this will help prevent condensation from forming on the cool surfaces in an unheated room; such condensation may be caused by warm, moist household air entering the room. (If you still get condensation in the room after sealing the door, your household air is too humid—take steps to reduce the amount of water vapor you release into the air in the heated regions of the home.)

Sometimes tacking blankets of insulation onto the interior walls of a stored room may also be worthwhile, to retard the flow of heat through the walls. This will take the thermal isolation of the room one step further. If you go about the storage process correctly, during cold weather the stored room should be much cooler than the rest of the house, while in hot weather it should be much warmer. The greater the difference between temperatures in the stored room and the normal temperatures maintained in the rest of the house, the greater your energy savings will be.

There are limits to how successful your Btu-trimming will be. For example, if the exterior walls of your house are already very well insulated, the savings you can expect from your efforts will be proportionately smaller. The law of diminishing returns makes each extra expenditure for energy conservation a longer-term investment.

These built-in limits may be a good thing, because if you are *too* successful at sealing off a room, you can run into problems. Be sure there are no plumbing runs in any of the walls of the stored room, for example; these could freeze if room temperatures drop too far. Another problem is harder to analyze. Large temperature swings occurring over a long period of time may cause expansion and contraction leading to cracks, leaks, and other undesirable consequences in the stored room. Very little firm data exists about the effect of such problems on the life expectancy of a building; what little data does exist has been generated in laboratory tests on separate building materials, not in tests of entire buildings. However, we do know that it is best to prevent thermal extremes in stored rooms by providing a small amount of heat. So be moderate in your efforts to isolate the stored room—don't try to block absolutely all heat flow between that room and the rest of the house.

Despite the potential problems, storing rooms can be highly effective. The technique is as old as architecture itself. In the days before sophisticated mechanical equipment, a large home was more than just a luxury: Its size was part of its climate-control system. Today we travel between climates; in bygone days, people migrated within the home—as the seasons changed, different segments of the house were closed off. In the second century B.C., a Roman named Vitruvius wrote *The Ten Books on Architecture*, the earliest surviving treatise on Western architecture. Vitruvius gave this advice about room placement:

Dining rooms for spring and autumn [should be] to the east; for when the windows face that quarter, the sun, as he goes on his career from over against them to the west, leaves such rooms at the proper temperature at the time when it is customary to use them. Summer dining rooms [should be] to the north, because that quarter is not, like the others, burning with heat during the solstice, for the reason that

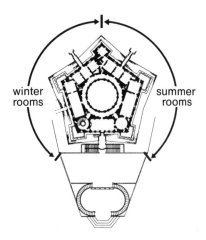

winter
rooms

summer
rooms

Figure 6-6. *An early example of storing rooms is the Palazzo Farnese. The residents lived in one suite of rooms during the warm months, then closed these rooms and moved to south-facing rooms for the cold months.*

it is unexposed to the sun's course, and hence it always keeps cool, and makes the use of the rooms both healthy and agreeable.

During the Renaissance, aristocratic families put this principle to work on a grand scale in buildings like the Palazzo Farnese, in Caprarola, Italy. This magnificent villa, designed in the mid-16th century, has a symmetrical plan that functioned as two distinct but equal houses during different seasons (see Figure 6-6).

Accessory Apartments

Apart from storing rooms, what else can be done with excess space in our homes? In some instances, you can look on such space as a source of revenue. Many people are doing this by creating "accessory apartments." When a relative or friend becomes a permanent resident in an existing house, no rent usually changes hands and no additional legal dwelling unit is created. If, however, you convert a section of your house into an apartment that you rent out, you could reap financial benefits. In Denmark, an accessory apartment is called a "kangaroo apartment"—a rather graphic description of how the apartment relates to the house proper, a small residence tucked into a larger residence's pouch.

Creating accessory apartments always has been reasonably common in urban neighborhoods, but it is now also becoming popular in the suburbs. The inner suburban rings—the communities lying closest to urban centers—have been particularly affected. As transportation costs have risen, the shorter commute to and from these communities and the easier access to mass transportation they offer have attracted a new round of residential development. Much of this development has focused on the rehabilitation and remodeling of single-family homes, often including the creation of additional bedrooms and entire apartments. Data from the 1980 census indicate that between 1970 and 1980, as many as 2.5 million single-family houses may have been renovated to create accessory apartments.

The Statistics Division of the National Association of Home Builders has predicted that an average of 500,000 accessory apartments will be created annually throughout the 1980s, for a total of 5 million such apartments in ten years. This is an enormous number when it is put into perspective. For instance, there was a total of about 1.1 million housing starts in 1982, not including accessory apartments. If the number of housing starts holds constant during the next few years, we can see that the half-million accessory apartments created each year will add almost 50 percent to the available stock of new housing. Clearly, we are looking at a major housing trend.

An accessory apartment is legally and practically very different from shared housing, in which kitchens and other major facilities are used in common by several occupants. Invariably, an accessory apartment has a private entrance, kitchen, and bathroom facilities. Even more important than the physical differences are the legal ones—when you construct an accessory apartment, you become a landlord with all the opportunities and responsibilities this entails.

Accessory apartments offer several real advantages to different segments of the community. Elderly homeowners can use rental income from such units to retain a home they otherwise might have been forced to sell because of the rising cost of living. Moreover, they and their tenants can benefit from a degree of companionship and security. Single parents and other individuals with limited incomes might be able to afford a home for the first time: The rental income they receive would help offset their mortgage payments. On occasion, elderly relatives of the homeowners could benefit. Such relatives often do not want to accept "charity," so they decline to move in with family members. An accessory apartment could enable them to maintain their financial independence and dignity while enjoying the advantages of physical proximity to the family.

Unfortunately, accessory apartments are illegal in many localities, usually because of zoning restrictions that have been put on the books to prevent overcrowding. The communities fear that greater population density will depress property values and decrease the desirability of their neighborhoods. Unfortunately, these knee-jerk reactions wholly overlook the quality of the new construction and the manner in which it might occur. Greater population density is not, in itself, anything to fear. After all, some of the most desirable and expensive residential addresses in the world—Park Avenue in New York City or Hyde Park in

London, to give just two examples—have enormously high densities. The real question is whether adequate amenities are provided to support the population. Are there sufficient parking, recreational, and shopping facilities to meet the needs of additional occupants? If there are, then increased population density *per se* is not a problem.

The American Planning Association issued a report in 1981 titled "Accessory Apartments: Using Surplus Space in Single-Family Houses." The report urges local officials and planners to revise codes that prohibit accessory apartments. It notes that "there are 18.3 million American homeowners with households of two persons or less living in homes of five rooms or more. Fifty-seven percent of homeowners 55 years of age and over live in such circumstances. . . .These underused housing resources are increasingly being looked at by homeowners as a source of income and services."

In some parts of the country, new homes are being marketed with accessory apartments already designed into their floor plans. A small family can be very comfortable in the main part of the home while receiving income from the apartment. Later, if circumstances warrant, the accessory apartment can be folded back into the home to provide more living area.

Variations on the concept of the accessory apartment are appearing in some communities. "Granny flat" is an Australian term for a concept known increasingly in North America as "echo housing"—an acronym for "elder cottage housing opportunities." Echo housing consists of small, removable cottages placed in rear or side yards to permit older people to live independently yet near the homes of their sons or daughters. A dwelling of this sort does add to the overall square footage of the occupied structures on a site but not to the extent that a full-scale retirement home would.

Other new forms of housing also are evolving, inspired by conditions similar to those that have fostered the accessory apartment. In the new-housing market, particularly on the West Coast, the so-called "mingles" co-ownership home has been gaining popularity. A mingles has two separate master bedroom suites but only one kitchen, dining area, and main living area. In such an arrangement, two unrelated occupants can live in the house and retain ownership advantages. The occupants have their private sleeping areas and they share the rest of the house. Such an arrangement is especially suited to many first-time and low-income home-buyers who otherwise might be priced out of the housing market.

The architectural possibilities of these various new living arrangements are only beginning to be explored. Too often, the design strategy has been to build a conventional house and then graft on a few additional entrances or walls. Perhaps the future will see a richer suburban landscape as the new living arrangements give rise to new, more authentic designs.

PART 3

Chapter 7

PUTTING IT ALL TOGETHER

This chapter gives you an opportunity to study how several successful architects and designer/builders have dealt with the constraints and opportunities of compact-home design. The 11 homes in this chapter were selected because they are excellent structures that, among their other virtues, employ many space-saving principles. Good designers do not isolate one concern and address it separately from all others; they balance the many goals in each building program, seeking a synthesis that will permit all of these goals to be realized. In this spirit, the homes presented here respond simultaneously to many design considerations, not only to the need for compactness.

The homes we will look at differ dramatically from one another in complexity, style, and cost. They were designed for different regions of the country with dissimilar climates and varied architectural traditions. Some of them were designed with specific families in mind; others were produced for the general housing market. It should not be surprising that they look very different from each other nor that they range from the relatively humble to the relatively opulent, reflecting different levels of amenities and craftsmanship. Some contain highly personal details that you would want to modify in your own home, but each has a lesson to offer.

You will benefit most from these examples if you look beyond the superficial differences of exterior decoration and focus instead on how the spaces in the homes are arranged. You will discover homes in which the spaces are arranged linearly; homes in which they are stacked; and homes in which they are clustered. You will find one-, two-, and even three-story homes. By comparing these arrangements, you should be able to judge which type suits your needs best. This is an important initial step on the road to planning your own modest mansion.

Each of the 11 homes is represented by one or more floor plans, an exploded isometric drawing, and several photographs. All of the floor plans are presented at the same scale (one inch equals 16 feet) so size comparisons between homes can be made easily. Similarly, all the isometric drawings are reproduced at a consistent scale. The text accompanying the illustrations guides you through each house, pointing out space-saving strategies and also more general architectural principles and details.

Triple A House
Architects: R. E. Hulbert & Partners
Location: Vancouver, British Columbia, Canada
Size: 640 square feet (basic plan, with upstairs allowing
    500 more square feet)

Affordable, accessible, and adaptable—these are the key words that apply to this Canadian house. Developed as a prototype for the Vancouver division of the Housing and Urban Development Association of Canada, the Triple A is intended to be sold as low-cost housing. Its compact, rectangular floor plan enables neighborhoods of these units to be clustered tightly together for high-density development. This saves acreage and reduces costs.

In its basic model, the Triple A is finished only on the first floor, yielding a total of 640 square feet of living space. There is one bedroom, one bathroom, an open-plan kitchen/dining/living area, and no basement. This configuration is particularly suited to the needs of the elderly, the handicapped who cannot negotiate stairs, and the "starter" homebuyers who cannot afford the high mortgage rates required by large homes.

But the most impressive feature of this house is that it squarely addresses the problem of changing family size and needs. When a growing family requires more space, the upstairs area can be finished as a work space or family room, or it can be partitioned into several bedrooms. With this flexibility, the Triple A can support a wide range of family sizes.

Photo 7-1. *A model Triple A House built in downtown Vancouver. Note the wing walls and column, which give the home a larger presence.*

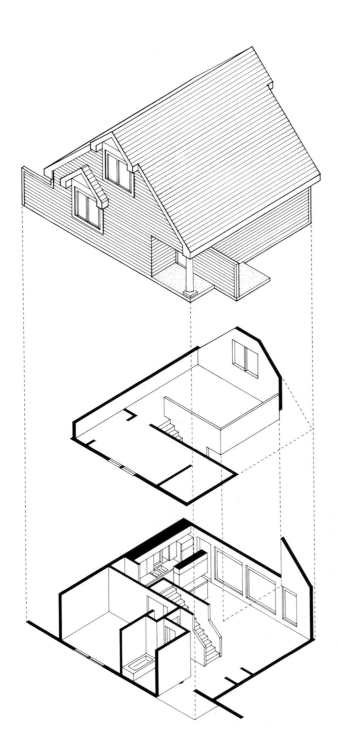

Figure 7-1. *Exploded isometric drawing of the Triple A.*

Figure 7-2. *Plan of the Triple A first floor. Containing 640 square feet, this floor has a bedroom, bathroom, kitchen, and open-plan living/dining area.*

1. Bedroom
2. Kitchen
3. Living/Dining Area
4. Entry
5. Bathroom

a

b

c

Figure 7-3. *The upper floor of the home can be finished in several ways.*

1. Bedroom
2. Dressing Room
3. Bathroom
4. Den
5. Study/Guest Room

Even more remarkable is how well the first-floor plan can respond to a second-floor renovation. If all the bedrooms are moved to the second floor, the first floor can be converted easily into a highly functional arrangement of common rooms. The original master bedroom can be converted readily to a dining room that will be accessible from the kitchen. With the dining area removed from the open-plan family room, the kitchen can be enlarged and enclosed, while the resulting living/family room will become more generous and private. During such transformations, the Triple A remains very space efficient, for its basic configuration includes little dedicated circulation space and no corridors at all. As the home is altered, little if any additional circulation space is required.

As you approach the Triple A from the street, you may be reminded of a child's drawing of a house with a gable roof, a single door, and a few large windows. But a second glance reveals that a great deal more is going on. Exterior details have been carefully selected to manipulate our perception of the home's size. For example, the front facade of the house extends horizontally in wing walls—further emphasized by horizontal siding—to create an impression of great width when seen from the street. A large decorative column—far larger than is required structurally—marks the entry to the home. The visual impact of the entry is further reinforced by a recessed porch that provides shelter from the plentiful Canadian snow. These details—like the surprisingly large windows—give the small home great presence.

Upon entering the house, you are presented with a continuous view from the entry hall across the living area and through a strategically placed picture window to the landscape beyond. A feeling of spaciousness is thus achieved. An open stairwell just off the entry hall leads to the second floor. In some variations of the basic configuration, the second floor is converted into a loft: Part of the living area is beneath this loft and part is open all the way to the finished inner surface of the roof. This openness reinforces the sense of spaciousness.

In all cases, the use of parallel-chord trusses for the roof structure allows the entire upper floor to be available for habitation. Parallel-chord trusses, which normally are used in floors, take up very little space; their use in the Triple A's roof structure reflects the designers' ingenuity. Between the trusses, there is ample room

Photo 7-2. *In the basic Triple A model, the kitchen is slightly separated from the living/dining area.*

for the substantial insulation required for energy efficiency in cold climates. The house also incorporates other energy-saving features, such as R-28 insulation in the perimeter walls and an air-to-air heat exchanger.

Photo 7-3. *Parallel-chord trusses (normally intended for floor construction) are used in the roof structure.*

Hurd Residence
Architect: Turner Brooks
Location: Starksboro, Vermont
Size: 1,000 square feet

This house commands a rolling site in northern Vermont. Gazing at it from across the adjacent field, you are confronted by the gable end of what appears to be a large house with a generous porch. But as you walk around the house, you realize that your first impressions were mistaken. This is actually a modestly sized home with big ideas.

Studying the house more closely, you spot various clues indicating that things are perhaps not what they first seemed. You realize the large columns that visually anchor the corners of the home are considerably larger than necessary. (They are essentially decorative, surrounding standard square posts that extend downward, forming piles for the home's foundation.) Moreover, the

Photo 7-4. *The Hurd Residence has a large front porch with massive columns that give the compact structure a large presence. The subtle placement of variously sized windows adds to the home's attractiveness.*

apparently simple facade of the house turns out not to be straight at all, but a wandering wall in search of a plumb line.

You enter from a small porch at the northeast corner of the house. An interior-view window in the kitchen affords surveillance of the front door while the rest of the kitchen wall defines an entry hall. Living and dining take place in one large room that adjoins the porch. From inside this room, you can appreciate that the quirky porch wall actually defines zones of activity—making implied rooms—within the large open-plan space. A pair of large sliding glass doors extends the living area out to the porch, which provides a transition zone between the domesticity of the house and the undisturbed natural setting.

The master bedroom on the north side is a saddlebag-like extension jutting from the simple form of the home. It is flanked by smaller saddlebags that contain the entry porch and bathroom. The bathroom is conveniently located to service both the master bedroom and the living area on the first floor.

A stairway leads to the second floor. There, a large landing occupies the center of the gable—it can be used as an additional bedroom, a study, or a den. An oversized window, of the grand scale befitting the gable end of the house, provides plenty of south light to the room. In the smaller rooms to either side—which can be used for storage or additional living space—headroom is restricted by the steeply sloping roof. Nevertheless, all of the volume under the roof is used.

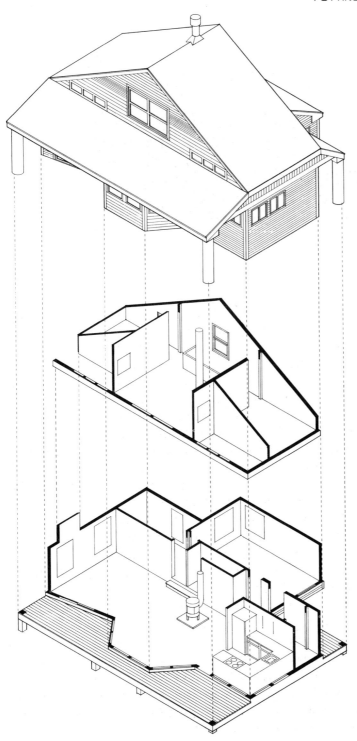

Figure 7-4. *Exploded isometric drawing of the Hurd Residence.*

Figure 7-5. *Hurd Residence floor plans. a. The lower floor has an open-plan living/dining area, plus the kitchen, bathroom, and master bedroom. b. Two small storage areas and a landing/bedroom occupy the upper floor.*

1. Bedroom
2. Kitchen
3. Living/Dining Area
4. Entry
5. Bathroom
6. Landing/Bedroom
7. Storage

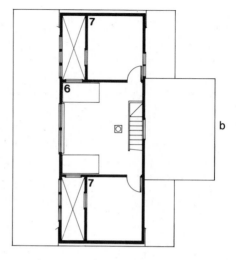

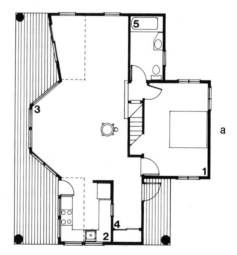

Light is shared among rooms. For example, a row of stubby windows in the two-story space adjacent to the smaller second-story rooms provides light for the kitchen and living spaces on the first floor as well as for the upstairs rooms. This wash of natural light brightens the home. A cut-out opening at the base of the stairwell supplies further visual release as you descend the stairs.

Photo 7-5. *The home feels surprisingly spacious. This view shows the interior as seen from the kitchen looking into the living/dining area.*

The open-plan living/dining room provides an ideal location for the woodstove that serves as the central heating system for the house: The open stairwell allows warm air to rise into the second-floor rooms. While not overtly solar heated, this house—like many of the houses in this chapter—benefits from solar "tempering." Sunlight floods through the ample south-facing windows, while the relatively small north, east, and west windows minimize window heat losses. And because summer can get hot even in Vermont, operable windows provide cross-ventilation throughout the house.

The design of the Hurd Residence owes a clear debt to the "shingle-style" regional tradition of New England. But in its willingness to adapt traditional solutions to contemporary living patterns, it is thoroughly modern, meriting detailed study by the contemporary small-home designer.

Gordon Residence
Designer/Builder: Bruce Gordon
Location: Free Union, Virginia
Size: 460 square feet

By any standards, the Gordon Residence is compact; at 460 square feet, it is one of the smallest homes in this book. But it is

Photo 7-6. *The Gordon Residence nestles among trees in the Virginia woods. This view is from the southwest.*

also one of the best examples of putting design principles to work to make good use of limited space.

The house is essentially one large room with cantilevered alcoves that provide special nooks for sitting and sleeping. Only the bathroom is a separate, enclosed space. Nevertheless, because the zones of the house overlap and there is plentiful window area to provide light and view, the house feels surprisingly spacious.

The house is perched on a steeply sloping site, supported by a pole foundation with a compact footprint. Where the grade drops off, space opens up under the house for storage, a pressure tank, a washing machine, and a water heater.

You enter the house from a porch on the north wall, protected by an ample roof overhang under which firewood is stored in the

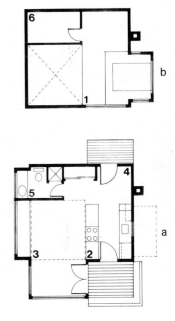

Figure 7-6. *Exploded isometric drawing of the Gordon Residence.*

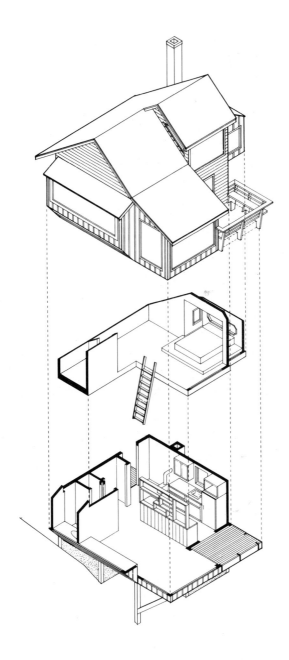

Figure 7-7. *Floor plans of the Gordon Residence. a. The first floor is essentially a single room. The deck on the south side can be reached through the kitchen area or through the main living area. b. The upstairs sleeping loft is reached via an adjustable ladder.*

1. Bedroom
2. Kitchen
3. Living/Dining Area
4. Entry
5. Bathroom
6. Storage

Photo 7-7. *The deck on the south side of the house has built-in seating that is slightly cantilevered to free more deck space.*

winter. The deck on the south side of the house is surrounded by built-in benches that take the place of chairs. The walls on the south side of the house have generous windows to provide solar tempering and a spectacular view of the Moormans River nearby.

An adjustable ladder leads to a loft, a cupola-shaped protrusion from the main roof of the house. The bed itself extends into a cantilevered "shed" hung off the east wall of the house. The roof of the shed is made entirely of a single 200-pound sheet of safety glazing to provide an unobstructed view of the stars. Large windows in the walls of the bed loft allow extended views to the landscape.

A walk-through galley kitchen leads to the southern deck. The kitchen area is visually separated from the 10-foot by 15-foot living/dining area by a wooden lattice of see-through shelving that provides storage without obstructing light and view. In a similar way, light is transmitted through the glass shelving that runs between wall cabinets in front of the kitchen window. Adjacent to the kitchen, a woodstove with an exterior chimney supplies heat for the entire house. The bathroom is stocked with space-saving features. For example, the bathroom mirror is hidden in the back of a framed picture that swings out from the wall to the left of the sink. The tight 30-inch-square shower stall has a glass exterior wall—a luxury possible only in this remote location—to provide a more spacious feeling.

Space-efficiency techniques are exemplified throughout the house: The bottoms of the exposed ceiling joists in the kitchen are just seven feet six inches off the floor; a four-foot-wide hall closet is the only full-height clothes storage area in the house; a windowseat/couch doubles as a guest bed; and the ship's ladder leading to the sleeping loft has a handrail that folds flat.

The Gordon Residence is also a tour de force of recycling. The kitchen cabinets are built from the floorboards of old bowling alley lanes, and the paneling is old barn siding. Many of the doors and windows are secondhand, as are the ceiling joists.

Gordon says, "If you are designing a small house, you have to plan a space for each possession. Not providing for one necessary chair, a television, or a stereo may leave you with a serious problem later. Although small-house design forces attention to space-related details, it also allows some unusual design freedoms.

For example, a ratio of 50 percent glass-to-floor area is practical only in such a small house, where a woodstove can provide all the heat."

Photo 7-8. *The compact sleeping loft feels quite large due to the extensive (and varied) windows and skylights.*

Hog Hill House
Architects: Bentley/LaRosa/Salasky Design
Location: East Holden, Maine
Size: 1,400 square feet

The Hog Hill House sits on a country road at the eastern edge of an undulating 26-acre site in Maine. Much like a traditional New England barn, it is partially embedded in the earth,

Photo 7-9. *The unique roof form of the Hog Hill House is evident in this view, shot from the southwest.*

with a primary entrance on the uphill side to the east and with access to the fields from the "stalls" below. In this case, however, the stalls have been transformed into bedrooms, making excellent use of what otherwise might have been only basement storage space.

The simple rectangular floor plan of the Hog Hill House is capped by a complex, warped-gable roof that gives the house its unique character. The house appears to be flapping a pair of oversized wings—a Canada goose that landed in Maine for the summer. The roof form was constructed by keeping the ridge beam level while gradually increasing the height of the side walls from east to west. The rafters sit on the sloping plate atop the walls. The house is at once a fantasy and a homage to the traditional "shingle-style" houses that proliferate in the region.

Entering the house from a small, covered porch facing the road, you step into an open-plan space with a kitchen area on your right and a dining area on your left. Above you is a loft that functions as a study and music room or as a play space for children. The underside of the loft's floor forms a seven-foot ceiling

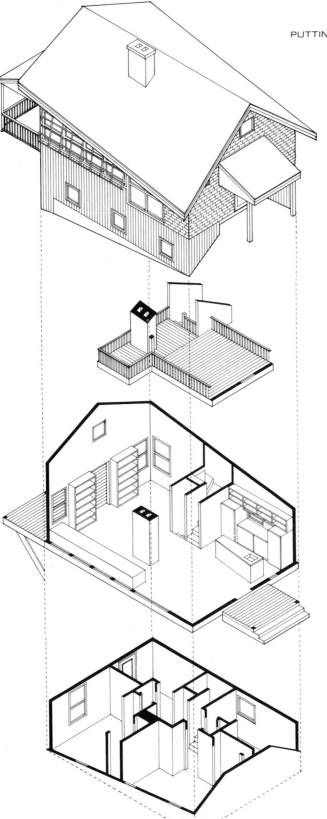

Figure 7-8. *Exploded isometric drawing of the Hog Hill House.*

Figure 7-9. *Floor plans of the Hog Hill House. a. Bedrooms are located on the lower level. b. The main level has an open plan. c. The loft perches above the dining area.*

1. Bedroom
2. Kitchen
3. Living Area
4. Dining Area
5. Bathroom
6. Loft

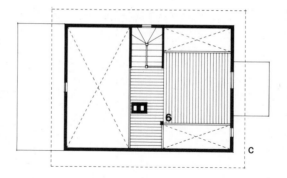

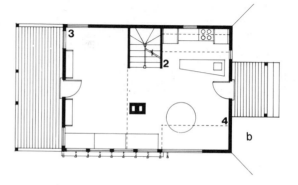

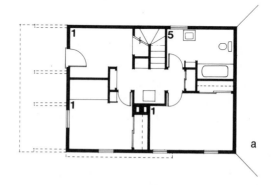

that defines the dining area. Exposed beams give an appearance of added dimension to this intimate ceiling, under which a dining table is comfortably situated, adjacent to the entry. The symbolic limit of the dining area is signaled by the chimney of the

Photo 7-10. *Generous south-facing windows give light and warmth to the home's dining and living areas.*

woodstove—it rises from the first floor up through the loft and out the roof.

As you leave the dining area, you become aware of the higher, expressive ceiling that shelters the all-purpose living area. A covered porch extends from this portion of the house and provides an excellent view of the rolling landscape. Built-in bookcases along the west wall and couches along the lower section of the south wall free the center of the room for a variety of activities. Sometimes during parties or ceremonial occasions, this area might become additional dining space; sometimes it might act as overflow space for a porch gathering; sometimes it might simply be a place for several people to congregate near the woodstove for quiet conversation.

From the main floor, you can descend to a small hallway linking the bedrooms on the lower level. They share a single bathroom that is conveniently located below the kitchen so that plumbing can be stacked. The bedroom on the northwest corner of the lower level has an exterior door at grade level and could be converted to a utility space or an entry vestibule.

Photo 7-11. *A cozy loft (serving, among other purposes, as a child's play area) fits under the warped roof.*

Solar-design considerations have not been overlooked. Large, south-facing windows brighten the living and dining areas on the main floor as well as the two primary bedrooms on the floor below; these windows also provide direct-solar gain for winter heating. The south-facing picture window in the dining area provides a splendid view of the forest from the table. A sunscreen set out from the exterior wall is designed to support shade-producing morning glories; it shields the windows on the main floor from the sun during the summer. To reduce heat losses, north-facing windows are limited.

Trubek and Wislocki Houses
Architects: Venturi, Rauch and Scott Brown
Location: Nantucket, Massachusetts
Size: Trubek—1,040 square feet, excluding porch
      Wislocki—1,495 square feet, excluding porch

Perched confidently in a field beside a bay on Nantucket, this pair of vacation homes was designed for related families with limited budgets. Each is a lesson in compact planning. In both designs, tightly interlocked rooms are arranged inside ordinary building forms clothed in not-quite-so-ordinary facades. The wood shingles, wood trim, and peaked roofs appear traditional enough, but the oversized windows and subtle asymmetries are a clue that something else is going on. These homes demonstrate that modest mansions can be, to use a phrase coined by the architect, "complex and contradictory."

Rarely will you find houses whose every square inch is so carefully studied and refined. Built in the early 1970s, these homes are well known in architectural circles for their contribution to contemporary design theory—they heralded a new era in which designers are again being encouraged to learn from the styles and details of the past as well as to look toward the future.

As you approach the houses from the land, you notice that they are angled toward each other, subtly acknowledging each other's presence while keeping a comfortable distance. In each house, the ground floor is primarily one large common space for living and dining, serviced by a small kitchen alcove. From this common space, a large covered porch extends toward the water. On the second floor, the smaller house has three bedrooms and a (continued on page 206)

Photo 7-12. *This view shows the Trubek House (left) and the Wislocki House (right) as you arrive from the inland side.*

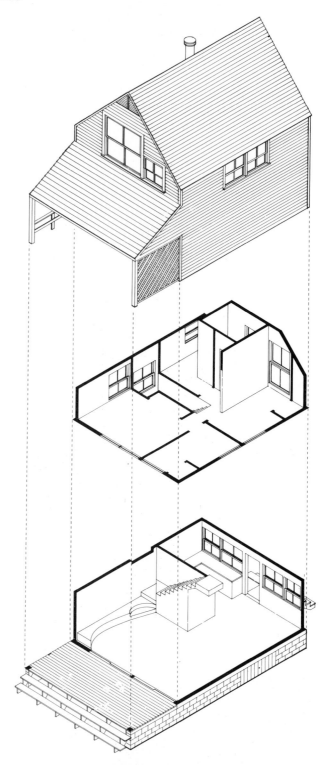

Figure 7-10. *Exploded isometric drawing of the Trubek House.*

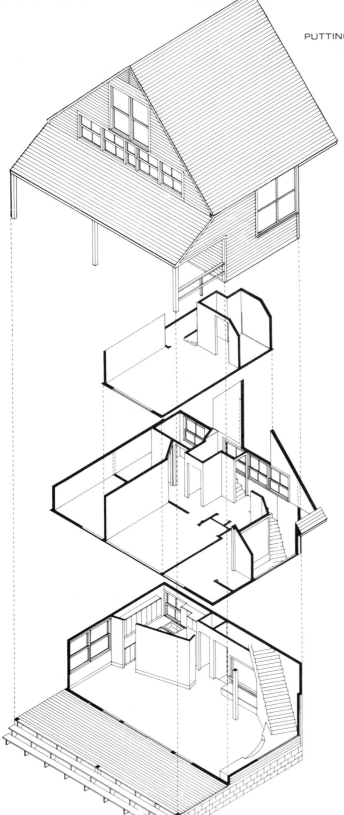

Figure 7-11. *Exploded isometric drawing of the Wislocki House.*

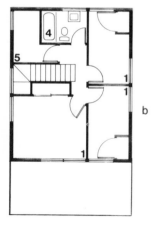

b

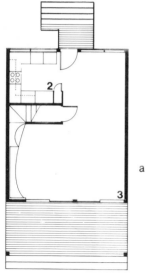

a

Figure 7-12. *Floor plans of the Trubek House. a. The first floor has an essentially open plan, with the kitchen partially enclosed behind the stairway. b. Three small bedrooms, a bathroom, and storage space are tucked into the second story.*

1. Bedroom
2. Kitchen
3. Living/Dining Area
4. Bathroom
5. Storage

large closet that can function in a pinch as a fourth bedroom. The larger home has three bedrooms and a bathroom on the second floor, while the master bedroom and bathroom are tucked under the eaves on the third floor.

The bedrooms in the Trubek House are organized around a small hall at the top of the stairway that rises from the first floor. Circulation space is kept to an absolute minimum. Each bedroom occupies a corner of the rectangular plan and benefits from windows on adjacent walls for cross-ventilation. The sloping roof-plane slices the bedrooms—which have been shrunk almost to the legal minimums—reducing headroom at the exterior wall. Large windows brighten and expand the otherwise tight bedrooms.

In the larger Wislocki House, the second-story bedrooms line up along the bay side of the house to afford an excellent view of the water. Headroom in the two outer bedrooms is restricted. However, the low roof eave provides storage and closet space at the perimeter wall, and it yields sufficient headroom for the stairwell that leads from the first floor. Cut-out interior windows share light and view between rooms and relieve the tight dimensions. For instance, the smallest bedroom is rewarded with a large cut-out opening that permits a view of the bay and the other house through the huge window in the stairwell.

In both houses, there is a playful and masterly dialogue between what windows seem to say on the outside and what they are really doing on the inside. For example, the semicircular Palladian-inspired window on the entrance facade of the larger house appears to belong to a single room. In fact, half of the window is located high in the stairwell that leads from the second floor to the master bedroom suite on the third floor. The other half of the window springs from the floor of the master bathroom. In the smaller home, the large four-square window on the second floor of the entrance facade is similarly deceptive. Half of this window is located in one of the small bedrooms, while the other half illuminates the bathroom. These large window patterns keep the house facades from being patchworks of many small windows, and they provide visual variety in the homes' interiors—always a desirable quality in compact dwellings.

The ground floors of both houses are designed to maximize the sense of space. In both houses, segments of curves are incorporated into the plans to lead the eye outside the walls of the rooms

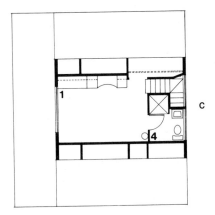

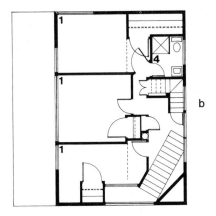

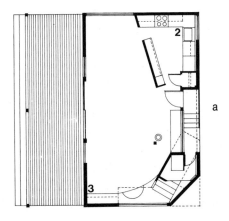

Figure 7-13. *Floor plans of the Wislocki House. a. The first floor consists of living/dining space and a separate kitchen. b. Each bedroom on the second floor has a view of the water. c. Another bedroom—also with a commanding view—is on the upper level.*

1. Bedroom
2. Kitchen
3. Living/Dining Area
4. Bathroom

Photo 7-13. *The houses as seen from the water side. Both houses have sheltered porches facing the water. The Wislocki House is in the foreground.*

Photo 7-14. *The living/dining area on the first floor of the Wislocki House. The kitchen is behind the angled wall.*

and to suggest that the rooms are only part of a much larger domain. These curves also lead you to the base of the stairways and make the transition from first floor to second more gracious.

For all the similarities between the two houses, there are also a great many instructive differences. In a basic way, they are organized quite differently. The smaller house has its long axis at right angles to the water. You enter this house through a small porch extending from the main volume of the house—you can see straight through the porch and the house to the water beyond. In the larger house, the greater square footage allows a more complex entrance sequence. Here you enter through an entrance vestibule carved into the facade. Immediately, you are forced to turn right and ascend a short flight of stairs to reach the main floor, where you are given a view of the water. The axis of this house runs parallel to the water. Service spaces—stairs, baths, closets—are grouped together on the entrance wall so that on both the main floor and the second floor, the primary rooms abut the bay-side wall and thus provide a water view.

Photo 7-15. *The Trubek House's entrance facade.*

La Vereda, Model Two
Designer/Builders: Susan and Wayne Nichols
Location: Santa Fe, New Mexico
Size: 1,270 square feet, excluding garage

La Vereda is a planned unit development (PUD) of 19 passive-solar homes on a ten-acre tract in Santa Fe, New Mexico. This difficult site is cut by three deep arroyos and is studded with piñon pines. The homes reflect the contemporary Southwest adobe style so prevalent in New Mexico, although most of their walls are not masonry but wood frame covered with stucco. Homebuyers at La Vereda can choose among four house designs, including Model Two (on page 211). While each model is different, all are space efficient and are designed with the same principle in mind—they squeeze space from bathrooms and bedrooms and use these gains to enlarge the open-plan living/dining areas.

All the homes at La Vereda are nestled at least three feet into the ground on the north, east, and west sides. This lowers their profiles, and it provides thermal buffering for part of the exterior walls while still allowing the south walls to gather solar heat. In

Photo 7-16. *In this view from the southwest, you can see the Trombe walls on the south side of Model Two at La Vereda.*

fact, efficient thermal performance is an important goal at La Vereda. A Model Two home receives about 75 percent of its heat from the sun through the use of Trombe walls (116 square feet), direct-gain south-facing windows (55 square feet), and south-facing clerestory windows (116 square feet). Altogether, there are 287 square feet of south-facing glass in this design—a considerable quantity for a home with just 1,270 square feet of floor area. The solar energy that enters the home is stored in the Trombe walls, a tile-covered concrete floor slab, masonry stem walls, and the masonry-lined north wall that is illuminated from above by the second-story clerestory windows.

Model Two's designers also understand that energy conservation must come before solar collection. Consequently, on the east, west, and north sides of the home there are relatively few windows, a feature that reduces window heat losses. The 2×6 wood-frame exterior walls are filled with five and one-half inches of batt insulation, and an additional three-quarter-inch of urethane sheathing is attached on the outside, resulting in an R-value of 33. The masonry stem walls of the foundation in the sunken

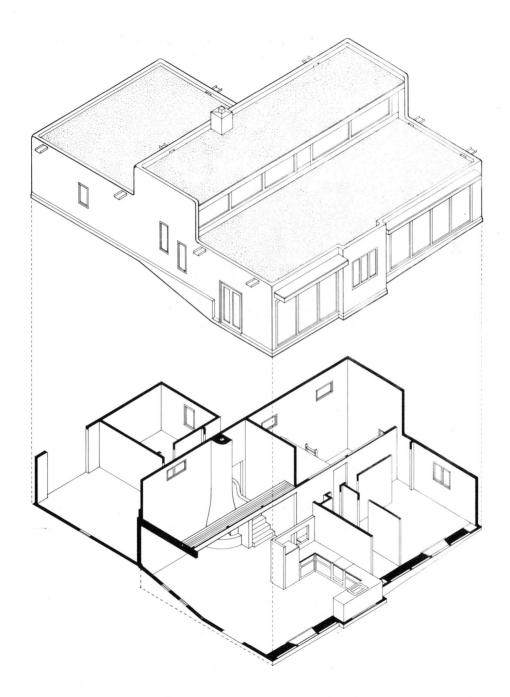

Figure 7-14. *Exploded isometric drawing of La Vereda, Model Two.*

Figure 7-15. *Floor plans of La Vereda, Model Two. a. The first floor has two bedrooms, a kitchen, a bathroom, and a living/dining area. b. A loft is located in the clerestory space.*

1. Bedroom
2. Kitchen
3. Living/Dining Area
4. Entry
5. Bathroom
6. Loft
7. Work Room
8. Garage

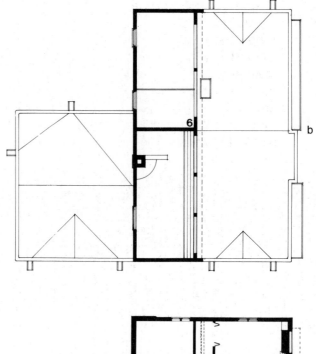

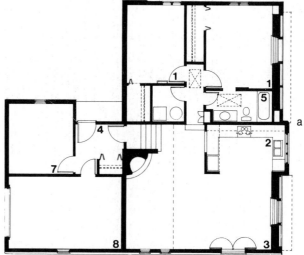

portion of the home are sheathed on the exterior with two inches of polystyrene to bring the mass of the walls inside the home's environmental envelope for thermal storage.

You might think that the opaque Trombe walls covering much of the southern side of the home would make the rooms too dark, but such fears are unjustified. The direct-gain windows and the ample clerestory windows provide plenty of light and give the living area an airy, spacious feeling. This effect is amplified by the ceiling height in the relatively large living/dining area. The floor of this room is two steps down from the bedroom "wing," so the ceiling is effectively higher—yet the flat-roof construction of the home is not altered.

Model Two has a compact master bedroom of about 150 square feet, an equally snug secondary bedroom of about 100

Photo 7-17. *The open-plan living/ dining area is bathed with light coming from the clerestory windows. Note the stairway to the storage loft.*

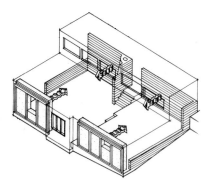

Figure 7-16. *La Vereda's solar heating system: The Trombe walls stand on the home's south side while the clerestory allows sunlight to reach the north wall. Thus, warmth radiates into the home from both directions. (Courtesy of Communico)*

square feet, and a sleeping loft in the northern clerestory space with access from the secondary bedroom. A central location and two separate entrances allow a single bathroom to service the entire home. As the family grows, this may be tight, so the design permits the garage area, which is easily accessible through the air-lock vestibule, to be converted into additional living and bathroom space.

The design abounds with details intended to increase the apparent size of the home. For example, exposed-beam ceilings increase the apparent ceiling height; most walls not used for thermal storage are painted or plastered in light colors; and a strategically placed see-through window in the kitchen alcove provides a visual release for anyone in the entrance foyer—it gives a view through the kitchen window into the landscape beyond. La Vereda may look like a strictly regional solution to compact-home design, but its lessons can be applied in all geographic regions.

Terrazas Del Sol
Architect: James M. Wehler
Location: Ranchos de Taos, New Mexico
Size: 960 square feet

Terrazas Del Sol is a community of nine condominiums in northern New Mexico. At first glance, it looks similar to the La Vereda Model Two. But a closer examination shows how subtle design differences can create significantly different living opportunities.

Each home at Terrazas Del Sol contains two bedrooms, a U-shaped kitchen, one all-purpose bathroom with a separate vanity area, and an open-plan living/dining area. Located at 7,000 feet above sea level in a sunny but cold climate, these homes take energy efficiency and solar design seriously. Fuel costs are kept low by direct-gain south-facing windows and by solar "plenums" that provide domestic water heating, active-solar space heating, and natural lighting.

The site plan of this development is particularly interesting. Groups of three homes are clustered together, sharing an outside entry terrace to which the homes connect in a pinwheel pattern. For this to be possible, one of the three homes must have its front

Photo 7-18. *The rooftop solar plenum is clearly visible in this view of a Terrazas Del Sol home, seen from the southeast.*

door on its west wall, one on its north wall, and one on its east wall. The homes thus are oriented toward different points of the compass, yet they all have the same basic plan with only slight modifications, and they all benefit from solar heating.

How can this be? The solution is that the footprint of each home is almost symmetrical (30 feet by 32 feet). Therefore, the basic design can be rotated or reversed as the entry condition dictates. Ample windows and the solar plenums face the sun in any of the configurations. In some cases, the living/dining area has extra south windows; in the other cases, the secondary bedroom is the beneficiary. Either way, plenty of warming sunlight enters each home, and the open plan allows the warmth to

Figure 7-17. *Exploded isometric drawing of Terrazas Del Sol.*

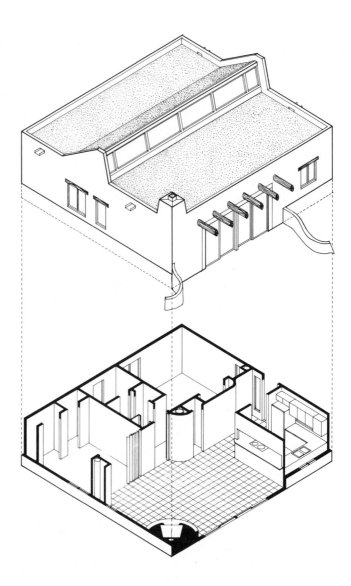

Figure 7-18. *Floor plan of Terrazas Del Sol. The virtually square shape of the home permits solar heating no matter which direction the house faces.*

1. Bedroom
2. Kitchen
3. Living/Dining Area
4. Entry
5. Bathroom

circulate. The solar plenum is positioned differently on homes with different orientations—it either straddles the central axis of the home or it runs perpendicular to it.

All the walls at each home are bermed except whichever wall faces south: It is left exposed to the sun. In the words of the architect, "Landscaped berms were constructed to modulate an otherwise flat terrain, to control drainage, to define space, and to give a sense of privacy and 'place.'" The berms also lower the profile of the home and, from a distance, make the home seem larger.

Spatially, every room is asked to do double duty, because each home relies heavily on the principle of overlapping space. For example, the second bedroom—separated from the living/dining area by a folding partition—can be opened up during the day to become a den for television viewing or a play room for children. The primary circulation space of each home doubles as usable square footage in the living/dining area, with the result that there is no enclosed corridor at all. Consequently, at almost every location in the home—except in the master bedroom—you are guaranteed a spacious 30-foot clear dimension in at least one direction. A strategically placed corner fireplace can be seen from most parts of the home, thus acting as a unifying focal point.

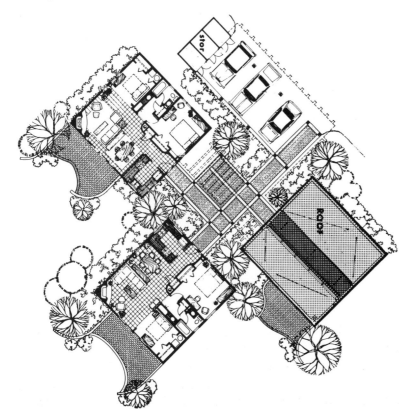

Figure 7-19. *The houses are arranged in a pinwheel pattern, oriented toward different points of the compass. (Courtesy of James M. Wehler)*

Photo 7-19. *The living/dining area in a slightly modified two-bedroom version of the design. Note the exposed-beam ceiling and the light from the solar plenum.*

The tile-covered slab-on-grade foundation performs two duties, functioning both as a decorative floor and as thermal storage for the direct-gain windows. Even the solar plenum is versatile, collecting solar energy, preheating the home's hot water, and allowing daylight to pass through a skylight that is fitted into its base. This brightens the center of the rather deep, potentially dark, near-square floor plan.

The design is rich with other space-saving amenities. For example, outside storage for each pinwheel of homes is grouped together to help define the parking area; exposed "vigas" (traditional beams) provide a feeling of greater ceiling height; walls are painted white; and outside terraces extend comfortably from the living rooms through large sliding-glass doors. The homes are arranged so that, despite their proximity, each patio has privacy.

Stone Home
Architects: Jersey Devil (Steve Badanes and John Ringel)
Location: Princeton, New Jersey
Size: 500 square feet (approximate)

The Stone Home is what results when you unleash an innovative design/build team on the renovation of a 150-year-old stone smokehouse. The project called for the construction of a poolside vacation home on the client's existing property. Motivated by steep energy prices, the client—a surgeon—decided he wanted a hideaway in his own backyard, an excellent retreat for a doctor "on call" during the weekend.

Despite the home's very small size, all the basics are provided: a small but fully equipped kitchen, a bathroom with stall shower, and a heater in the form of a woodstove. The detailing picks up the client's interest in boating, and it also, as architect Steve Badanes points out, "gets somewhat involved in an eye, ear, nose, and throat motif."

With barely 500 square feet of interior space, the house is very compact—almost nautical in its meticulous use of space. Two-foot-thick stone walls leave an interior dimension of only 14 feet by 21 feet. You enter the house—which is partially embedded in the ground on its sloping site—at an intermediate level and either go up half a flight of stairs to a sleeping loft or go down half a flight to the all-purpose room. Irregularly shaped steps, which function almost like a piece of furniture in the room, decrease the footprint of the stairwell. (Of course, you should think carefully before building irregular stairs; they can be hazardous.) The minimal amount of space under the stairs is put to good use: It

Photo 7-20. *Sitting quietly beside a swimming pool, the Stone Home gives few exterior clues to the unique forms inside.*

Figure 7-20. *Exploded isometric drawing of the Stone Home.*

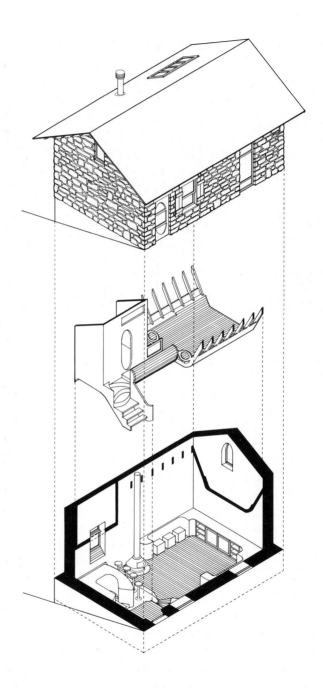

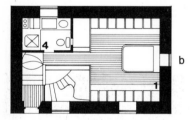

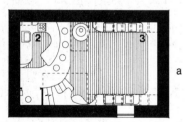

Figure 7-21. *Floor plans of the Stone Home. a. The first floor is a multipurpose living/cooking/dining area. b. A bathroom is at the head of the stairs and a wooden "hammock" provides sleeping quarters.*

1. Bedroom
2. Kitchen
3. Living Area
4. Bathroom

Photo 7-21. *The loft sleeping "hammock" is reached via a bridge that is flanked by a pair of metaphorical eyeglasses.*

houses mechanical equipment (a water heater and the electrical service panel), and it provides storage space.

A narrow, 18-inch bridge connects the bathroom landing to the sleeping loft, which is open to the living space below and appears suspended from the walls of the smokehouse like a gigantic wooden hammock. A series of four skylights in the sloped ceiling floods both the loft and the living space with light. Real hammocks sometimes are suspended from the loft structure to accommodate overnight guests.

On the lower level, a kitchen with a countertop dining area occupies the low-ceilinged space under the bathroom. A window that is shared by both the bathroom and the kitchen provides light for the kitchen alcove. In the remaining portion of the first floor, built-ins abound: bookshelves, cabinets, and cubbyholes are sprinkled liberally throughout the home in unlikely places. Many of these were created improvisationally by the design/build team during the construction process.

The Stone Home is proof of the proposition that a modest mansion can afford to be handcrafted. Laminated plywood handrails, flocked rubber-ball doorstops, and a pleated-velour door with jalousie window are but a few of the details that make this home special.

Photo 7-22. *This construction shot of the loft shows the curved structure from below. Note the skylights overhead.*

Photo 7-23. *The curving shapes in the kitchen area call to mind nautical architecture.*

Bohlin Residence
Architects: Bohlin Powell Larkin Cywinski
Location: northeast Pennsylvania
Size: 1,950 square feet

A huge arrow piercing the forest, the Bohlin Residence creates a strong horizontal counterpoint to the verticality of the trees surrounding it. The house is raised on irregularly spaced piles, some of which extend through the house and mimic the massive tree trunks nearby. For access, a long pedestrian bridge extends the domain of the house and connects it to the sloping ground.

In a previous chapter, we indicated that even a large house can benefit from the principles of space efficiency. The Bohlin Residence proves the point. At almost 2,000 square feet, it is anything but small—yet it provides several valuable spatial lessons. To give just one example, the space immediately under the home's shed roof is used particularly well. At the north eave of the roof on the second floor, space has been found for compact built-in bookcases that alternate with low storage units and cut-out windows through which light can be shared with the lower floor.

The rooms in the house are strung out in a line, an arrangement calling for a long, potentially wasteful corridor. But in this home, the corridor always becomes part of something else—here it is part of the pantry system of the kitchen, there it is the landing for the stairwell, elsewhere it forms a library lined with built-in bookcases—and, finally, it is swallowed by the master bedroom at the west end of the house.

Floor-to-ceiling windows, which use an industrial glazing system, dissolve the corner of the living room and visually extend the common area at the east end of the house into the forest. You feel as if you are sitting in the treetops. Naturally, a price must be paid for this large north-facing window area during the winter. But the home has plentiful south-facing glass to partially compensate—generous two-story windows in the living area and stairwell.

A family room that doubles as a guest bedroom overhangs part of the living/dining area, creating an implied room for dining below. This dining "room" is further delineated by being

(continued on page 226)

Photo 7-24. *A pedestrian bridge marks the entry to the long, narrow Bohlin Residence.*

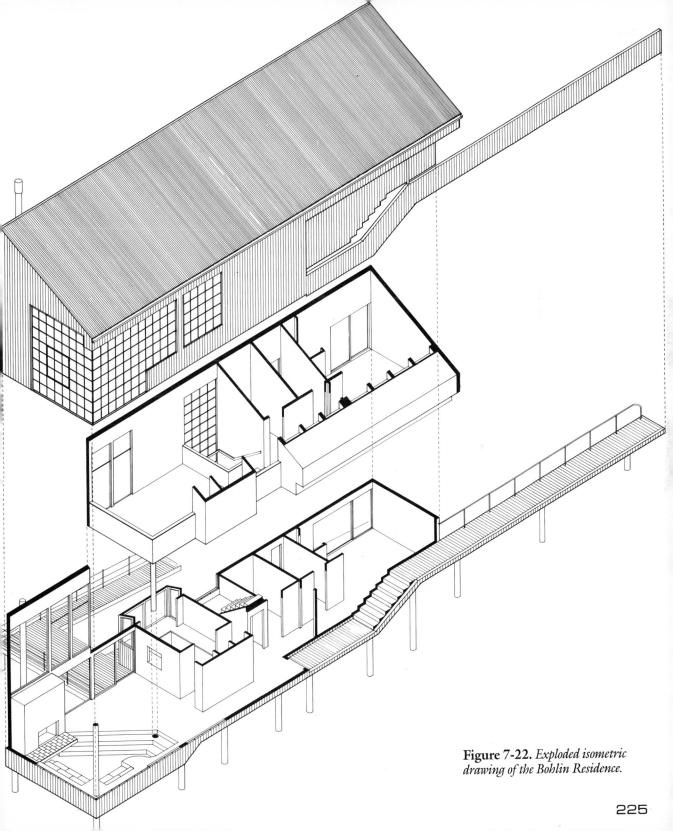

Figure 7-22. *Exploded isometric drawing of the Bohlin Residence.*

225

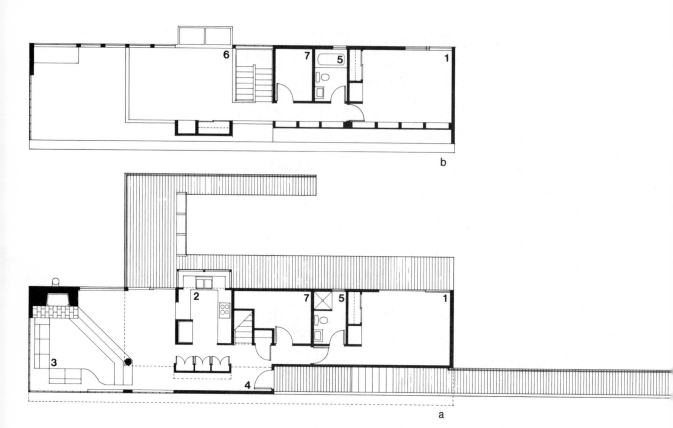

Figure 7-23. *a. The Bohlin Residence is arranged along a corridor that is productively incorporated into each room on the first floor. b. A family room/guest room, bathroom, bedroom, and storage space are on the upper floor.*

1. Bedroom
2. Kitchen
3. Living/Dining Area
4. Entry
5. Bathroom
6. Family Room
7. Storage/Multiuse Space

two steps up from the living "room." The steps can be used for additional seating around the fireplace, supplementing the built-in couches that line the wall of the living area. A column that supports the family room punctuates the end of the circulation corridor and announces the start of the main living area.

The kitchen is efficiently organized in a compact U-shape. It bulges out of the taut skin of the home's south wall; the glazed roof of this shed-shaped extension ensures a bright working space for the sink area. In good weather, outside dining is encouraged by a system of wood decks that extends off the south side of the house.

Photo 7-25. *The northeast corner of the house is almost entirely glass, offering a magnificent view from indoors and creating a striking image from outdoors.*

The Bohlin Residence is a dramatic solution suited to its dramatic site. While your site and budget may be more humble, do not be dissuaded from learning the spatial lessons this home has to offer.

Photo 7-26. *A column marks the beginning of the "living room." The space is carefully detailed, with built-in couches and the impressive window system.*

Cottage Court House
Architects: Orr & Taylor
Location: Point Washington, Florida
Size: 990 square feet (excluding porch and roof
    deck)

The Cottage Court House is one of a number of houses designed for Seaside, a large development in the Florida panhandle city of Point Washington. In defiance of typical unrestrained suburban sprawl, this new village is organized compactly, with pedestrian walkways, orderly street grids, a village center, and distinct residential precincts that are to be designed by different architects. The Cottage Court House is the predominant house type in one of the precincts.

(continued on page 232)

Photo 7-27. *The Cottage Court House, just 16 feet wide, is topped by a distinctive crow's nest.*

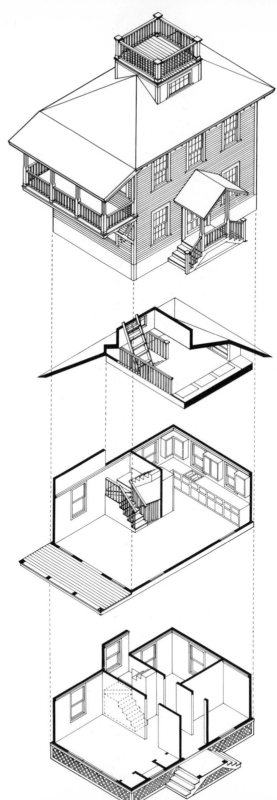

Figure 7-24. *Exploded isometric drawing of the Cottage Court House.*

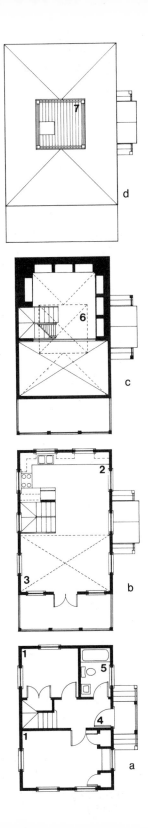

Figure 7-25. *Floor plans of the Cottage Court House. a. The first floor has two bedrooms and a bath. b. The second floor has the kitchen and open-plan living/dining space. c. A loft is tucked under the roof. d. A hatch gives access to the rooftop crow's nest.*

1. Bedroom
2. Kitchen
3. Living/Dining Area
4. Entrance Foyer
5. Bathroom
6. Loft
7. Crow's Nest

The Cottage Court House can be approached on foot from the neighborhood's main pedestrian thoroughfare, a walkway down the center of the block. The narrow end of the 16-foot-wide house faces the walkway. To enter the house, you walk around to the side, where a slightly elevated, roofed porch protects the front door. The same entry is used if you arrive at the house by car and park—as the site plan dictates—in the rear.

With its narrow plan and its side-porch entrance, the Cottage Court House applies the organization of the Charleston "single" house, discussed in Chapter 2. Like the single, the Cottage Court House is only one room wide, which facilitates cross-ventilation in Seaside's hot and humid climate. In fact, almost every room has windows on three sides for maximum air flow. In

Photo 7-28. *The house and its neighbors are linked by a walkway that runs down the middle of the block.*

keeping with the house's architectural style, the windows are double-hung with multiple panes.

Upon entering the house, you find yourself in a small foyer off which two bedrooms and a full bathroom open. A winding stairway leads from the foyer to the common rooms on the second floor. This arrangement is a reminder of the ceremonial central hall and grand staircases of courtly antebellum mansions. But here the customary location of common rooms and bedrooms is inverted, with the living areas upstairs and the bedrooms on the first floor, where nighttime temperatures are lower.

On the second floor, the stairwell divides the kitchen area from the living/dining area, creating a place for a dining table at the stair landing. The living/dining area is compact, but it benefits from a large porch to which it is connected by a pair of glass doors. The benign climate makes outdoor living possible during most of the year. Reminiscent of New Orleans balconies, the porch overlooks the pedestrian walkway and encourages interaction between neighbors. Delicate Victorian-style detailing gives both porch and house a light, airy character. The structural members are chamfered to reduce their massiveness, and open lattice-work is used under the porch eaves and around the crawl-space foundation.

The main stairway with its open railing leads from the second floor to a loft tucked under the hipped roof. The loft, which can be used as a den or guest bedroom, covers only the kitchen and dining area, leaving the living area as a sloping one-and-a-half-story space that feels quite large. Cleverly lighted by two dormer windows at the base of the roof deck, the loft makes good use of the low headroom under the roof eaves: Built-in drawers for storage are located there. From the loft, a ladder provides access through a flush floor hatch to a private crow's nest that affords a view of the water nearby.

From entry porch to crow's nest, the Cottage Court House stands upright and proud. It is both a necessary response to today's need for compact, affordable housing and a genteel reminder of the benefits to be reaped by tapping our rich architectural heritage for inspiration in house design.

Appendix 1

CONSTRUCTION REGULATIONS

Through the years, the nation has developed a sometimes bewildering array of building codes (laws that ensure adequate construction practices), zoning ordinances (laws that allow municipalities to control the use of land within their jurisdictions), housing codes (laws that regulate minimum living conditions in completed dwellings), and Minimum Property Standards (guidelines that establish acceptable practices for government-financed construction and government-insured mortgages). This welter of regulations can make residential design seem like an excursion through a minefield. But the situation is actually not as bad as it may appear. In fact, most building codes and housing codes, as well as the national Minimum Property Standards, are easily met today. In most circumstances, only local zoning ordinances present serious potential problems.

One of the first pieces of legislation to establish space standards for American housing was passed in 1901. In response to unconscionable overcrowding and poor sanitation in working-class slums, New York State adopted the Tenement House Act. Among other provisions, this law stipulated that at least 400 cubic feet of air space had to be provided for each adult and 200 cubic feet for each child. In a typical home of today, this would translate into 50 square feet of floor space per adult and 25 square feet per child. If we apply these standards to the average new home built in 1981, which had 1,600 square feet of floor area, we

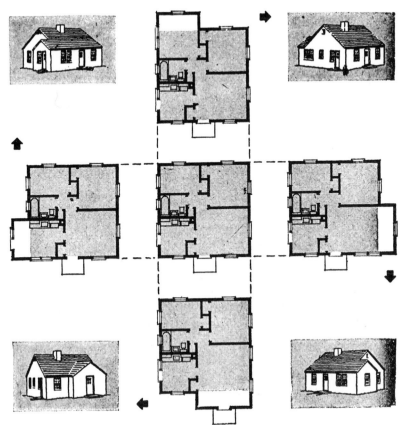

Figure A1-1. *In the past, home size frequently was measured in cubic feet rather than square feet. Here a small 9,216-cubic-foot home is shown. Note how a small addition made to any side—increasing the volume to 9,944 cubic feet—affects the home's character. (Source: Federal Housing Administration)*

reach the amazing conclusion that the house should be able to accommodate 20 adults plus 24 children. This gives some idea of the overcrowding that must have existed at the turn of the century, if these standards represented an improvement over the prevailing conditions.

A complete analysis of housing standards in the United States was, until recently, hampered by a lack of reliable housing data. Although a census has been conducted every ten years since the founding of the country, it was not until the latter half of the 19th century that the census included housing information. At first, census questions about household size were expressed in terms of the number of rooms occupied. This led to discussions of home size in terms of occupants per room. For example, the United States Census Bureau uses a figure of more than 1.51

people per room as a measure of "overcrowding." This measure is obviously inadequate, however, without some knowledge of actual room size. Nevertheless, this type of statistic has had great influence on national housing policy and popular perceptions of our housing needs.

After World War II, the census was modified to describe housing in terms of square footage, and organizations such as the Federal Housing Administration began to compile their own records. From that time on, dependable information on the size of new housing has been collected, as well as information on housing costs. Today's building codes, zoning ordinances, and Minimum Property Standards—the three types of regulations having the greatest relevance for small-home design—generally have been promulgated with the benefit of these data.

Building Codes

In most locations, the absolute minimum size of a permanent dwelling is limited by a local building code. Such codes are legal documents that attempt to safeguard the "public health, safety, and general welfare" as they relate to the construction and occupancy of buildings. In addition to size, the codes generally cover fire protection, structural design, exits, sanitary facilities, light, and ventilation.

People frequently confuse building codes with zoning ordinances. This confusion arises because in most communities the codes and ordinances are enforced by the same agency. There is an essential difference, however. Whereas building codes are intended to ensure minimum standards of health and safety, zoning ordinances are conceived with an eye toward community planning.

There are several different model building codes on which communities base their own codes; you should check to determine which code applies in the area where you plan to build. Under the One and Two Family Dwelling Code (discussed below), it is possible to build a permanent dwelling of only 200 square feet (exterior dimensions). This is probably the smallest permanent home that can be built legally in the United States. Nevertheless, in many underdeveloped countries, even this bare-minimum dwelling would be expected to provide shelter for an extended family.

If your area follows the One and Two Family Dwelling Code, you shouldn't run into any code problems concerning the size of your planned compact home. Study your local code carefully, however, to avoid unpleasant surprises when permit-approval time rolls around.

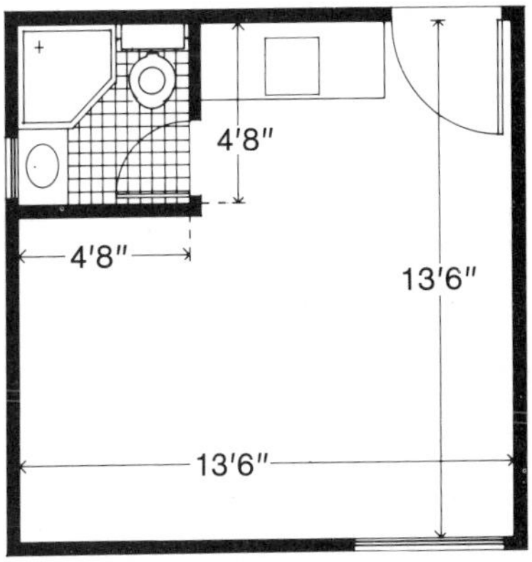

Figure A1-2. *The smallest permanent dwelling permissible under the One and Two Family Dwelling Code.*

Zoning Ordinances

The biggest potential problems for the designer of a modest mansion are often caused by local zoning ordinances. In some localities, zoning regulations require that detached dwelling units meet or exceed prescribed minimum square footages. Sometimes the ordinances also stipulate how many stories a house must be and what percentage of the site it must cover.

Restrictive zoning ordinances are fairly widespread. For instance, a recent study indicates that about 25 percent of all Connecticut towns have ordinances that require single-family houses to contain at least 1,000 square feet of floor space. The towns in Connecticut can prescribe the minimum size of private homes because of a state law that permits zoning "with a view to conserving the value of buildings." In other words, the towns can outlaw very small homes if they believe such homes would lower the value of the other homes in the community. Some people consider this to be discrimination against owners and would-be owners of inexpensive homes. At present, the Connecticut chapter of the National Association of Home Builders is testing the constitutionality of such zoning. The result might well have national consequences, for it may curtail the ability of local governments to legislate house sizes.

Just as with building codes, you should be sure to study local zoning ordinances before building a home. Usually you will have to submit your building plans for an approval process in which both building codes and zoning ordinances are enforced. If your plans differ from the legal requirements, you may be able to obtain a variance that will allow you to erect the home you want. Otherwise, you'll have to conform to the local rules.

Minimum Property Standards

The existence of federal Minimum Property Standards dates from the inception of the Federal Housing Administration (FHA) in 1934. The FHA was one of the many alphabet agencies created by the Roosevelt administration; its original charge was to encourage investment in housing construction by insuring financial institutions against losses on approved mortgage loans. An FHA appraisal of a property was required to qualify for an insured mortgage. The agency developed its Minimum Property Standards to help appraisers determine how resalable the properties in question were.

The 1973 edition of the Minimum Property Standards has been particularly influential. The origins of the size stipulations included in these standards are difficult to trace, however. In general, there has been surprisingly little practical research into the uses of space in rooms other than kitchens and bathrooms. From the studies that have been conducted—such as the work by the University of Illinois Small Home Council on efficiency in the kitchen, and the research by Alexander Kira on the anthropometrics of the bathroom—some very useful rules of thumb have emerged for organizing space efficiently in these two areas of the house. But few, if any, such rules exist for other household areas.

History does reveal that in 1950, the American Public Health Association (APHA), a nonprofit organization of health care professionals, issued space standards for homes. APHA was motivated by concerns about the minimal area provided in much of the "economy housing" built immediately after World War II. When developing its standards, the APHA staff "defined activities generally performed in dwellings and calculated the space which was needed to perform these activities." But precisely how this was done is impossible to determine from current literature and appears to be lost to posterity.

APHA published its standards in terms of total square feet per household. It recommended 750 square feet for a two-person household, 1,000 square feet for a three-person household, and so forth, up to 1,500 square feet for a six-person household. These standards called for about 25 percent more space than was provided in the better public housing projects of the day, and they specified about double the space of the "economy housing" that met the FHA minimum standards at that time. Subsequently, new FHA standards were developed that more closely conformed to the APHA standards, and these ultimately formed one basis for the 1973 Minimum Property Standards. When the 1973 standards were published, they quickly assumed great importance throughout the housing industry. In effect, Washington began regulating the size of American homes.

In the deregulatory environment of the early 1980s, federal policy was changed. The 1982 edition of the Minimum Property Standards dropped the "marketability and livability" provisions, many of which had to do with minimum allowable room size. The introduction of the 1982 standards states, "This . . . will be the last revision [of the Minimum Property Standards]. The content of this revision is reduced in substance and in bulk. It reflects the policy of the Department [of Housing and Urban Development] to move away from imposing Federal standards where market forces, local requirements and nationally recognized standards developed in the private sector serve to achieve the same goals." Today, the federal government is moving toward the implementation of a privately developed consensus code, the One and Two Family Dwelling Code, as a national standard; it emphasizes health and safety concerns rather than room dimensions. The result of these changes is a lack of any institutionalized national standards for the size of houses. Indeed, it is likely that the Minimum Property Standards will be eliminated entirely.

DIMENSIONAL STANDARDS

This appendix is an illustrated summary of widely accepted standards for the dimensions of residential structures—it is a yardstick against which you can measure a compact home. You should find it particularly helpful during the schematic phase of the design process, for the minimum dimensions shown may jar you into acknowledging shortcomings in your design. If you are going to use dimensions smaller than those suggested here, you should have a good reason for doing so and a good idea of how your design can accommodate the activities calculated for the spaces in question.

For the most part, the dimensions listed here are not legal minimums but practical standards that can be interpreted differently by different compilers. Therefore, you should not be surprised by any discrepancies you may find between these dimensions and those listed in other reference books. When a dimension cited in this appendix is based on a code requirement, the applicable code or standard is cited. The following abbreviations are used:

MPS 1973: *Minimum Property Standards*, 1973 edition
MPS 1982: *Minimum Property Standards*, 1982 edition
OTFDC: *One and Two Family Dwelling Code*, 1983 edition

As we indicated in Appendix 1, the One and Two Family Dwelling Code may wholly supplant the Minimum Property Standards. Nevertheless, the dimensions specified in MPS are still worth attention because—to a certain extent—they reflect the demands of the marketplace: They have shaped many people's perceptions of their housing needs. Thus, the standards given here include information from both MPS 1973 and MPS 1982.

We will list dimensions by room type and by activity. Minimum total room sizes are not emphasized, because in many modest-mansion designs, rooms will be combined, making simple minimum room sizes meaningless—minimum total sizes for living rooms and dining rooms will be irrelevant if you plan to create a combined living/dining area. Thus, we will emphasize the minimum space requirements for various activities and for standard-size furniture and appliances. To determine how large a particular area in your home should be, you should determine what activities will occur there and what furniture or appliances will be placed there. If you are designing around unique fixtures or furniture, you should modify the space requirements accordingly.

For each room type, you will find a general discussion, a list of important dimensions, and a list of additional comments. In most cases, a range of dimensions is listed for each piece of furniture or for each appliance, and in some cases an average or typical value is given as well. The following conventions are observed: "Depth" is always measured front to back; "length" or "width" is measured side to side.

Bedrooms/Sleeping Areas

Discussion

The provision of special rooms for sleeping seems to have appeared in Western architecture in about the 11th century. The notion of the bed as a separate piece of furniture to be used solely for sleeping is a later innovation, dating from approximately the 16th century. In that era, the bed was simply a straw-filled sack. At bedtime, one would stretch out the sack wherever space was available and literally hit the hay.

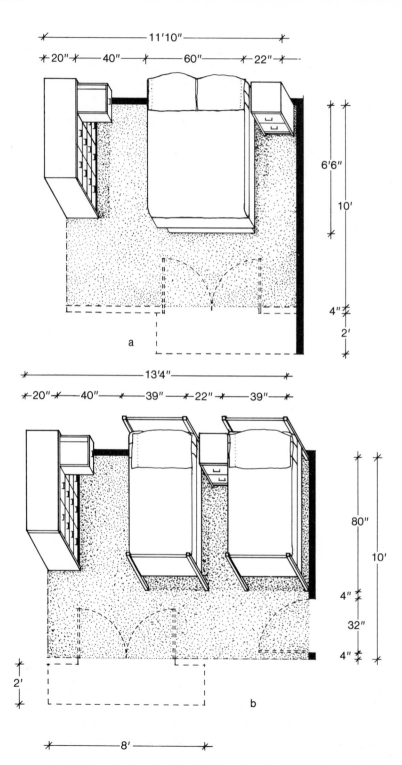

Figure A2-1. *Schematic bedroom layouts with (a) double bed and (b) twin beds. Recommended clearances and dimensions are shown.*

The most important factor in determining minimum bedroom dimensions is the size of the bed or beds for which you are designing. Because a modern bed is so large compared to the dimensions of most rooms, the proportions of a bedroom are very important. If the proportions are wrong, you may have difficulty fitting a bed in even a reasonably spacious room. One- and two-bed arrangements are depicted in Figure A2-1, indicating the clearances required between beds and nearby closets and furniture with drawers.

Important Dimensions

Mattresses:
    crib (average) . . . . 27″ by 48″
    single . . . . 39″ by 75″ or 80″
    double . . . . 54″ by 75″
    queen . . . . 60″ by 80″ or 84″
    king . . . . 76″ by 80″ or 84″
Dresser:
    depth . . . . 18″ to 22″
      average depth . . . . 18″
    length . . . . highly variable
      average length . . . . 52″
Nightstand:
    depth . . . . 15″ to 20″
    length . . . . 14″ to 26″
Closet Space:
    depth (minimum) . . . . 24″
    length:
      master bedroom . . . . 60″ (MPS 1973)
        preferable minimum . . . . 96″
      other bedrooms . . . . 36″ (MPS 1973)
        preferable minimum
        per person . . . . 48″
      hanging height (minimum) . . . . 60″

Clearances

• Provide 36″ to 40″ clearance from a bed to a closet or to furniture that has drawers or hinged doors.

• Most codes require the minimum width of a habitable room to be 7′ (see Table A2-1). For a separate master bedroom, a 9′4″ minimum width is preferable.

• Provide 48″ clearance on one side of each bed so you can vacuum under the bed with an upright vacuum cleaner.

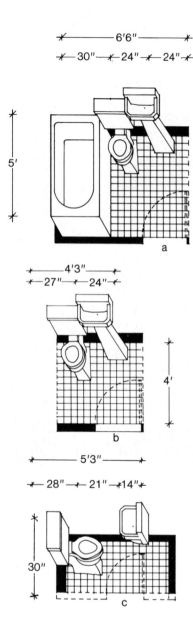

Figure A2-2. *Schematic layouts for (a) three-fixture bathroom with plumbing in one wall, (b) two-fixture bathroom with plumbing in one wall, and (c) two-fixture bathroom with plumbing in opposite walls.*

Additional Comments

• By most codes, all habitable rooms must be at least 70 square feet in plan.

• Paragraph R-211.2 of OTFDC and paragraph 402-3.1 of MPS 1982 both state, "Every sleeping room shall have at least one operable window or exterior door approved for emergency egress or rescue. . . . Where windows are provided as a means of egress or rescue they shall have a sill height of not more than 44 inches above the floor. All egress or rescue windows . . . must have a minimum net clear opening of 5.7 square feet. The minimum net clear opening height dimension shall be 24 inches. The minimum net clear opening width dimension shall be 20 inches."

• See the standards for light and ventilation listed under General Standards, Additional Comments, below.

Bathrooms

Discussion

In 1837, when Queen Victoria ascended the throne of England, there were no bathrooms in Buckingham Palace, and it was not until 1851 that the White House in Washington, D.C., acquired its first bathroom. Thomas Crapper improved on primitive water closets with his "Valveless Water Waste Preventer," which became a popular fixture in England in the late 19th century. By the start of the 20th century, the bathroom was on its way to becoming the important sanctuary it is today.

A master bathroom generally contains at least three fixtures: a lavatory (sink), a water closet (toilet), and a bathtub or shower stall. Secondary bathrooms may have only one or two fixtures. Bathroom layout depends considerably on whether the plumbing is clustered in one wall or distributed among several walls. Because bathroom fixtures, particularly lavatories and base cabinets, come in many different sizes, you should try to design around the specific fixtures you plan to use; the dimensions given below should be employed for schematic-design purposes only. Figure A2-2 represents three minimum bathroom configurations.

Important Dimensions

Bathtub:
standard . . . . 30″ by 60″
short . . . . 30″ by 54″
Shower Stall: . . . . 30″ by 30″
Toilet (average one-piece unit):
depth . . . . 28″
width . . . . 22″ to 24″
Lavatory:
depth . . . . 14″ to 20″
average depth . . . . 18″
width . . . . 18″ to 27″
average width . . . . 22″
Bathroom Door (width): . . . . 24″ to 28″
Medicine Cabinet: . . . . 20″ by 30″.

Clearances

• Provide 15″ between the center line of a toilet and an adjacent fixture or wall.

• Provide 21″ between a bathtub and a wall or door.

• Provide 14″ between the center line of a lavatory and an adjacent fixture or wall.

Additional Comments

• Allow at least 35 square feet of floor space for a three-fixture bathroom.

• Section R-208.2 of OTFDC states, "Each water closet compartment shall be not less than 30 inches in width and there shall be not less than 21 inches clear space in front of each water closet."

• Sections 403-2.2 of the MPS 1982 and R-204.3 of OTFDC both state, "Bathrooms . . . shall be provided with aggregate glazing area in windows of not less than three square feet, one-half of which must be operable. Exception: The glazed areas are not required where artificial light and an approved mechanical ventilation system is [sic] provided. . . ."

• See the light and ventilation standards listed under General Standards, Additional Comments, below.

Kitchens

Discussion

When discussing early American architecture, folklorists some-times refer to the "gender-specific hearth area." The first time you hear this phrase, you do not immediately realize that they are referring to the kitchen. Today, the kitchen is the province of all household members, not just the wife. What's more, with the domestic-technology revolution of the mid-20th century, the kitchen has evolved from the simple hearth to become a highly sophisticated nerve center for the home. It is invariably the most complex and the most expensive room to build and the one that needs the most efficient planning.

The kitchen can be divided into three (or sometimes four) distinct zones: the sink center, the refrigerator center, the cooking

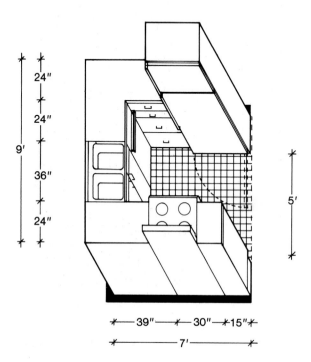

Figure A2-3. *Basic kitchen layouts showing recommended clearances and dimensions.*

center, and the food-preparation center. Most people are familiar with the concept of the kitchen "triangle"—the distance between the sink, refrigerator, and stove. The total distance along the three legs of the triangle should be more than 13 feet and less than 22 feet, with no leg shorter than 4 feet.

Space must be allocated for the major kitchen appliances. The floor or counter space required for each appliance varies with the make and model. If the kitchen is planned before the appliances are selected, use average values from the list below. Otherwise, use the actual dimensions.

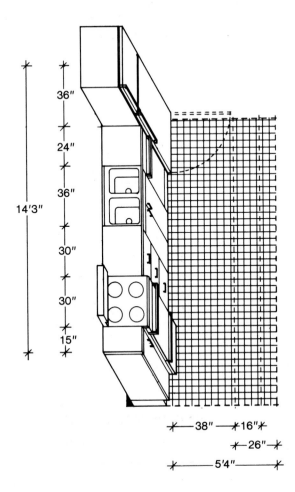

36"
30"
10'6"
36"
24"

60"
10'6"
30"
36"

24"   54"   24"
8'6"

36"
24"
12' 36"
24"
24"

5'

10'

24" 15" 30" 15"
7'

Important Dimensions

Refrigerator:
13 cubic feet . . . . 29″ to 31″ deep
24″ to 31″ wide
19 cubic feet . . . . 24″ to 29″ deep
31″ to 36″ wide
26 cubic feet . . . . 24″ to 28″ deep
41″ to 48″ wide

Sink:
single bowl (average) . . . . 21″ deep
24″ wide
double bowl (average) . . . . 21″ deep
36″ wide

Dishwasher:
average . . . . 24″ deep by
24″ wide

Single-Oven Range:
depth . . . . 24″ to 27″
average depth. . . . . 24″
width . . . . 20″ to 40″
average width . . . . 30″

Base Cabinets:
typical countertop height . . . . 36″
cabinet depth . . . . 24″
minimum required length . . . . 72″

Wall Cabinets:
height above counter. 15″ (24″ at sink)
cabinet depth . . . . 12″
typical cabinet height . . . . 30″

Counter Space (linear inches):
on latch side of refrigerator . . . . 15″
adjacent to range/oven . . . . 15″
food preparation area . . . . 30″
on one side of sink . . . . 18″
on the other side of sink . . . . 24″

Clearances

• Provide 60″ between base cabinets or appliances opposite each other to allow people to walk past, or provide 48″ to let them edge past.

• Provide 15″ between counters and wall cabinets; increase this to 24″ at sinks.

• Provide 15″ of counter space between a refrigerator or range and the next appliance.

Additional Comments

• There are four basic types of kitchen layouts: U-shaped, corridor, one-wall, and L-shaped. One important factor in selecting a layout is preventing unnecessary circulation through the kitchen work area: People should not continually obstruct the chef. For this reason, the U-shaped kitchen is often the most popular.

• Prefabricated kitchen cabinets come in 3-inch increments of length, usually starting at either 9 inches or 12 inches.

• Wall cabinets typically have three shelves.

• The counter space requirements listed are minimum values. In homes with several bedrooms or large families, additional space should be provided.

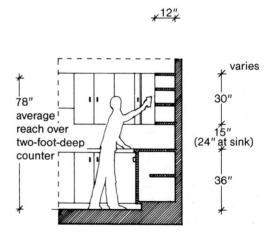

Figure A2-4. *Section of a typical cabinet arrangement showing recommended dimensions.*

Family Rooms/Dens/Living Rooms

Discussion

In the modest mansion, there is apt to be one room that is intended for general activities—everything except bathing, cooking, and sleeping. The family room is as good a name for this area as

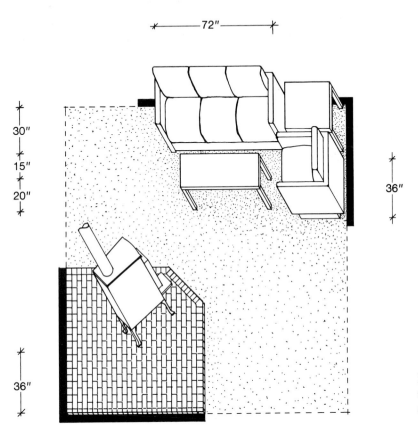

Figure A2-5. *Schematic living room layout showing recommended clearances and dimensions.*

anything else. Because the uses to which this room is put are so variable, its possible shape and size also cover a wide range. The best approach is to determine what the primary activities in the room will be, then design specific settings within the room for these activities. Figure A2-5 depicts two corners of a typical family room.

Important Dimensions

Arm Chair:
    depth . . . . 28" to 34"
    width . . . . 28" to 36"
Piano:
    baby grand . . . . 53" by 55"
Sofa:
    depth (average) . . . . 30"
    length . . . . 48" to 112"
Typical Sofa Bed:
    depth (closed) . . . . 36"
    depth (extended) . . . . 91"
    length . . . . 78"
Woodstove:
    depth . . . . 25" to 32"
    width . . . . 14" to 17"
Desk:
  average office type:
    depth . . . . 30"
    length . . . . 60"
  minimum house type:
    depth . . . . 20"
    length . . . . 42"

Clearances

• For fire safety, there should be at least 36" of clearance between a woodstove and unprotected combustible surfaces (National Fire Protection Association recommended minimum).

• Provide 26" of clearance between high partitions for one person to pass between them; double this for two people.

• Provide 24" of clearance where circulation occurs between furniture.

• Provide at least 60" of clearance between a television set and seating intended for television viewing.

Additional Comments

• As you plan the furnishings for your family room, bear in mind that informal conversation is usually limited to a distance of ten feet.

• Circulation should be separated from activity centers. For example, do not put a conversation zone where people must pass through it when entering or leaving the room.

• Seating intended for television viewing should be placed within 45 degrees of the screen; viewing the screen from a more oblique angle is uncomfortable.

Dining Area

Discussion

The era of the separate dining room is drawing to a close. In the long history of house design, the dining room is a rather late innovation and an early casualty. The dining room did not evolve as a separate area until the second half of the 18th century in France, Italy, and Germany. England lagged behind; in fact, forks were not even introduced into England until the 17th century. Today, the pendulum is swinging back: Forks may be here to stay, but dining areas are being merged once again into general living spaces.

In a modest mansion, dining generally will occur in part of an open-plan living/dining space. The key is to be sure your

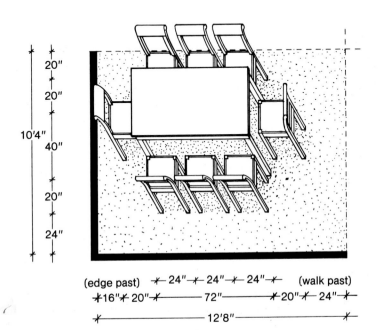

Figure A2-6. *Schematic dining room layout showing recommended clearances and dimensions.*

20"
20"
10'4" 40"
20"
24"

(edge past) — 24"— 24"— 24"— (walk past)
16"— 20"— 72" — 20"— 24"—
12'8"

design can accommodate an adequately sized dining table with sufficient chair locations and reasonable clearances around the table. Whenever possible, base your design on the actual dimensions of the furniture you will be using. Figure A2-6 summarizes the dimensions necessary for comfortable dining and the clearances required to serve all sides of the table. Of course, your table need not be located near a room corner like the diagram suggests, but you should still respect necessary clearances to other furniture or obstructions.

Important Dimensions

Tables:
> rectangular:
>> for four to six people . . . . 36″ to 40″ by 48″
>> for six to eight people . . . . 36″ to 40″ by 72″
> circular:
>> for four people . . . . 36″ diameter
>> for six people . . . . 48″ diameter

Chairs:
> armless (side chair, average) . . . . 20″ by 22″
> armchair (average) . . . . 23″ by 23″

Clearances
- Provide 16″ for people to edge past someone who is seated.
- Provide 24″ for people to walk past someone who is seated.
- Provide 18″ to 24″ leg clearance under the table.
- Provide 24″ of table edge for each person seated at the table.

Additional Comments
- A side of the table may be positioned against a wall; in this case, provide 14 inches from the wall to the center line of the first chair.
- For armchairs, add two inches to the clearances shown in Figure A2-6.

General Standards

Discussion
There are many standards that apply more to the house as a whole than to any particular room. Some of these standards are grouped in this section.

Important Dimensions

Stairs:

width (minimum)	36″ clear (OTFDC)
headroom (minimum)	78″
riser (maximum)	8¼″
run (tread minimum)	9″
handrail height	30″ to 34″

Doors (width):

main house door	36″ minimum
bath	24″ minimum
interior passage	30″ minimum
service	32″ minimum

Ceiling Heights (see Table A2-1):

habitable rooms	90″
baths/utility/halls	84″

Closets:

depth:

clothes	24″ to 28″
linen	16″ to 20″

length:

for six suits or eight dresses	allow 12″

walk-in:

length	72″
depth	60″

Laundry:

side-by-side washer/dryer	60″ length

Corridors:

minimum width (hallway or access to an exit)	36″ (OTFDC)
minimum height	84″

Wheelchair:

width	25″
length	42½″
corridor for wheelchair	40″ wide
	(MPS 1982)

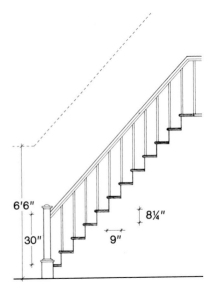

Figure A2-7. *Typical stairway layout showing recommended clearances and dimensions.*

Additional Comments

• Light and ventilation: Section 403-2.2 of MPS 1982 and section R-204.1 of OTFDC both state, "All habitable rooms shall be provided with aggregate glazing area of not less than 8 percent of the floor area of such rooms. One-half of the required area of glazing shall be operable."

• There are several rules of thumb for determining interior-stair riser-to-tread ratios. Two of the most popular are:

1. 1 riser + 1 tread = 17 to 18 inches
2. 2 risers + 1 tread = 24 to 25 inches

Site Work

Discussion

The relationship between a house and its site is one of the most important factors in residential design. Unfortunately, this relationship is often overlooked or underappreciated. Do not forget to pay careful attention to site improvements.

Important Dimensions

Exterior Stairs (more than 30" high, MPS 1982):

riser (maximum)	6"
(minimum)	3"
tread (minimum)	12"

Driveways:

width	8' (MPS 1982)

Garages:

one-car garage:

depth	20' minimum
width	10' minimum
preferable	23' by 13'

two-car garage:

depth	20' minimum
width	18'4" minimum
preferable	23' by 24'

garage hinged doors:

width	8', 8'6", or 9'

Car Sizes:

small	15'5" by 5'10"
compact	16'11" by 6'3"
standard	17'9" by 6'8"
large	18' by 6'8"

Additional Comments

• For safety reasons, exterior stairs must have more than one step.

• Section R-215.2 of OTFDC states, "Porches, balconies, or raised floor surfaces located more than 30 inches above the floor or grade below shall have guardrails not less than 36 inches in height."

• A rule of thumb for the riser-to-tread ratio for exterior stairs is: 2 risers + 1 tread = 26 inches.

• Check local codes for house setback requirements.

Table A2-1

Selected Current Size Standards

Subject	MPS 1982 *last edition*	One and Two Family Dwelling Code 1983 edition
Minimum Kitchen Size	50 square feet	50 square feet
Habitable Room	none	"Every dwelling unit shall have at least one habitable room which shall have not less than 150 square feet of floor area."
Other Habitable Rooms	none	"Other habitable rooms shall have an area of not less than 70 square feet." "Habitable rooms, except kitchens, shall be not less than 7 feet in any horizontal dimension."
Ceiling Height	none	"Habitable rooms, except kitchens, shall have an average ceiling height of not less than 7'6" in at least 50 percent of their required area with no portion less than 5 feet in height." "All other rooms, including hallways and corridors, shall have a ceiling height of not less than 7 feet measured to the lowest projection from the ceiling."

Table A2-2

Minimum Room Sizes for
Residential Units
Based on MPS 1973, revised May 1979

Name of Room	Unit with 1 Bedroom	Unit with 2 Bedrooms	Unit with 3 Bedrooms	Unit with 4 Bedrooms	Smallest Dimension
			Square Footage		
Separate Rooms					
Living Room	160	160	170	180	11'
Dining Room	80	80	95	110	8'
Master Bedroom	120	120	120	120	9'4"
Other Bedrooms	NA	80	80	80	8'
Total Area, Bedrooms	120	200	280	360	
Combined Spaces					
Living/Dining	180	180	200	220	
Living/Dining/Kitchen	220	220	250	280	
Kitchen/Dining	100	100	110	100	

ANNOTATED BIBLIOGRAPHY

The following publications are suggested for further reading on the general subject of housing and the specific topic of compact-house design. The titles are listed under the chapters to which they are most closely related. Each citation is followed by a brief comment about the publication.

Chapter 1

Farallones Institute. *The Integral Urban House.* San Francisco: Sierra Club Books, 1979. A case for the viability of autonomous, sustainable urban living.

Hall, Edward T. *The Hidden Dimension.* Garden City, N.Y.: Doubleday & Co., 1966. An anthropologist examines man's use of space.

Harrison, Henry S. *Houses: The Illustrated Guide to Construction, Design, and Systems.* Chicago: National Association of Realtors, 1973. An excellent resource for the beginning homebuyer.

Moore, Charles, and Gerald Allen. *Dimensions: Space, Shape and Scale in Architecture.* New York: Architectural Record Books, 1976. A ". . . series of architectural walking tours" in the style of *The Place of Houses.*

Sale, Kirkpatrick. *Human Scale.* New York: Coward, McGann & Geoghegan, 1980. A call for human scale in all aspects of society, not only buildings.

U.S. Department of Commerce. *U.S. Census Statistics. Series C-20,25, etc./Annual Housing Survey.* Also, "Statistics from Colonial Times." Superintendent of Documents, U.S. Government Printing Office, Washington, DC 20402. The basic federal data on housing.

Winnick, Louis. *American Housing and Its Use: The Demand for Shelter Space.* New York: John Wiley, 1957. An analysis of census housing data; the data are now old, but the interpretation is still interesting.

Chapter 2

Byam, Wally. *Trailer Travel Here and Abroad.* New York: David McKay Co., 1960. A history of recreational vehicles from the founder of the Airstream Company.

Engel, H. *The Japanese House: A Tradition for Contemporary Architecture.* Rutland, Vt.: Charles E. Tuttle Co., 1964. An excellent, well-illustrated summary of traditional Japanese residential building techniques.

Fish, Gertrude Sipperly, ed. *The Story of Housing.* New York: Macmillan Publishing Co., 1979. A detailed survey of housing history in the United States from the point of view of federal intervention.

Harvey, Thomas. "Mail-Order Architecture in the Twenties." *Landscape*, vol. 25, no. 3. An informative article on the history of standard-plan, stock-design houses.

Itoh, Teiji. *Traditional Domestic Architecture of Japan.* New York: John Weatherhill, 1972. Wonderful photographs of traditional Japanese houses.

Jones, Robert T. *Small Homes of Architectural Distinction: A Book of Suggested Plans Designed by the Architects' Small House Service Bureau, Inc.* New York: Harper & Brothers Publishers, 1929. An interesting source of historical house plans.

Kahn, Lloyd, ed. *Shelter II.* New York: Random House, 1978. Tidbits of information on vernacular housing.

Koch, Carl. *At Home with Tomorrow.* New York: Rinehart & Co., 1958. Interesting chapters on prefabricated housing, including the Lustron, Techbuilt, and Acorn houses.

Macintosh, Duncan. *The Modern Courtyard House: A History.* London: Architectural Association, Paper No. 9, 1973. An art-historical text loaded with 20th-century courtyard plans.

Morse, Edward S. *Japanese Homes and Their Surroundings.* New York: Dover Publications, 1961. A modern reprint of a classic 1885 description of the traditional Japanese house.

Perin, Constance. "The Social Order of Environmental Design" in *Designing for Human Behavior.* Edited by Jon Lang et al. Stroudsburg, Pa.: Dowden, Hutchinson & Ross, 1974. Dwelling size and livability are investigated to "exemplify specific questions about accepted definitions of the universe of human behavior."

Rapoport, Amos. *House Form and Culture.* Englewood Cliffs, N.J.: Prentice-Hall, 1969. A convincing discussion by an anthropologist on the reasons homes look the way they do.

Schoenauer, Norbert. *Introduction to Contemporary Indigenous Housing.* Montreal: Reporter Books, 1973. A summary of nonurban, contemporary, indigenous housing.

Sherwood, Roger. *Modern Housing Prototypes.* Cambridge: Harvard University Press, 1978. A formal examination of prototypical multifamily housing projects.

Talib, Kaizer. *Shelter in Saudi Arabia.* London: Academy Editions, 1984. Good examples of vernacular housing from the Middle East.

Wright, Gwendolyn. *Building the Dream.* New York: Pantheon Books, 1981. A social history of housing in America through the eyes of an architectural historian.

Chapter 3

Battelle Laboratory. *Basic Homes Program.* Superintendent of Documents, U.S. Government Printing Office, Washington, DC 20402. Report from a study to investigate the "feasibility of developing low-cost basic homes to low-income rural families."

De Vido, Alfredo. *Designing Your Client's Home.* New York: Whitney Library of Design, 1983. Architects explain in a case-study format how they design homes.

Moore, Charles, Gerald Allen, and Donlyn Lyndon. *The Place of Houses.* New York: Holt, Rinehart & Winston, 1974. Must reading for the serious residential designer, offering conceptual ideas about house design.

U.S. Department of Housing and Urban Development. *Minimum Property Standards: One and Two Family Dwellings, 1973 Edition.* Superintendent of Documents, U.S. Government Printing Office, Washington, DC 20402 (out of print). The last Minimum Property Standards edition having room-size standards.

———. *Manual of Acceptable Practices, 1973 edition (revised 1978).* Superintendent of Documents, U.S. Government Printing Office, Washington, DC 20402. Back-up data and information to better understand the 1973 Minimum Property Standards.

———. *Minimum Property Standards: One and Two Family Dwellings, 1982 Edition.* Superintendent of Documents, U.S. Government Printing Office, Washington, DC 20402. This revision of the Minimum Property Standards may well be the last.

Walker, Lester. *American Shelter.* Woodstock, N.Y.: The Overlook Press, 1981. An encyclopedic and delightfully illustrated survey of American residential style.

Walker, Lester, and Jeff Milstein. *Designing Houses.* Woodstock, N.Y.: The Overlook Press, 1979. An illustrated guide that teaches the layman how to design a personal dwelling.

Chapter 4

Burch, Monte. *Building Small Barns, Sheds and Shelters.* Pownal, Vt.: Garden Way, 1983. Basic information on constructing simple structures, particularly those with pole foundations.

Bureau of Naval Personnel. *Basic Construction Techniques for Houses and Small Buildings Simply Explained.* New York: Dover Publication, 1972. Good information from an unlikely source in this reprint of a United States government publication.

Dietz, Albert. *Dwelling House Construction*. 4th ed. Cambridge: MIT Press, 1974. Long a basic text on residential construction practices.

Gallo, Frank J., and Regis I. Campbell. *Small Residential Structures*. New York: John Wiley & Sons, 1984. A manual on residential and small commercial construction techniques.

Hornbostel, Caleb, and William J. Hornung. *Materials and Methods for Contemporary Construction*. 2d ed. Englewood Cliffs, N.J.: Prentice-Hall, 1982. A general guide to building construction.

R. S. Means Co. *Means Square Foot Costs*. 6th annual ed. Kingston, Mass.: R. S. Means Co., 1985. A helpful guide to estimating new home construction costs.

Parker, Harry. *Simplified Design of Structural Timber*. 3d ed. New York: John Wiley & Sons, 1979. A handy, succinct reference for wood construction, including safe-load tables.

Schwolsky, Rick, and James I. Williams. *The Builder's Guide to Solar Construction*. New York: McGraw-Hill, 1982. Sound information on passive-solar design construction techniques.

Small Homes Council. *Current House Construction Practices*. Champaign, Ill.: University of Illinois, 1982. Brief, no-nonsense discussion of residential construction techniques.

Steven Winter Associates, *The Passive Solar Construction Handbook*. Emmaus, Pa.: Rodale Press, 1983. A source of passive-solar construction details.

U.S. Department of Housing and Urban Development. *Reducing Home Building Costs with OVE Design and Construction*. Guideline 5, 1979. With the NAHB Research Foundation. Superintendent of Documents, U.S. Government Printing Office, Washington, DC 20402. Optimum value engineered building system is explained; details for minimum-cost, stripped-down construction practices.

Wade, Alex. *A Design and Construction Handbook for Energy-Saving Houses*. Emmaus, Pa.: Rodale Press, 1980. A handy design and construction handbook for the owner/builder.

Chapter 5

Birren, Faber. *Color and Human Response.* New York: Van Nostrand Reinhold, 1978. A personal interpretation of how individuals respond to color.

————. *Color, Form, and Space.* New York: Reinhold Publishing, 1961. More on the effect of color on spatial perception.

Friedmann, Arnold, John F. Pile, and Forrest Wilson. *Interior Design: An Introduction to Architectural Interiors.* Rev. ed. New York: Elsevier, 1976. An introduction to interior design for aspiring design professionals.

Heschong, Lisa. *Thermal Delight in Architecture.* Cambridge: MIT Press, 1979. An inspiring argument for organizing space around thermal phenomena, with many examples of thermal "implied rooms."

Hills, Nicholas, and Barty Phillips. *Setting Up Home.* London: Design Council, 1978. Interior-design ideas from the British perspective.

New York Times Magazine, Part II. "Luxury in Limited Spaces." 17 April 1983. Articles and advertising on compact-design ideas.

Small Homes Council. *Indoor Storage, 1975.* Champaign, Ill.: University of Illinois, 1975. A brief but useful guide to storage design.

Sunset Books and Sunset Magazine. *Complete Home Storage.* Menlo Park, Calif.: Lane Publishing Co., 1984. Lots of pictures of complete storage schemes at a reasonable price.

Chapter 6

Better Homes and Gardens. *Stretching Living Space.* Des Moines, Iowa: Better Homes and Gardens, 1983. Information on interior design.

Clark, Sally, and Lois Perschetz. *Making Space.* New York: Clarkson N. Potter, 1983. Space-saving interior design, primarily for apartments and lofts.

Hare, Patrick H. "Accessory Apartments: Using Surplus Space in Single-Family Houses." American Planning Association, 1981. 1313 East 60th Street, Chicago, IL 60637. The legal aspects of accessory apartments, including a sample ordinance.

Shafer, Paul, and Jean Weiner. *Small Space Design: Remodeling Apartments for Multiple Uses.* New York: Van Nostrand Reinhold, 1984. A design-and-build team offers examples of compact interior design for apartments.

Chapter 7

Armstrong, Leslie. *The Little House.* New York: Macmillan Publishing Co., 1979. A case study, with details, of a "little house."

Conran, Terence. *The Bed and Bath Book.* New York: Crown Publishers, 1978. A complete and copiously illustrated source of bed and bath design ideas.

Dickinson, Duo. *Adding On.* New York: McGraw-Hill, 1985. A well-illustrated guide to "affordable residential additions."

Metz, Don, ed. *The Compact House Book.* Pownal, Vt.: Garden Way, 1983. Thirty-three compact home designs are presented schematically.

Sumichrast, Michael. *The Complete Book of Home Buying.* Rev. ed. 1982. New York: Bantam Books. An excellent reference for the novice homebuyer.

Urban Land Institute. *Housing for a Maturing Population.* Washington, D.C.: Urban Land Institute (ULI), 1983. A survey of the design and policy issues that affect housing for a maturing population.

———. *Affordable Housing: Twenty Examples from the Private Sector.* Washington, D.C.: ULI, 1982. A survey of trends in affordable-housing design.

Yorke, F. R. S., and Penelope Whiting. *The New Small House.* London: The Architectural Press, 1953. A well-photographed compilation of high-quality post-World War II small homes.

Appendixes

Agan, Tessie, and Elaine Luchsinger. *The House: Principles/Resources/Dynamics.* Philadelphia: J. B. Lippincott Co., 1965. Out of date today, but a good historical summary of post-World War II housing expectations and standards.

American Public Health Association, Committee on the Hygiene of Housing. *Construction and Equipment of the Home.* Chicago: Public Administration Service, 1951. Performance standards for residential building environments.

————. *Planning the Home for Occupancy.* Chicago: Public Administration Service, 1950. The definitive work in its day on residential space standards—the basis for much of the size standards in the MPS.

Council of American Building Officials. *One and Two Family Dwelling Code.* Country Club Hills, Ill.: Building Officials and Code Administrators International, 1983. An attempt to standardize requirements by using a compilation of data from several national model codes.

Kira, Alexander. *The Bathroom.* New York: Viking Press, 1976. An anthropometric study of the bathroom and its appliances.

McCullough, Helen E. "Space Design for Household Storage." Bulletin 557, 1952, University of Illinois. Agricultural Experiment Station. Helpful storage hints, even if a bit outdated.

McCullough, K. P., R. H. Smith, A. L. Wood, and A. Woolrich. "Space Standards for Household Activities." Bulletin 686, University of Illinois. Agricultural Experiment Station. An early effort to quantify residential space requirements.

Macsai, John, et al. *Housing.* 2d ed. New York: John Wiley & Sons, 1982. Standards for single-family and multifamily residential design.

Ramsey, Charles G., and Harold R. Sleeper. *Architectural Graphic Standards.* 7th ed. New York: John Wiley & Sons, 1981. The architect's bible for dimensional standards.

St. Marie, Satenig S. *Homes Are for People*. New York: John Wiley & Sons, 1973. A home economist describes principles for home furnishing.

General

Allen, Edward. *How Buildings Work*. New York: Oxford University Press, 1980. An excellent summary—in a simple, graphic format—of what a building does and how it does it; a must for novice designers.

Handlin, David P. *The American Home: Architecture and Society, 1815–1915*. Boston: Little, Brown & Co., 1979. A historical account of the evolution of the American home within American society.

Harris, Cyril M. *Dictionary of Architecture and Construction*. New York: McGraw-Hill, 1975. A concise reference source of definitions of architectural and building terminology.

Hayden, Delores. *The Grand Domestic Revolution: A History of Feminist Designs for American Homes, Neighborhoods and Cities*. Cambridge: MIT Press, 1981. A primarily social history of American house design from the feminist perspective.

Sanderson, Richard L. *Codes and Code Administration*. Chicago: Building Officials Conference of America, 1969. Several good introductory chapters on the history, rationale, and structure of building codes.

Whittick, Arnold. *The Small House: Today and Tomorrow*. London: Crosby Lockwood and Son, 1947. The English know how to write about building techniques, although the data in this book are now old.

Wright, Gwendolyn. *Moralism and the Model Home*. Chicago: University of Chicago Press, 1980. See particularly Chapter 8, "The Minimal House."

Zinseer, William. *On Writing Well: An Informal Guide to Writing Nonfiction*. 2d ed. New York: Harper & Row, Publishers, 1980. Nothing to do with houses, but a must for the novice nonfiction author.

Magazine List

A number of magazines consistently include articles that address the subject of compact or affordable house design. Among them are:

Better Homes and Gardens
Fine Homebuilding
Home
Housing
Metropolitan Home
New Shelter
Progressive Architecture
Solar Age

Photograph Credits

Kevin Gilson: photos 5-8a & b
Susan Mortell Gordon: photos 3-10, 5-13a & b, 7-6, 7-7, 7-8
Helcermanas-Benge Photo: photos 7-1, 7-2, 7-3
Eliza Hicks: photo 5-14
Timothy Hursley © The Arkansas Office: photos 7-9, 7-10, 7-11
Michael Jantzen: photos 5-10a & b
Howard N. Kaplan: photo 5-16
Courtesy of Kelbaugh & Lee: photos 3-18a & b, 4-13, 5-4, 5-15
Douglas Kelbaugh: photos 3-9, 3-12, 4-2, 4-14
Mark Lenny: photo 0-1b
Norman McGrath: photo 5-5
Mitch Mandel: photos 1-3b, 3-15
Courtesy of the Metropolitan Museum of Art, Gift of
    Mrs. Russell Sage, 1909: photo 5-11
Keith Meyer/*New York Times:* photos 5-12a & b
Alison Miksch: photos 4-8a, 6-4
Joseph W. Molitor: photos 4-1, 7-24, 7-25, 7-26
Robert Perron: photos 3-7a & b, 5-3
Kristen Peterson: photos 2-7a & b
Donald Prowler: photos 0-1a, 2-1, 2-4
John Randolph: photos 3-11, 3-14, 4-5
Courtesy of Rodale Photo Department: photo 3-2
Steve Rosenthal: photo 4-4
Patti Seip: photos 1-2, 4-3
Sally Shenk: photo 3-3
Tim Snyder: photo 4-6
Courtesy of the University of Pennsylvania: photos 2-5a & b, 3-4
Kevin Wilkes: photos 0-2, 4-10
Tom Wilson: photos 1-1, 5-9a & b

INDEX

Page numbers in italic type indicate tables.

A

Aalto, Alvar, 146
Acoustics, 134–35
Additions. *See also* Extending space
    enclosed, 76
    to garages, 176
    size of, 72
Aediculae, 143
American Institute of Architects
    (AIA), 37
American Public Health Association
    (APHA), 238–39
Apartments, accessory
    advantages of, 181
    in Australia, 182
    in Denmark, 180
    difference of, from shared
        housing, 181
    legality of, 181–82
    trend toward, 180–82
Appliances. *See also* Furniture
    built-in, 68
    dimensional standards of
        bathroom, *245*

    kitchen, *249*
    laundry, *255*
    living room, *252*
    movable, 151
    selection of, 146
Architects' Small House Service
    Bureau, 37
Architecture, modern movement in,
    34–35. *See also specific designs of
    compact homes*
Artificial light, 138, 140
Attached housing developments, 81
Attics
    bedrooms in, 166–70
    eliminating, 52
    found space in, 66–67
    storage in, 133–34

B

Badanes, Steve, 218–19. *See also*
    Stone Home
Balconies, 76, 256
Barcelona Chair, 145–46

Baseboards, 126–27
Basements
    bedrooms in, 170–73
    eliminating, 52
    full, 91
    in Trinity houses, 23
Bathrooms
    in closets, 174
    dimensional standards of, 244–45
    master, 244
    and movable furniture, 150–51
    secondary, 244
    storage in, 133–34
Bays. *See* Windows, bay
Beam-and-deck ceiling, 100
Bedrooms
    in attics, 166–70
    in basements, 170–73
    combining, 61–62, 64
    dimensional standards of, 241,
        243–44
    eliminating, 53
    finding, 163–66
    in garages, 173–74
    as implied rooms, 142–43

minimum sizes of, *258*
and movable furniture, 148-50
shrinking, 47
Bentley/LaRosa/Salasky Design, 197.
See also Hog Hill House
Bohlin Powell Larkin Cywinski, 223.
See also Bohlin Residence
Bohlin Residence
living spaces in, 223, 226-27
site of, 223
Breuer, Marcel, 146
Brick, for house construction, 11
Brooks, Turner, 60, 189. *See also*
Hurd Residence
Building codes
description of, 236-37
for stairways, 114
Building program, 43

C

Cape Cods, 21
Ceilings
dimensional standards of, *255*
exposed, 100-101
and joist depth, 99-100
lights in, 68
sloped, 104-6
space above, 68
structure of, 99
variation of exposed, 101
Charleston single house, 32
Chimneys, 121
Closets
dimensional standards of, *255*
improvement of, 174
Cogeneration plants, shared, 83
Colonials, 21, 118
Color, 151-53
Combining space
advantages of, 57
in Dekhan Home, 61
disadvantages of, 57-59
examples of, 56-57, 65
and furniture, 65
in Glazebrook House, 60
of rooms with same activities,
60-61, 64

of rooms with same function,
61-62, 64
social factors of, 57
in "Stayin' Alive" house, 59
technical factors of, 57
trend toward, 56
Compact homes. *See also specific
designs of; specific strategies of designing*
case for, 1-5
completing, 130-31
construction of
bays in, 114-15
ceilings in, 99-101
corridors in, 116-17
dimensions and, 86-90
doors and, 109-11
dormers in, 114-15
exterior walls in, 94-96
finishes and, 118-19
floors in, 99-101
footprint, minimizing,
92-93
foundation in, 90-92
interior walls in, 96-99
picking up inches and, 93-94
roofs in, 103-6
stairways in, 111, 113-14
trim and, 118-19
windows and, 106-9
design benefits of
and expression, 15-17
opportunities for, 17-18
and quality vs. quantity,
14-15
and do-it-yourselfers, 16-17
early designers of, 33
economic benefit(s) of
affordability as, 5-6
and energy consciousness,
6-8
sustainability as, 8-11
evolutionary process of, 18
goals of
design excellence, 41-42
and large- and small-scale
elements, 44
objective, 43
and personal needs, 43
subjective, 43-44

and symbolism, 42-43
and visual clues, 44
and homeownership, 6
and 1969 recession, 4
opportunities for, 19
planning of, 41
recent
custom homes as, 32-36
mass-produced housing as,
36-40
social benefits of
and family, new American,
11-12
as status symbol, 11-14
and standard-size homes, 17-18
strategies for, 44-84
traditional
courtyard houses as, 29-32
igloos as, 26-29
Japanese houses as, 24-26
Trinity houses as, 21-23
trend toward, 4, 13
Complete-spectrum light bulbs, 138,
140
Computers, in home, 13-14
Condominiums, 82-83. *See also*
Terrazas Del Sol
Construction regulations
and building codes, 236-37
and data on housing, 235-36
history of, 234-35
and home improvement
in attics, 166
in basements, 172-73
and Minimum Property
Standards, 238-39
and zoning ordinances, 237
Conversions. *See* Home
improvement
Cooling systems, 127-28
Corridors
central, 117
dimensional standards of, *255*
eliminating, 116-17
use of, 116
Cost penalty of decreasing home size,
89-90
Cottage Court House
entry to, 233

Cottage Court House *(continued)*
    exterior of, 232
    living spaces of, 233
    site of, 228-29
Courtyard houses
    construction of, 29, 31
    design of, 29
    exterior spaces of, 31-32
    interior spaces of, 31
Crawlspaces, 92
Custom homes
    definition of, 32-33
    designers of, 33-36

D

Dead space, 67-68
Decks, 76, 89. *See also* Balconies;
    Porches
Dekhan Home, 61
Dens. *See* Living rooms
Design. *See also specific strategies of*
    excellence, 41-42
    goals of, 41-44
Dimensional standards. *See also*
    Dimensions
    of bathrooms, 244-45
    of bedrooms, 241, 243-44
    of dining rooms, 253-54
    explanation of, 240-41
    general, 254-55
    of kitchens, 246-47, 249-50
    of living rooms, 250-53
    and minimum room sizes, *258*
    and selected current size
      standards, *257*
    of site work, 256
    of stairways, *255-56*
Dimensions. *See also* Dimensional
    standards
    cost penalty of decreasing, 89-90
    difficulties in calculating, 87-88
    exterior, 87
    interior, 87
    and setup time, 89-90
    and square footage, 86-87
Dining rooms
    dimensional standards of, 253-54

eliminating, 52-53
    minimum sizes of, *258*
Doors
    dimensional standards of, *255*
    functions of, 109
    sliding glass, 79
    swing of, 110-11
    and wasted space, 109-10
Dormers
    in attics, 169
    definition of, 114-15
    functions of, 114
Dymaxion houses, 37

E

Electrical systems, 128-29
Electric heat, 126-27
Eliminating space
    advantages of, 56
    as corridor(s), 116-17
    drawbacks of, 55-56
    as parts of rooms, 53-54
    in starter homes, 54-55
    as whole rooms, 52-53
Empty-nesters, 12
Energized exterior walls, 129
Energy conservation, 6-8. *See also*
    Solar heating systems
Extending space
    impulse for, 72
    methods of, 72
    physically
      with additions, 72, 76
      with balconies, 76
      with landscaping, 77
      with porches, 76
      with roof decks, 76
    visually
      using windows, 77-79

F

Family rooms. *See* Living rooms
Federal Housing Administration
    (FHA), 238-39
Fences, as extension, 72

Finding space. *See* Found space
Finishing strategy(ies)
    color as, 151-53
    exterior, 118-19
    materials for, 156-57, 159
    mirrors as, 153-55
    pattern, 153
    shape, 153
    trim as, 155-56
Fireplaces, 121
Floor(s)
    of basements, 171-72
    of garages, 173-74
    trusses, 101
Footprint, home's
    definition of, 92
    minimizing, 92-93
Foundation
    crawlspace, 92
    full basement as, 91
    selection of, 90-91
    slab-on-grade, 91-92
Found space
    in attics, 66-67
    definition of, 66
    expense of creating, 70-71
    in kitchens, 68
    outside, 70
    in partition walls, 68
    search for, 66
    in stair landings, 67-68
    for storage, 69-70
    in trusses, 66-67
    in vertical dimensions of room,
      67
Fuller, Buckminster, 37-38
Furnishing strategy(ies)
    implied rooms as, 140-44
    movable furniture as, 146,
      148-51
    and selection of furniture,
      144-46
Furniture. *See also* Appliances
    dimensional standards of
      in bathroom, *245*
      in bedroom, *243*
      in dining room, *254*
      in kitchen, *249*
      in living room, *252*

materials for, 146
movable, 148-51
multifunction, 65
selection of
    rules for, 144-45
    styles and, 145-46

G

Gable shape, 42
Garages
    additions to, 176
    bedrooms in, 173-74
    dimensional standards of, *256*
    storage in, 133-34
    ventilation in, 174
Gas minifurnaces, 120
Gateway, entry, 76
Glazebrook House, 60
Goldberger, Paul, 12-13
Gordon, Bruce, 193. *See also* Gordon
    Residence
Gordon Residence
    design of, 196-97
    entry to, 194, 196
    living spaces of, 196
    and recycling, 196
    site of, 194
    size of, 193-94
Granny flat, 182
Greenhouses, 61, 125
Gropius, Walter, 33, 35

H

Heaters
    portable space, unvented, 120-21
    water, 129
Heating, ventilating, and air-
    conditioning systems (HVAC),
    178. *See also* Cooling systems;
    Heating systems
Heating systems
    and cutting off space, 177-80
    electric, 126-27
    gas, 120-21

new oil, 120-21
selection of, 119
solar, 123-25
superinsulation and, 125-26
woodstoves and, 121
Heat loss. *See also* Insulation
    through exterior surfaces, 7-8, *7*
    from flues, 70
Heat pumps, 126-27
Hitchcock, Henry-Russell, 33
Hog Hill House
    entry to, 198
    living spaces of, 198, 200-201
    site of, 197
    solar design in, 202
Homebuilding industry
    growth of, 1
    and new homes, 2-4
    and new households, 12
Home improvement
    attics and, 166-70
    basements and, 170-73
    bedrooms for, finding, 163-74,
      176
    closets and, 174
    garages and, 173-74
    vs. moving, 160-62
    space and
      cutting off, 177-83
      making, 162-63
      new, 174-76
Homeownership
    commitment to, national, 5
    and compact homes, 6
    dream of, 1, 6
Households
    age of, 12
    change in, 11
    occupants in, 3
    size of, 10-12, *10*
House(s). *See also* Compact homes;
    Custom homes; Mass-produced
    housing; New homes; *specific
    designs of*
    Cape Cod, 21
    Colonial, 21, 118
    computers in, 13-14
    expansion of, 54-55
    gross size of, 87

large, 12
manufactured, 39-40
minimum room sizes for, *257-58*
minimum three-bedroom, *50*
offices in, 13
personalizing, 16
private zone in, 164
public zone in, 164
ranch, 46, 87-88
selection of, 15
shrinkage of, 54-55
size of
    calculating, 87-88
    cost penalty and, 89-90
starter, 54-56
Housing payments. *See* Mortgage(s)
Housing recession, 4
Hurd Residence
    entry to, 190
    exterior of, 189-90
    heating of, 193
    light in, 192
    living spaces of, 190
    open plan of, 193
    site of, 189

I

Igloos
    construction of, 28
    design of, 26-27
    interior spaces in, 28-29
    size of, 27-28
Implied rooms
    and beds, 142-43
    and behavior patterns, 143-44
    definition of, 141-42
    example of, 143-44
    exterior, 144
    ideas for, 144
    purpose of, 142
Insulation. *See also* Heating systems
    of attics, 167, 169-70
    of basements, 171-72
    and bays, 115
    and cutting off space, 178
    and dormers, 115
    and exterior walls, 95-96

Insulation (*continued*)
    and slab-on-grade foundation,
      123
    and sloped ceilings, 105–6
International Style, 34–35

J

Japanese house, traditional
    design of, 24–25
    flexibility of, 26
    floor of, 25
    rooms in, 25–26
Jersey Devil, 218. *See also* Stone Home
Joists, 99–100

K

Kangaroo apartment, 180
Kelbaugh, Douglas, 14
Kerosene minifurnaces, 120
Kira, Alexander, 238
Kitchens
    dimensional standards of,
      246–47, 249–50
    found space in, 68
    in igloos, 28
    minimum sizes of, *258*

L

Landscaping, 77
La Vereda, Model Two
    design of, 214
    heating system of, 210, 212
    living spaces of, 212–14
    site of, 209–10
LeCorbusier, 33, 35–36, 47–48
Light sources
    artificial, 138, 140
    control of, 140
    natural, 136–38
    recessed, 68
    types of, 136
Living rooms
    dimensional standards of, 250–53
    eliminating, 52

minimum sizes of, *258*
shrinking, 52
Lumber, for house construction, 8–10

M

Manufactured houses, 39–40
Mass-produced housing
    and cost of houses, 36–37
    and Depression, 37
    and Fuller (Buckminster), 37–38
    and recreational vehicles, 39
    and stock pan, 37
Means Square Foot Costs, 90
Mies Van der Rohe, 33, 35, 145–46
Mingles homes, 182–83. *See also*
    Condominiums
Minifurnaces, 120
Minimum Property Standards (MPS).
    See also Construction regulations
    and American Public Health
      Administration, 238–39
    and dimensional standards, 241
    and Federal Housing
      Administration, 238–39
    1982 edition of, 239
    1973 edition of, 238
    and shrinking space, 48–49
Miniwarehouses, 83
Mirrors, 153–55
Mobile homes, 39
Mortgage(s)
    FHA, 238
    payments, 6
    rates, 1–2
Mount Vernon, 54
Murphy, William K., 148
Murphy bed, 148–50

N

National Association of Home
    Builders (NAHB)
    and apartments, accessory,
      180–81

and combined rooms, 64
    and remodeling, 5
    and resources for house
      construction, 8–10
    Statistics Division of, 180–81
Natural light, 136–38
Natural resources, consumption of,
    8–11
New homes
    cost of, 2, *2*
    size of, 3–4, *3,* 6
Nichols, Susan, 209. *See also* La
    Vereda, Model Two
Nichols, Wayne, 209. *See also* La
    Vereda, Model Two

O

Offices, home, 13
Oil furnace, 119
One and Two Family Dwelling
    Code, 239, 241
OPEC oil embargo (1973), 6
Open plan. *See also* Combining space
    and plumbing systems, 128
    trend toward, 56
Orr & Taylor, 228. *See also* Cottage
    Court House

P

Palazzo Farnese, 180
Parallel-chord trusses, 118
Piazzas, 32. *See also* Porches
Picking up inches, 93–94
Planned unit developments (PUDs),
    81. *See also* La Vereda, Model Two;
    Shared space
Plumbing cores, 37
Plumbing systems, 128–29
Plywood siding, 118
Porches
    in Charleston single house, 32
    cost estimates of, 89
    dimensional standards of, 256
    as extensions, 76
    improvements of, 176

Portable heaters, 120-21
Power plants, shared, 83

R

R. E. Hulbert & Partners, 185. *See also* Triple A House
Radiant panels, 126-27
Ranch homes, 46, 87-88
Recessed light fixtures, 68
Recreational vehicles, 39
Recycling, 196
Remodeling, 5. *See also* Home improvement
Ringel, John, 218. *See also* Stone Home
Roof(s)
    decks on, 76
    found space in, 70
    pitched, 104
    and sloped ceilings, 104-6
    trusses, 66-67, 104
    types of, 103

S

Scale, human, 43-44
Scully, Dan, 59
Setup time, 89-90
Shared space. *See also* Condominiums; Planned unit developments
    in Europe, 81
    and facilities, 83
    and new technologies, 83
    trend toward, 81-83
    and two units in one building, 83-84
Shelter, need for, 1
Shingle-style houses, 193
Shrinking space
    and dimensions, 48
    by lowering ceilings, 47
    and Minimum Property Standards, 48-49
    partially, 46-47
    proportionally, 45-46
    trade-offs of, 49

Shutters, 118
Siding, 118
Skylights. *See* Windows
Slab-on-grade construction, 91-92, 123
Solar heating systems
    active-solar water, 123
    passive, 123-25
Sound isolation, 134-35
Space. *See also* Combining space; Eliminating space; Extending space; Found space; Shared space; Shrinking space
    cutting of
        in accessory apartments, 180-83
        for storing rooms, 177-80
    and finishes, 156-57
    horizontal, 54
    for kitchen appliances, 247
    making, 162-63
    maximizing, 93-94
    and mirrors, 153-55
    and movable furniture, 148-51
    new, 174, 176
    storage
        compartments and, 133
        locations for, 133-34
        rules for, 131-33
        size standards for, 48
    vertical, 54
Spatial strategies
    and light sources, 136-38, 140
    and sound isolation, 134-35
    and storage, 131-34
Square footage
    costs and, 90
    figures, 86-87
    maximizing, 14
Stair landings, 67-68
Stairways
    building codes for, 114
    dead space around, 67-68
    dimensional standards of, 255-56
    dimensions of, 113-14
    riser-to-tread ratio, 113
    selection of, 113
    space for, 111
    types of, 111

Standardized house plans, 37
Starter houses, 54-56
"Stayin' Alive" house, 59
Stencils, painted, 159
Stock plans, 37
Stone Home
    living spaces in, 219, 221
    site of, 218-19
    size of, 219
Storage, 69-70. *See also* Found space; Space
    compartments, 133
    rules for, 131-33
Storing rooms, 177-80
SunTop design, 33
Superinsulation, 125-26. *See also* Insulation

T

Taxes, 5
Tenement House Act, 234
Terrazas Del Sol
    design of, 218
    living spaces in, 217-18
    site of, 214-15
    solar heating of, 214-16
Trailers, 39
Trellis, 76-77
Trim
    at ceiling height, 155-56
    eliminating, 156
    functions of, 155
    interior molding, 155
    oversized, 156
    selection of, 118-19
Trinity house
    facade of, 21
    floor of, 21
    popularity of, 23
    size of, 21-22
    stairways in, 113
Triple A House
    basic model of, 185
    entry to, 188
    exterior of, 188
    flexibility of, 185-86
    and found space, 67

Triple A House *(continued)*
    insulation of, 188–89
    living spaces of, 188
    purpose of, 185
    site of, 185
Trombe wall, 124–25, 212–13
Trompe l'oeil, 152
Trubek and Wislocki Houses
    comparison of, 209
    exteriors of, 203
    living spaces in, 203, 206, 209
    site of, 202–3
Trusses
    floor, 101
    parallel-chord, 188
    roof, 66–67, 104

U

University of Illinois Small Home
    Council, 238

V

Ventilation. *See also* Cooling systems
    forced, 127–28
    in garages, 174
    and sloped ceilings, 104–6

Vent stack, 128
Venturi, Rauch and Scott Brown, 202.
    See also Trubek and Wislocki
    Houses
Vinyl siding, 118
Vitruvius, 179–80

W

Walls
    of basements, 171–72
    exterior
        energized, 129
        and insulation, 95–96
        masonry, 95
        and maximizing space,
            93–94
        in past, 94–95
        recent, 95
        and superinsulation, 126
    and home improvement, 165–66
    interior
        functions of, 96
        height of, 97–99
        thickness of, 96–97
        and wasted space, 97
    and light sources, 138, 140
    sound-blocking, 135
Wasted space. *See also* Space

of door swing, 109
    elimination of, 54, 56
    in interior walls, 97
Water heaters, 129
Wehler, James M., 214. *See also*
    Terrazas Del Sol
Whole-house fans, 128
Wilkes House, 117
Windows. *See also* Skylights
    in attics, 169
    in basements, 172–73
    bay, 114–15
    design of, 106
    double-hung, 106–7, 109
    as extensions, 77–79
    functions of, 78
    light from, 136–38
    picture, 72
    selection of, 109
    types of, 109
    ventilation from, 127–28
Woodstoves
    dimensional standard of, *252*
    as heating system, 121
Wright, Frank Lloyd, 33–34, 47–48

Z

Zoning ordinances, 237